Henry A. (Henry Augustin) Beers

From Chaucer to Tennyson

With 29 Portraits And Selections from Thirty Authors

Henry A. (Henry Augustin) Beers

From Chaucer to Tennyson
With 29 Portraits And Selections from Thirty Authors

ISBN/EAN: 9783744725804

Printed in Europe, USA, Canada, Australia, Japan

Cover: Foto ©ninafisch / pixelio.de

More available books at **www.hansebooks.com**

Chautauqua Reading Circle Literature

FROM
CHAUCER TO TENNYSON

WITH TWENTY-NINE PORTRAITS

AND

SELECTIONS FROM THIRTY AUTHORS.

BY

HENRY A. BEERS

Professor of English Literature in Yale University.

FLOOD AND VINCENT
The Chautauqua-Century Press
MEADVILLE PENNA
150 FIFTH AVE. NEW YORK
1894

PREFACE.

IN so brief a history of so rich a literature, the problem is how to get room enough to give, not an adequate impression—that is impossible—but any impression at all of the subject. To do this I have crowded out every thing but *belles lettres.* Books in philosophy, history, science, etc., however important in the history of English thought, receive the merest incidental mention, or even no mention at all. Again, I have omitted the literature of the Anglo-Saxon period, which is written in a language nearly as hard for a modern Englishman to read as German is, or Dutch. Cædmon and Cynewulf are no more a part of English literature than Vergil and Horace are of Italian. I have also left out the vernacular literature of the Scotch before the time of Burns. Up to the date of the union Scotland was a separate kingdom, and its literature had a development independent of the English, though parallel with it.

In dividing the history into periods, I have followed, with some modifications, the divisions made by Mr. Stopford Brooke in his excellent little *Primer of English Literature.* A short reading course is appended to each chapter.

HENRY A. BEERS.

CONTENTS.

CHAPTER I.

PAGE

FROM THE CONQUEST TO CHAUCER, 1066–1400...................... 7

CHAPTER II.

FROM CHAUCER TO SPENSER, 1400–1599.......................... 31

CHAPTER III.

THE AGE OF SHAKSPERE, 1564–1616.............................. 56

CHAPTER IV.

THE AGE OF MILTON, 1608–1674................................ 92

CHAPTER V.

FROM THE RESTORATION TO THE DEATH OF POPE, 1660–1744......... 121

CHAPTER VI.

FROM THE DEATH OF POPE TO THE FRENCH REVOLUTION, 1744–1789... 143

CHAPTER VII.

FROM THE FRENCH REVOLUTION TO THE DEATH OF SCOTT, 1789–1832... 164

CHAPTER VIII.

FROM THE DEATH OF SCOTT TO THE PRESENT TIME, 1832–1893........ 197

APPENDIX... 223

LIST OF PORTRAITS.

WILLIAM SHAKSPERE . . . . *Frontispiece.*

Facing page

GEOFFREY CHAUCER, EDMUND SPENSER, FRANCIS BACON, JOHN MILTON 60

JOHN DRYDEN, JOSEPH ADDISON, ALEXANDER POPE, JONATHAN SWIFT 141

SAMUEL JOHNSON, OLIVER GOLDSMITH, WILLIAM COWPER, ROBERT BURNS. 157

WILLIAM WORDSWORTH, GEORGE GORDON BYRON, PERCY BYSSHE SHELLEY, JOHN KEATS 164

ROBERT SOUTHEY, SIR WALTER SCOTT, SAMUEL TAYLOR COLERIDGE, THOMAS BABINGTON MACAULAY 197

THOMAS CARLYLE, JOHN RUSKIN, WILLIAM MAKEPEACE THACKERAY, CHARLES DICKENS 205

GEORGE ELIOT (MARY ANN EVANS), JAMES ANTHONY FROUDE, ROBERT BROWNING, ALFRED TENNYSON . . . 213

FROM CHAUCER TO TENNYSON.

CHAPTER I.

FROM THE CONQUEST TO CHAUCER.

1066–1400.

THE Norman conquest of England, in the 11th century, made a break in the natural growth of the English language and literature. The Old English or Anglo-Saxon had been a purely Germanic speech, with a complicated grammar and a full set of inflections. For three hundred years following the battle of Hastings this native tongue was driven from the king's court and the courts of law, from Parliament, school, and university. During all this time there were two languages spoken in England. Norman French was the birth-tongue of the upper classes and English of the lower. When the latter got the better of the struggle, and became, about the middle of the 14th century, the national speech of all England, it was no longer the English of King Alfred. It was a new language, a grammarless tongue, almost wholly stripped of its inflections. It had lost half of its old words, and had filled their places with French equivalents. The Norman lawyers had introduced legal terms; the ladies and courtiers words of dress and courtesy. The knight had imported the vocabulary of war and of the chase. The master-builders of the Norman castles and cathedrals contributed technical expressions proper to the architect and the mason. The art of cooking was French. The naming of the living animals, *ox, swine, sheep, deer,* was left to the Saxon churl who had the herding of them, while the dressed meats, *beef, pork, mutton, venison,* received their baptism from the table-talk of his Norman master. The four orders of begging friars, and especially the Franciscans or Gray Friars, introduced into England in 1224, became intermediaries between the high and the low. They went about preaching to the poor, and in their sermons they intermingled French with English. In their hands, too, was almost all the science of the day; their *medicine, botany,* and *astronomy* displaced the old nomenclature of *leechdom, wort-cunning* and *star-craft.* And, finally, the translators of French poems often found it easier to transfer a foreign word bodily than to seek out a native synonym, particularly when the former supplied them with a rhyme. But the innovation reached even to the commonest words in every-day use, so that *voice* drove out *steven, poor* drove out *earm,* and *color, use,* and *place* made good their footing beside *hue, wont,* and *stead.* A great part of the English words that were left were so changed in spelling and pronunciation as to be practically new. Chaucer stands, in date, midway between King Alfred and Alfred Tennyson, but his English differs vastly more from the former's than from the latter's. To Chaucer, Anglo-Saxon was as much a dead language as it is to us.

The classical Anglo-Saxon, moreover, had been the Wessex dialect, spoken and written at Alfred's capital, Winchester. When the French had displaced this as the language of culture, there was no longer a "king's English" or any literary standard. The sources of modern standard English are to be found in the East Midland, spoken in Lincoln, Norfolk, Suffolk, Cambridge, and neighboring shires. Here the old Anglian had been corrupted by the Danish settlers, and rapidly threw off its inflections when it became a spoken and no longer a written language, after the Conquest. The West Saxon, clinging more tenaciously to ancient forms, sank into the position of a local dialect; while the East Midland, spreading to London, Oxford, and Cambridge, became the literary English in which Chaucer wrote.

The Normans brought in also new intellectual influences and new forms of literature. They were a cosmopolitan people, and they connected England with the Continent. Lanfranc and Anselm, the first two Norman archbishops of Canterbury, were learned and splendid prelates of a type quite unknown to the Anglo-Saxons. They introduced the scholastic philosophy taught at the University of Paris, and the reformed discipline of the Norman abbeys. They bound the English Church more closely to Rome, and officered it with Normans. English bishops were deprived of their sees for illiteracy, and French abbots were set over monasteries of Saxon monks. Down to the middle of the 14th century the learned literature of England was mostly in Latin, and the polite literature in French. English did not at any time altogether cease to be a written language, but the extant remains of the period from 1066 to 1200 are few and, with one exception, unimportant. After 1200 English came more and more into written use, but mainly in translations, paraphrases, and imitations of French works. The native genius was at school, and followed awkwardly the copy set by its master.

The Anglo-Saxon poetry, for example, had been rhythmical and alliterative. It was commonly written in lines containing four rhythmical accents and with three of the accented syllables alliterating.

> *Reste* hine thâ *rúm*-heort; *ré*ced hlîfade
> *Ge*áp and *gó*ld-fâh, *gä*st inne swâf.

> Rested him then the great-hearted; the hall towered
> Roomy and gold-bright, the guest slept within.

This rude, energetic verse the Saxon *scóp* had sung to his harp or *glee-beam*, dwelling on the emphatic syllables,

passing swiftly over the others, which were of undeter-
mined number and position in the line. It was now displaced by the smooth metrical verse with rhymed endings,
which the French introduced and which our modern poets
use, a verse fitted to be recited rather than sung. The old
English alliterative verse continued, indeed, in occasional use
to the 16th century. But it was linked to a forgotten
literature and an obsolete dialect, and was doomed to give
way. Chaucer lent his great authority to the more modern
verse system, and his own literary models and inspirers were
all foreign, French or Italian. Literature in England began
to be once more English and truly national in the hands of
Chaucer and his contemporaries, but it was the literature of
a nation cut off from its own past by three centuries of
foreign rule.

The most noteworthy English document of the 11th and
12th centuries was the continuation of the Anglo-Saxon
chronicle. Copies of these annals, differing somewhat among
themselves, had been kept at the monasteries in Winchester,
Abingdon, Worcester, and elsewhere. The yearly entries are
mostly brief, dry records of passing events, though occasionally they become full and animated. The fen country of Cambridge and Lincolnshire was a region of monasteries. Here
were the great abbeys of Peterborough and Croyland and
Ely minster. One of the earliest English songs tells how the
savage heart of the Danish king Cnut was softened by the
singing of the monks in Ely.

> Merie sungen muneches binnen Ely
> Tha Cnut chyning reu ther by;
> Roweth, cnihtes, noer the land.
> And here we thes muneches sang.

> Merrily sung the monks in Ely
> When King Canute rowed by.
> 'Row boys, nearer the land,
> And let us hear these monks' song.'

It was among the dikes and marshes of this fen country that the bold outlaw Hereward, "the last of the English," held out for some years against the conqueror. And it was here, in the rich abbey of Burgh or Peterborough, the ancient Medeshamstede (meadow-homestead), that the chronicle was continued nearly a century after the Conquest, breaking off abruptly in 1154, the date of King Stephen's death. Peterborough had received a new Norman abbot, Turold, "a very stern man," and the entry in the chronicle for 1070 tells how Hereward and his gang, with his Danish backers, thereupon plundered the abbey of its treasures, which were first removed to Ely, and then carried off by the Danish fleet and sunk, lost, or squandered. The English in the later portions of this Peterborough chronicle becomes gradually more modern, and falls away more and more from the strict grammatical standards of the classical Anglo-Saxon. It is a most valuable historical monument, and some passages of it are written with great vividness, notably the sketch of William the Conquerer put down in the year of his death ·(1086) by one who had "looked upon him and at another time dwelt in his court." " He who was before a rich king, and lord of many a land, he had not then of all his land but a piece of seven feet. . . . Likewise he was a very stark man and a terrible, so that one durst do nothing against his will. . . . Among other things is not to be forgotten the good peace that he made in this land, so that a man might fare over his kingdom with his bosom full of gold unhurt. He set up a great deer preserve, and he laid laws therewith that whoso should slay hart or hind, he should be blinded. As greatly did he love the tall deer as if he were their father."

With the discontinuance of the Peterborough annals, English history written in English prose ceased for three hundred years. The thread of the nation's story was kept up in Latin chronicles, compiled by writers partly of English

and partly of Norman descent.   The earliest of these, such
as Ordericus Vitalis, Simeon of Durham, Henry of Huut-
ingdon, and William of Malmesbury, were contemporary
with the later entries of the Saxon chronicle.   The last
of them, Matthew of Westminster, finished his work in
1273.   About 1300, Robert, a monk of Gloucester, composed
a chronicle in English verse, following in the main the
authority of the Latin chronicles, and he was succeeded by
other rhyming chroniclers in the 14th century.   In the
hands of these the true history of the Saxon times was
overlaid with an ever-increasing mass of fable and legend.
All real knowledge of the period dwindled away until
in Capgraves's *Chronicle of England*, written in prose in
1463–1464, hardly any thing of it is left.   In history as in
literature the English had forgotten their past, and had
turned to foreign sources.   It is noteworthy that Shakspere,
who borrowed his subjects and his heroes sometimes from
authentic English history, sometimes from the legendary
history of ancient Britain, Denmark, and Scotland—as in
Lear, Hamlet, and Macbeth, respectively—ignores the Saxon
period altogether.   And Spenser, who gives in the second
book of his *Faerie Queene* a *resumé* of the reigns of
fabulous British kings—the supposed ancestors of Queen
Elizabeth, his royal patron—has nothing to say of the real
kings of early England.   So completely had the true
record faded away that it made no appeal to the imaginations of our most patriotic poets.   The Saxon Alfred had
been dethroned by the British Arthur, and the conquered
Welsh had imposed their fictitious genealogies upon the
dynasty of the conquerors.

   In the *Roman de Rou*, a verse chronicle of the dukes of
Normandy, written by the Norman Wace, it is related that
at the battle of Hastings the French *jongleur*, Taillefer,
spurred out before the van of William's army, tossing his
lance in the air and chanting of "Charlemagne and of

Roland, of Oliver and the peers who died at Roncesvals."
This incident is prophetic of the victory which Norman
song, no less than Norman arms, was to win over England.
The lines which Taillefer sang were from the *Chanson de
Roland,* the oldest and best of the French hero sagas. The
heathen Northmen, who had ravaged the coasts of France
in the 10th century, had become in the course of one hundred
and fifty years completely identified with the French. They
had accepted Christianity, intermarried with the native
women, and forgotten their own Norse tongue. The race
thus formed was the most brilliant in Europe. The warlike,
adventurous spirit of the vikings mingled in its blood with
the French nimbleness of wit and fondness for display. The
Normans were a nation of knights-errant, with a passion for
prowess and for courtesy. Their architecture was at once
strong and graceful. Their women were skilled in em-
broidery, a splendid sample of which is preserved in the
famous Bayeux tapestry, in which the conqueror's wife,
Matilda, and the ladies of her court wrought the history of
the Conquest.

This national taste for decoration expressed itself not only
in the ceremonious pomp of feast and chase and tourney, but
likewise in literature. The most characteristic contribution
of the Normans to English poetry were the metrical romances
or chivalry tales. These were sung or recited by the minstrels, who were among the retainers of every great feudal
baron, or by the *jongleurs,* who wandered from court to
castle. There is a whole literature of these *romans d'
aventure* in the Anglo-Norman dialect of French. Many of
them are very long—often thirty, forty, or fifty thousand
lines—written sometimes in a strophic form, sometimes in
long Alexandrines, but commonly in the short, eight-syllabled
rhyming couplet. Numbers of them were turned into English verse in the 13th, 14th, and 15th centuries. The translations were usually inferior to the originals. The French

trouvere (finder or poet) told his story in a straightforward,
prosaic fashion, omitting no details in the action and unroll-
ing endless descriptions of dresses, trappings, gardens, etc.
He invented plots and situations full of fine possibilities by
which later poets have profited, but his own handling of them
was feeble and prolix.   Yet there was a simplicity about the
old French language and a certain elegance and delicacy in
the diction of the *trouveres* which the rude, unformed English failed to catch.

The heroes of these romances were of various climes: Guy
of Warwick, and Richard the Lion Heart of England,
Havelok the Dane, Sir Troilus of Troy, Charlemagne, and
Alexander.   But, strangely enough, the favorite hero of
English romance was that mythical Arthur of Britain, whom
Welsh legend had celebrated as the most formidable enemy
of the Sassenach invaders and their victor in twelve great
battles.   The language and literature of the ancient Cymry
or Welsh had made no impression on their Anglo-Saxon
conquerors.   There are a few Welsh borrowings in the English speech, such as *bard* and *druid;* but in the old Anglo-
Saxon literature there are no more traces of British song and
story than if the two races had been sundered by the ocean
instead of being borderers for over six hundred years.   But
the Welsh had their own national traditions, and after the
Norman Conquest these were set free from the isolation of their
Celtic tongue and, in an indirect form, entered into the general literature of Europe.   The French came into contact
with the old British literature in two places: in the Welsh
marches in England and in the province of Brittany in
France, where the population is of Cymric race, and spoke,
and still to some extent speaks, a Cymric dialect akin to the
Welsh.

About 1140 Geoffrey of Monmouth, a Benedictine monk,
seemingly of Welsh descent, who lived at the court of Henry
the First and became afterward bishop of St. Asaph, pro-

duced_in Latin a so-called *Historia Britonum,* in which it was told how Brutus, the great grandson of Æneas, came to Britain, and founded there his kingdom called after him, and his city of New Troy (Troynovant) on the site of the later London. An air of historic gravity was given to this tissue of Welsh legends by an exact chronology and the genealogy of the British kings, and the author referred, as his authority, to an imaginary Welsh book given him, as he said, by a certain Walter, Archdeacon of Oxford. Here appeared that line of fabulous British princes which has become so familiar to modern readers in the plays of Shakspere and the poems of Tennyson : Lear and his three daughters ; Cymbeline ; Gorboduc, the subject of the earliest regular English tragedy, composed by Sackville and acted in 1562; Locrine and his Queen Gwendolen and his daughter Sabrina, who gave her name to the river Severn, was made immortal by an exquisite song in Milton's *Comus* and became the heroine of the tragedy of *Locrine,* once attributed to Shakspere ; and above all, Arthur, the son of Uther Pendragon, and the founder of the Table Round. In 1155 Wace, the author of the *Roman de Rou,* turned Geoffrey's work into a French poem entitled *Brut d' Angleterre,* "brut" being a Welsh word meaning chronicle. About the year 1200 Wace's poem was Englished by Layamon, a priest of Arley Regis, on the border stream of Severn. Layamon's *Brut* is in thirty thousand lines, partly alliterative and partly rhymed, but written in pure Saxon English with hardly any French words. The style is rude but vigorous, and, at times, highly imaginative. Wace had amplified Geoffrey's chronicle somewhat, but Layamon made much larger additions, derived, no doubt, from legends current on the Welsh border. In particular, the story of Arthur grew in his hands into something like fullness. He tells of the enchantments of Merlin, the wizard ; of the unfaithfulness of Arthur's queen, Guenever, and the treachery of his nephew, Modred. His narration of the last

great battle between Arthur and Modred ; of the wounding
of the king — "fifteen fiendly wounds he had, one might in
the least three gloves thrust " — ; and of the little boat
with "two women therein, wonderly dight," which came to
bear him away to Avalun and the Queen Argante, "sheen-
est of all elves," whence he shall come again, according
to Merlin's prophecy, to rule the Britons ; all this left little, in essentials, for Tennyson to add in his *Passing of
Arthur.*

This new material for fiction was eagerly seized upon by
the Norman romancers.   The story of Arthur drew to itself
other stories which were afloat.   Walter Map, a gentleman
of the court of Henry II., in two French prose romances
connected with it the church legend of the Sangreal, or holy
cup, from which Christ had drunk at his last supper, and
which Joseph of Arimathea had afterward brought to England.   Then it miraculously disappeared and became thence-
forth the occasion of knightly quest, the mystic symbol of
the object of the soul's desire, an adventure only to be
achieved by the maiden knight, Galahad, the son of that
Launcelot who in the romances had taken the place of
Modred in Geoffrey's history as the paramour of Queen
Guenever.   In like manner the love-story of Tristan and
Isolde, which came probably from Brittany or Cornwall, was
joined by other romancers to the Arthur-saga.

Thus there grew up a great epic cycle of Arthurian
romance, with a fixed shape and a unity and vitality which
have prolonged it to our own day and rendered it capable of a deeper and more spiritual treatment and a more
artistic handling by such modern English poets as Tennyson in his *Idyls of the King*, Matthew Arnold, Swinburne, and many others.   There were innumerable Arthur
romances in prose and verse, in Anglo-Norman and conti-
nental French dialects, in English, in German, and in other
tongues.   But the final form which the saga took in mediæ-

val England was the prose *Morte Dartur* of Sir Thomas Malory, composed at the close of the 15th century. This was a digest of the earlier romances, and is Tennyson's main authority.

Beside the literature of the knight was the literature of the cloister. There is a considerable body of religious writing in early English, consisting of homilies in prose and verse, books of devotion, like the *Ancren Riwle* (Rule of Anchoresses), 1225, and the *Ayenbite of Inwyt* (Remorse of Conscience), 1340, in prose; the *Handlyng Sinne*, 1303, the *Cursor Mundi*, 1320, and the *Pricke of Conscience*, 1340, in verse; metrical renderings of the Psalter, the Pater Noster, the Creed, and the Ten Commandments; the Gospels for the Day, such as the *Ormulum*, or Book of Orm, 1205; legends and miracles of saints; poems in praise of virginity, on the contempt of the world, on the five joys of the Virgin, the five wounds of Christ, the eleven pains of hell, the seven deadly sins, the fifteen tokens of the coming judgment; and dialogues between the soul and the body. These were the work not only of the monks, but also of the begging friars, and in smaller part of the secular or parish clergy. They are full of the ascetic piety and superstition of the Middle Age, the childish belief in the marvelous, the allegorical interpretation of Scripture texts, the grotesque material horrors of hell with its grisly fiends, the vileness of the human body and the loathsome details of its corruption after death. Now and then a single poem rises above the tedious and hideous barbarism of the general level of this monkish literature, either from a more intensely personal feeling in the poet, or from an occasional grace or beauty in his verse. A poem so distinguished is, for example, *A Luve Ron* (A Love Counsel), by the Minorite friar, Thomas de Hales, one stanza of which recalls the French poet Villon's *Balade of Dead Ladies*, with its refrain—

> Mais ou sont les neiges d'antan?
> "Where are the snows of yester year?"
>
> Where is Paris and Heléyne
>   That weren so bright and fair of blee[1]
> Amadas, Tristan, and Idéyne
>   Yseudē and allē the,[2]
> Hector with his sharpē main,
>   And Cæsar rich in worldēs fee?
> They beth ygliden out of the reign[3]
>   As the shaft is of the clee.[4]

A few early English poems on secular subjects are also worthy of mention, among others, *The Owl and the Nightingale*, generally assigned to the reign of Henry III. (1216–1272), an *estrif*, or dispute, in which the owl represents the ascetic and the nightingale the æsthetic view of life. The debate is conducted with much animation and a spirited use of proverbial wisdom. *The Land of Cokaygne* is an amusing little poem of some two hundred lines, belonging to the class of *fabliaux*, short humorous tales or satirical pieces in verse. It describes a lubber-land, or fool's paradise, where the geese fly down all roasted on the spit, bringing garlic in their bills for their dressing, and where there is a nunnery upon a river of sweet milk, and an abbey of white monks and gray, whose walls, like the hall of little King Pepin, are "of pie-crust and pastry crust," with flouren cakes for the shingles and fat puddings for the pins.

There are a few songs dating from about 1300, and mostly found in a single collection (Harl. MS., 2253), which are almost the only English verse before Chaucer that has any sweetness to a modern ear. They are written in French strophic forms in the southern dialect, and sometimes have an intermixture of French and Latin lines. They are musical, fresh, simple, and many of them very pretty. They celebrate the gladness of spring with its cuckoos and throstle-cocks, its daisies and woodruff.

[1] Hue.   [2] Those.   [3] Realm.   [4] Bowstring.

When the nightingalē sings the woodēs waxen green;
Leaf and grass and blossom spring in Averil, I ween,
And love is to my hertē gone with a spear so keen,
Night and day my blood it drinks, my hertē doth me tene.[1]

Others are love plaints to "Alysoun" or some other lady whose "name is in a note of the nightingale;" whose eyes are as gray as glass, and her skin as "red as rose on ris."[2] Some employ a burden or refrain.

Blow, northern wind,
Blow thou me my sweeting,
Blow, northern wind, blow, blow, blow!

Others are touched with a light melancholy at the coming of winter.

Winter wakeneth all my care
Now these leavēs waxeth bare,
Oft I sigh and mournē sare
When it cometh in my thought
Of this worldes joy, how it goeth all to nought.

Some of these poems are love songs to Christ or the Virgin, composed in the warm language of earthly passion. The sentiment of chivalry united with the ecstatic reveries of the cloister had produced Mariolatry, and the imagery of the Song of Solomon, in which Christ wooes the soul, had made this feeling of divine love familiar. Toward the end of the 13th century a collection of lives of saints, a sort of English *Golden Legend*, was prepared at the great abbey of Gloucester for use on saints' days. The legends were chosen partly from the hagiology of the Church Catholic, as the lives of Margaret, Christopher, and Michael; partly from the calendar of the English Church, as the lives of St. Thomas of Canterbury, and of the Anglo-Saxons, Dunstan, Swithin—who is mentioned by Shakspere—and Kenelm, whose life is quoted by Chaucer in the *Nonne Preste's Tale*. The verse was

[1] Pain.   [2] Branch.

clumsy and the style monotonous, but an imaginative touch
here and there has furnished a hint to later poets. Thus the
legend of St. Brandan's search for the earthly paradise has
been treated by Matthew Arnold and William Morris.

About the middle of the 14th century there was a revival
of the Old English alliterative verse in romances like
William and the Werewolf, and *Sir Gawayne*, and in religious pieces such as *Clannesse* (purity), *Patience*, and *The
Perle*, the last named a mystical poem of much beauty, in
which a bereaved father sees a vision of his daughter among
the glorified. Some of these employed rhyme as well as
alliteration. They are in the West Midland dialect, although
Chaucer implies that alliteration was most common in the
north. "I am a sotherne man," says the parson in the
Canterbury Tales. "I cannot geste rom, ram, ruf, by my
letter." But the most important of the alliterative poems
was the *Vision of William concerning Piers the Plowman*.

In the second half of the 14th century French had ceased
to be the mother-tongue of any considerable part of the
population of England. By a statute of Edward III., in
1362, it was displaced from the law courts. By 1386 English
had taken its place in the schools. The Anglo-Norman
dialect had grown corrupt, and Chaucer contrasts the French
of Paris with the provincial French spoken by his prioress,
"after the scole of Stratford-atte-Bowe." The native English genius was also beginning to assert itself, roused in
part, perhaps, by the English victories in the wars of Edward
III. against the French. It was the bows of the English
yeomanry that won the fight at Crecy, fully as much as the
prowess of the Norman baronage. But at home the times
were bad. Heavy taxes and the repeated visitations of the
pestilence, or Black Death, pressed upon the poor and wasted
the land. The Church was corrupt; the mendicant orders
had grown enormously wealthy, and the country was eaten

up by a swarm of begging friars, pardoners, and apparitors.
That social discontent was fermenting among the lower
classes which finally issued in the communistic uprising of
the peasantry under Wat Tyler and Jack Straw.

This state of things is reflected in the *Vision of Piers
Plowman*, written as early as 1362, by William Langland, a
tonsured clerk of the west country. It is in form an allegory,
and bears some resemblance to the later and more famous
allegory of the *Pilgrim's Progress*. The poet falls asleep on
the Malvern Hills, in Worcestershire, and has a vision of a
"fair field full of folk," representing the world with its
various conditions of men. There were pilgrims and pal-
mers ; hermits with hooked staves, who went to Walsing-
ham—and their wenches after them—great lubbers and long
that were loth to work ; friars glossing the Gospel for their
own profit ; pardoners cheating the people with relics and
indulgences; parish priests who forsook their parishes—that
had been poor since the pestilence time—and went to London to sing there for simony ; bishops, archbishops, and dea-
cons, who got themselves fat clerkships in the Exchequer,
or King's Bench ; in short, all manner of lazy and corrupt
ecclesiastics. A lady, who represents holy Church, then
appears to the dreamer, explains to him the meaning of his
vision, and reads him a sermon the text of which is, "When
all treasure is tried, truth is the best." A number of other
allegorical figures are next introduced, Conscience, Reason,
Meed, Simony, Falsehood, etc., and after a series of speeches
and adventures, a second vision begins in which the seven
deadly sins pass before the poet in a succession of graphic
impersonations ; and finally all the characters set out on a
pilgrimage in search of St. Truth, finding no guide to direct
them save Piers the Plowman, who stands for the simple,
pious laboring man, the sound heart of the English common
folk. The poem was originally in eight divisions or
" passus," to which was added a continuation in three parts,

Vita Do Wel, Do Bet, and Do Best. About 1377 the whole was greatly enlarged by the author.

Piers Plowman was the first extended literary work after the Conquest which was purely English in character. It owed nothing to France but the allegorical cast which the *Roman de la Rose* had made fashionable in both countries. But even here such personified abstractions as Langland's Fair-speech and Work-when-time-is, remind us less of the Fraunchise, Bel-amour, and Fals-semblaunt of the French courtly allegories than of Bunyan's Mr. Worldly Wiseman, and even of such Puritan names as Praise-God Barebones, and Zeal-of-the-land Busy. The poem is full of English moral seriousness, of shrewd humor, the hatred of a lie, the homely English love for reality. It has little unity of plan, but is rather a series of episodes, discourses, parables, and scenes. It is all astir with the actual life of the time. We see the gossips gathered in the ale-house of Betun the brewster, and the pastry cooks in the London streets crying "Hote pies, hote! Good gees and grys.[1] Go we dine, go we!" Had Langland not linked his literary fortunes with an uncouth and obsolescent verse, and had he possessed a finer artistic sense and a higher poetic imagination, his book might have been, like Chaucer's, among the lasting glories of our tongue. As it is, it is forgotten by all but professional students of literature and history. Its popularity in its own day is shown by the number of MSS. which are extant, and by imitations, such as *Piers the Plowman's Crede* (1394), and the *Plowman's Tale*, for a long time wrongly inserted in the *Canterbury Tales*. Piers became a kind of typical figure, like the French peasant, *Jacques Bonhomme*, and was appealed to as such by the Protestant reformers of the 16th century.

The attack upon the growing corruptions of the Church was made more systematically, and from the stand-point of

---

[1] Pigs.

a theologian rather than of a popular moralist and satirist, by John Wiclif, the rector of Lutterworth and professor of divinity in Baliol College, Oxford. In a series of Latin and English tracts he made war against indulgences, pilgrimages, images, oblations, the friars, the pope, and the doctrine of transubstantiation. But his greatest service to England was his translation of the Bible, the first complete version in the mother-tongue. This he made about 1380, with the help of Nicholas Hereford, and a revision of it was made by another disciple, Purvey, some ten years later. There was no knowledge of Hebrew or Greek in England at that time, and the Wiclifite versions were made not from the original tongues but from the Latin Vulgate. In his anxiety to make his rendering close, and mindful, perhaps, of the warning in the Apocalypse, "If any man shall take away from the words of the book of this prophecy, God shall take away his part out of the book of life," Wiclif followed the Latin order of construction so literally as to make rather awkward English, translating, for example, *Quib sibi vult hoc somnium?* by *What to itself wole[1] this sweven?[2]* Purvey's revision was somewhat freer and more idiomatic. In the reigns of Henry IV. and V. it was forbidden to read or to have any of Wiclif's writings. Such of them as could be seized were publicly burned. In spite of this, copies of his Bible circulated secretly in great numbers. Forshall and Madden, in their great edition (1850), enumerate one hundred and fifty MSS. which had been consulted by them. Later translators, like Tyndale and the makers of the Authorized Version, or "King James's Bible" (1611), followed Wiclif's language in many instances ; so that he was, in truth, the first author of our biblical dialect and the founder of that great monument of noble English which has been the main conservative influence in the mother-tongue, holding it fast to many strong, pithy words and idioms that would else have been lost. In

[1] Will.   [2] Dream.

1415, some thirty years after Wiclif's death, by decree of the Council of Constance, his bones were dug up from the soil of Lutterworth chancel and burned, and the ashes cast into the Swift. "The brook," says Thomas Fuller, in his *Church History,* "did convey his ashes into Avon; Avon into Severn; Severn into the narrow seas; they into the main ocean. And thus the ashes of Wiclif are the emblem of his doctrine, which now is dispersed all the world over."

Although the writings thus far mentioned are of very high interest to the student of the English language and the historian of English manners and culture, they cannot be said to have much importance as mere literature. But in Geoffrey Chaucer (died 1400) we meet with a poet of the first rank, whose works are increasingly read and will always continue to be a source of delight and refreshment to the general reader as well as a "well of English undefiled" to the professional man of letters. With the exception of Dante, Chaucer was the greatest of the poets of mediæval Europe, and he remains one of the greatest of English poets, and certainly the foremost of English story tellers in verse. He was the son of a London vintner, and was in his youth in the service of Lionel, Duke of Clarence, one of the sons of Edward III. He made a campaign in France in 1359–60, when he was taken prisoner. Afterward he was attached to the court and received numerous favors and appointments. He was sent on several diplomatic missions by the king, three of them to Italy, where, in all probability, he made the acquaintance of the new Italian literature, the writings of Dante, Petrarch, and Boccaccio. He was appointed at different times comptroller of the wool customs, comptroller of petty customs, and clerk of the works. He sat for Kent in Parliament, and he received pensions from three successive kings. He was a man of business as well as books, and he loved men and nature no less than study. He knew his world; he " saw life steadily and saw it whole." Living

at the center of English social and political life, and resorting to the court of Edward III., then the most brilliant in
Europe, Chaucer was an eye-witness of those feudal pomps
which fill the high-colored pages of his contemporary, the
French chronicler, Froissart. His description of a tournament in the *Knight's Tale* is unexcelled for spirit and detail.
He was familiar with dances, feasts, state ceremonies, and
all the life of the baronial castle, in bower and hall : the
"trompes with the loude minstralcie," the heralds, the ladies,
and the squires. He knew—

> What hawkës sitten on the perch above,
> What houndës liggen [1] on the floor adown.

But his sympathy reached no less the life of the lowly; the
poor widow in her narrow cottage, and that "trewe swyn-
kere [2] and a good," the plowman whom Langland had made
the hero of his vision. He is, more than all English poets,
the poet of the lusty spring, of "Aprillë with her showrës
sweet" and the "foulës song;" of "May with all her flourës
and her green;" of the new leaves in the wood, and the
meadows new powdered with the daisy, the mystic Margue-
rite of his *Legend of Good Women*. A fresh vernal air
blows through all his pages.

In Chaucer's earlier works, such as the translation of the
Romaunt of the Rose (if that be his), the *Boke of the
Duchesse*, the *Parlament of Foules*, the *Hous of Fame*, as
well as in the *Legend of Good Women*, which was later, the
inspiration of the French court poetry of the 13th and 14th
centuries is manifest. He retains in them the mediæval
machinery of allegories and dreams, the elaborate descriptions of palaces, temples, portraitures, etc., which had been
made fashionable in France by such poems as Guillaume
de Lorris's *Roman de la Rose*, and Jean Machault's *La Fon-
taine Amoureuse*. In some of these the influence of Italian

---

[1] Lie.   [2] Laborer.

poetry is also perceptible. There are suggestions from Dante, for example, in the *Parlament of Foules* and the *Hous of Fame*, and *Troilus and Cresseide* is a free handling rather than a translation of Boccaccio's *Filostrato*. In all of these there are passages of great beauty and force. Had Chaucer written nothing else, he would still have been remembered as the most accomplished English poet of his time, but he would not have risen to the rank which he now occupies, as one of the greatest English poets of all time. This position he owes to his masterpiece, the *Canterbury Tales.* Here he abandoned the imitation of foreign models and the artificial literary fashions of his age, and wrote of real life from his own ripe knowledge of men and things.

The *Canterbury Tales* are a collection of stories written at different times, but put together, probably, toward the close of his life. The frame-work into which they are fitted is one of the happiest ever devised. A number of pilgrims who are going on horseback to the shrine of St. Thomas à Becket, at Canterbury, meet at the Tabard Inn, in Southwark, a suburb of London. The jolly host of the Tabard, Harry Bailey, proposes that on their way to Canterbury, each of the company shall tell two tales, and two more on their way back, and that the one who tells the best shall have a supper at the cost of the rest when they return to the inn. He himself accompanies them as judge and "reporter." In the setting of the stories there is thus a constant feeling of movement and the air of all outdoors. The little "head-links" and "end-links" which bind them together give incidents of the journey and glimpses of the talk of the pilgrims, sometimes amounting, as in the prologue of the *Wife of Bath,* to full and almost dramatic character-sketches. The stories, too, are dramatically suited to the narrators. The general prologue is a series of such character-sketches, the most perfect in English poetry. The portraits of the pilgrims are illuminated with the soft brilliancy and the minute loving fidelity of the miniatures in the old missals, and with the same quaint precision in traits of expression and in costume.   The pilgrims are not all such as one would meet nowadays at an English inn.   The presence of a knight, a squire, a yeoman archer, and especially of so many kinds of ecclesiastics, a nun, a friar, a monk, a pardoner, and a sompnour or apparitor, reminds us that the England of that day must have been less like Protestant England, as we know it, than like the Italy of some fifty years ago.   But however the outward face of society may have changed, the Canterbury pilgrims remain, in Chaucer's descriptions, living and universal types of human nature.   The *Canterbury Tales* are twenty-four in number.   There were thirty-two pilgrims, so that if finished as designed the whole collection would have numbered one hundred and twenty-eight stories.

Chaucer is the bright consummate flower of the English Middle Age.   Like many another great poet he put the final touch to the various literary forms that he found in cultivation.   Thus his *Knight's Tale*, based upon Boccaccio's *Teseide*, is the best of English mediæval romances.   And yet the *Rime of Sir Thopas*, who goes seeking an elf queen for his mate, and is encountered by the giant Sir Olifaunt, burlesques these same romances with their impossible adventures and their tedious rambling descriptions.   The tales of the prioress and the second nun are saints' legends.   The *Monk's Tale* is a set of dry, moral apologues in the manner of his contemporary, the "moral Gower."   The stories told by the reeve, miller, friar, sompnour, shipman, and merchant belong to the class of *fabliaux*, a few of which existed in English, such as *Dame Siriz*, the *Lay of the Ash*, and the *Land of Cokaygne*, already mentioned.   The *Nonne Preste's Tale*, likewise, which Dryden modernized with admirable humor, was of the class of *fabliaux*, and was suggested by a little poem in forty lines, *Dou Coc et Werpil*, by Marie de France, a Norman poetess of the 13th century.   It belonged, like the early English poem of *The Fox and the Wolf*, to the popular animal saga of *Reynard the Fox*. The *Franklin's Tale*, whose scene is Brittany, and the *Wife of Bath's Tale* which is laid in the time of the British Arthur, belong to the class of French *lais*, serious metrical tales shorter than the romance and of Breton origin, the best representatives of which are the elegant and graceful *lais* of Marie de France.

Chaucer was our first great master of laughter and of tears. His serious poetry is full of the tenderest pathos. His loosest tales are delightfully humorous and life-like. He is the kindliest of satirists. The knavery, greed, and hypocrisy of the begging friars and the sellers of indulgences are exposed by him as pitilessly as by Langland and Wiclif, though his mood is not, like theirs, one of stern, moral indignation, but rather the good-natured scorn of a man of the world. His charity is broad enough to cover even the corrupt sompnour, of whom he says,

> And yet in sooth he was a good felawe.

Whether he shared Wiclif's opinions is unknown, but John of Gaunt, the Duke of Lancaster and father of Henry IV., who was Chaucer's life-long patron, was likewise Wiclif's great upholder against the persecution of the bishops. It is, perhaps, not without significance that the poor parson in the *Canterbury Tales*, the only one of his ecclesiastical pilgrims whom Chaucer treats with respect, is suspected by the host of the Tabard to be a "loller," that is, a Lollard, or disciple of Wiclif, and that, because he objects to the jovial innkeeper's swearing "by Goddes bones."

Chaucer's English is nearly as easy for a modern reader as Shakspere's, and few of his words have become obsolete. His verse, when rightly read, is correct and melodious. The early English was, in some respects, "more sweet upon the tongue" than the modern language. The vowels had their broad Italian sounds, and the speech was full of soft gutterals and vocalic syllables, like the endings ën, ës, ë, which made feminine rhymes and kept the consonants from coming harshly together.

Great poet as Chaucer was, he was not quite free from the literary weakness of his time. He relapses sometimes into the babbling style of the old chroniclers and legend writers; cites "auctours" and gives long catalogues of names and objects with a *naïve* display of learning; and introduces vulgar details in his most exquisite passages. There is something childish about almost all the thought and art of the Middle Ages—at least outside of Italy, where classical models and traditions never quite lost their hold. But Chaucer's artlessness is half the secret of his wonderful ease in story-telling, and is so engaging that, like a child's sweet unconsciousness, one would not wish it otherwise.

The *Canterbury Tales* had shown of what high uses the English language was capable, but the curiously trilingual condition of literature still continued. French was spoken in the proceedings of Parliament as late as the reign of Henry VI. (1422–1471). Chaucer's contemporary, John Gower, wrote his *Vox Clamantis* in Latin, his *Speculum Meditantis* (a lost poem), and a number of *ballades* in Parisian French, and his *Confessio Amantis* (1393) in English. The last named is a dreary, pedantic work, in some fifteen thousand smooth, monotonous, eight-syllabled couplets, in which Grande Amour instructs the lover how to get the love of Bel Pucel.

———

1. Early English Literature. Bernhard ten Brink. Translated from the German by H. M. Kennedy. New York: Henry Holt & Co., 1883.

2. Morris and Skeat's Specimens of Early English. (Clarendon Press Series.) Oxford.

3. The Vision of William concerning Piers the Plowman. Edited by W. W. Skeat.   Oxford, 1886.

4. Chaucer's Canterbury Tales.   Tyrwhitt's Edition.   New York: D. Appleton & Co., 1883.

5. The Poetical Works of Geoffrey Chaucer.   Edited by Richard Morris.   London: Bell & Daldy (6 volumes.)

CHAPTER II.

FROM CHAUCER TO SPENSER.

1400–1599.

THE 15th century was a barren period in English literary history. It was nearly two hundred years after Chaucer's death before any poet came whose name can be written in the same line with his. He was followed at once by a number of imitators who caught the trick of his language and verse, but lacked the genius to make any fine use of them. The *manner* of a true poet may be learned, but his style, in the high sense of the word, remains his own secret. Some of the poems which have been attributed to Chaucer and printed in editions of his works, as the *Court of Love*, the *Flower and the Leaf*, the *Cuckow and the Nightingale*, are now regarded by many scholars as the work of later writers. If not Chaucer's, they are of Chaucer's school, and the first two, at least, are very pretty poems after the fashion of his minor pieces, such as the *Boke of the Duchesse* and the *Parlament of Foules*.

Among his professed disciples was Thomas Occleve, a dull rhymer, who, in his *Governail of Princes*, a didactic poem translated from the Latin about 1413, drew, or caused to be drawn, on the margin of his MS. a colored portrait of his "maister dere and fader reverent."

> This londës verray tresour and richesse
> Dethe by thy dethe hath harm irreparable
> Unto us done; hir vengeable duresse
> Dispoilēd hath this londe of the swetnésse
> Of Rhetoryk.

Another versifier of this same generation was John Lydgate, a Benedictine monk of the Abbey of Bury St. Edmunds,

in Suffolk, a very prolix writer, who composed, among other
things, the *Story of Thebes*, as an addition to the *Canterbury Tales*. His ballad of *London Lyckpenny*, recounting
the adventures of a countryman who goes to the law courts
at Westminster in search of justice—

> But for lack of mony I could not spede—

is of interest for the glimpse that it gives us of London street
life.

Chaucer's influence wrought more fruitfully in Scotland,
whither it was carried by James I., who had been captured
by the English when a boy of eleven, and brought up at
Windsor as a prisoner of state. There he wrote during the
reign of Henry V. (1413–1422) a poem in six cantos, entitled
the *King's Quhair* (King's Book), in Chaucer's seven-lined
stanza, which had been employed by Lydgate in his *Falls of
Princes* (from Boccaccio), and which was afterward called
the "rime royal," from its use by King James. The *King's
Quhair* tells how the poet, on a May morning, looks from
the window of his prison chamber into the castle garden full
of alleys, hawthorn hedges, and fair arbors set with

> The sharpë, greenë, sweetë juniper.

He was listening to "the little sweetë nightingale," when
suddenly casting down his eyes he saw a lady walking in
the garden, and at once his "heart became her thrall."
The incident is precisely like Palamon's first sight of Emily
in Chaucer's *Knight's Tale*, and almost in the very words of
Palamon the poet addresses his lady:

> Ah, sweet, are ye a worldly crēatúre
> Or heavenly thing in likeness of natúre?
> Or are ye very Nature, the goddéss,
> That have depainted with your heavenly hand
> This garden full of flowrës as they stand?

Then, after a vision in the taste of the age, in which the
royal prisoner is transported in turn to the courts of *Venus*,

Minerva, and *Fortune*, and receives their instruction in the duties belonging to Love's service, he wakes from sleep and a white turtle-dove brings to his window a spray of red gilly flowers, whose leaves are inscribed, in golden letters, with a message of encouragement.

James I. may be reckoned among the English poets. He mentions Chaucer, Gower, and Lydgate as his masters. His education was English, and so was the dialect of his poem, although the unique MS. of it is in the Scotch spelling. The *King's Quhair* is somewhat overladen with ornament and with the fashionable allegorical devices, but it is, upon the whole, a rich and tender love song, the best specimen of court poetry between the time of Chaucer and the time of Spenser. The lady who walked in the garden on that May morning was Jane Beaufort, niece to Henry IV. She was married to her poet after his release from captivity and became queen of Scotland in 1424. Twelve years later James was murdered by Sir Robert Graham and his Highlanders, and his wife, who strove to defend him, was wounded by the assassins. The story of the murder has been told of late by D. G. Rossetti, in his ballad, *The King's Tragedy.* The whole life of this princely singer was, like his poem, in the very spirit of romance.

The effect of all this imitation of Chaucer was to fix a standard of literary style, and to confirm the authority of the East-Midland English in which he had written. Though the poets of the 15th century were not overburdened with genius, they had, at least, a definite model to follow. As in the 14th century, metrical romances continued to be translated from the French, homilies and saints' legends and rhyming chronicles were still manufactured. But the poems of Occleve and Lydgate and James I. had helped to polish and refine the tongue and to prolong the Chaucerian tradition. The literary English never again slipped back into the chaos of dialects which had prevailed before Chaucer.

In the history of every literature the development of prose is later than that of verse. The latter being, by its very form, artificial, is cultivated as a fine art, and its records preserved in an early stage of society, when prose is simply the talk of men, and not thought worthy of being written and kept. English prose labored under the added disadvantage of competing with Latin, which was the cosmopolitan tongue and the medium of communication between scholars of all countries. Latin was the language of the Church, and in the Middle Ages churchman and scholar were convertible terms. The word *clerk* meant either priest or scholar. Two of the *Canterbury Tales* are in prose, as is also the *Testament of Love*, formerly ascribed to Chaucer, and the style of all these is so feeble, wandering, and unformed that it is hard to believe that they were written by the same man who wrote the *Knight's Tale* and the story of Griselda. *The Voiage and Travaile of Sir John Maundeville*—the forerunner of that great library of oriental travel which has enriched our modern literature—was written, according to its author, first in Latin, then in French, and, lastly, in the year 1356, translated into English for the behoof of "lordes and knyghtes and othere noble and worthi men, that conne [1] not Latyn but litylle." The author professed to have spent over thirty years in Eastern travel, to have penetrated as far as Farther India and the "iles that ben abouten Indi," to have been in the service of the Sultan of Babylon in his wars against the Bedouins, and, at another time, in the employ of the Great Khan of Tartary. But there is no copy of the Latin version of his travels extant; the French seems to be much later than 1356, and the English MS. to belong to the early years of the 15th century, and to have been made by another hand. Recent investigations make it probable that Maundeville borrowed his descriptions of the remoter East from many sources, and particularly from the narrative

[1] Know.

of Odoric, a Minorite friar of Lombardy, who wrote about 1330. Some doubt is even cast upon the existence of any such person as Maundeville. Whoever wrote the book that passes under his name, however, would seem to have visited the Holy Land, and the part of the "voiage" that describes Palestine and the Levant is fairly close to the truth. The rest of the work, so far as it is not taken from the tales of other travelers, is a diverting tissue of fables about gryfouns that fly away with yokes of oxen, tribes of one-legged Ethiopians who shelter themselves from the sun by using their monstrous feet as umbrellas, etc.

During the 15th century English prose was gradually being brought into a shape fitting it for more serious uses. In the controversy between the Church and the Lollards Latin was still mainly employed, but Wiclif had written some of his tracts in English, and, in 1449, Reginald Peacock, Bishop of St. Asaph, contributed, in English, to the same controversy, *The Repressor of Overmuch Blaming of the Clergy.* Sir John Fortescue, who was chief-justice of the King's Bench from 1442–1460, wrote during the reign of Edward IV. a book on the *Difference between Absolute and Limited Monarchy*, which may be regarded as the first treatise on political philosophy and constitutional law in the language. But these works hardly belong to pure literature, and are remarkable only as early, though not very good, examples of English prose in a barren time. The 15th century was an era of decay and change. The Middle Age was dying, Church and State were slowly disintegrating under the new intellectual influences that were working secretly under ground. In England the civil wars of the Red and White Roses were breaking up the old feudal society by decimating and impoverishing the baronage, thus preparing the way for the centralized monarchy of the Tudors. Toward the close of that century, and early in the next, happened the four great events, or series of events, which freed and widened men's minds, and, in a succession of shocks, overthrew the mediæval system of life and thought. These were the invention of printing, the Renaissance, or revival of classical learning, the discovery of America, and the Protestant Reformation.

William Caxton, the first English printer, learned the art in Cologne. In 1476 he set up his press and sign, a red pole, in the Almonry at Westminster. Just before the introduction of printing the demand for MS. copies had grown very active, stimulated, perhaps, by the coming into general use of linen paper instead of the more costly parchment. The scriptoria of the monasteries were the places where the transcribing and illuminating of MSS. went on, professional copyists resorting to Westminster Abbey, for example, to make their copies of books belonging to the monastic library. Caxton's choice of a spot was, therefore, significant. His new art for multiplying copies began to supersede the old method of transcription at the very head-quarters of the MS. makers. The first book that bears his Westminster imprint was the *Dictes and Sayings of the Philosophers*, translated from the French by Anthony Woodville, Lord Rivers, a brother-in-law of Edward IV. The list of books printed by Caxton is interesting, as showing the taste of the time, since he naturally selected what was most in demand. The list shows that manuals of devotion and chivalry were still in chief request, books like the *Order of Chivalry, Faits of Arms*, and the *Golden Legend*, which last Caxton translated himself, as well as *Reynard the Fox*, and a French version of the *Æneid*. He also printed, with continuations of his own, revisions of several early chronicles, and editions of Chaucer, Gower, and Lydgate. A translation of *Cicero on Friendship*, made directly from the Latin, by Thomas Tiptoft, Earl of Worcester, was printed by Caxton, but no edition of a classical author in the original. The new learning of the Renaissance had not, as yet, taken much hold in England.

Upon the whole the productions of Caxton's press were mostly of a kind that may be described as mediæval, and the most important of them, if we except his edition of Chaucer, was that "noble and joyous book," as Caxton called it, *Le Morte Dartur*, written by Sir Thomas Malory in 1469, and printed by Caxton in 1485. This was a compilation from French Arthur romances, and was by far the best English prose that had yet been written. It may be doubted, indeed, whether, for purposes of simple story telling, the picturesque charm of Malory's style has been improved upon. The episode which lends its name to the whole romance, the death of Arthur, is most impressively told, and Tennyson has followed Malory's narrative closely, even to such details of the scene as the little chapel by the sea, the moonlight, and the answer which Sir Bedwere made the wounded king, when bidden to throw Excalibur into the water, "'What saw thou there?' said the king. 'Sir,' he said, 'I saw nothing but the waters wap and the waves wan.'"

> I heard the ripple washing in the reeds
> And the wild water lapping on the crag.

And very touching and beautiful is the oft-quoted lament of Sir Ector over Launcelot, in Malory's final chapter : "'Ah, Launcelot,' he said, 'thou were head of all Christian knights; and now I dare say,' said Sir Ector, 'thou, Sir Launcelot, there thou liest, that thou were never matched of earthly knight's hand; and thou were the courtiest knight that ever bare shield ; and thou were the truest friend to thy lover that ever bestrode horse ; and thou were the truest lover of a sinful man that ever loved woman; and thou were the kindest man that ever strake with sword; and thou were the goodliest person that ever came among press of knights ; and thou were the meekest man and the gentlest that ever ate in hall among ladies; and thou were the sternest knight to thy mortal foe that ever put spear in the rest.'"

Equally good, as an example of English prose narrative, was the translation made by John Bourchier, Lord Berners, of that most brilliant of the French chroniclers, Chaucer's contemporary, Sir John Froissart. Lord Berners was the English governor of Calais, and his version of Froissart s *Chronicles* was made in 1523–1525, at the request of Henry VIII. In these two books English chivalry spoke its last genuine word. In Sir Philip Sidney the character of the knight was merged into that of the modern gentleman. And although tournaments were still held in the reign of Elizabeth, and Spenser cast his *Faerie Queene* into the form of a chivalry romance, these were but a ceremonial survival and literary tradition from an order of things that had passed away. How antagonistic the new classical culture was to the vanished ideal of the Middle Age may be read in *Toxophilus*, a treatise on archery published in 1545, by Roger Ascham, a Greek lecturer in Cambridge, and the tutor of the Princess Elizabeth and of Lady Jane Grey: "In our forefathers' time, when papistry as a standing pool covered and overflowed all England, few books were read in our tongue saving certain books of chivalry, as they said, for pastime and pleasure, which, as some say, were made in monasteries by idle monks or wanton canons: as one, for example, *Morte Arthure*, the whole pleasure of which book standeth in two special points, in open manslaughter and bold bawdry. This is good stuff for wise men to laugh at or honest men to take pleasure at. Yet I know when God's Bible was banished the court, and *Morte Arthure* received into the prince's chamber."

The fashionable school of courtly allegory, first introduced into England by the translation of the *Romaunt of the Rose*, reached its extremity in Stephen Hawes's *Passetyme of Pleasure*, printed by Caxton's successor, Wynkyn de Worde, in 1517. This was a dreary and pedantic poem, in which it is told how Graunde Amoure, after a long series of adventures and instructions among such shadowy personages as Verite, Observaunce, Falshed, and Good Operacion, finally won the love of La Belle Pucel. Hawes was the last English poet of note whose culture was exclusively mediæval. His contemporary, John Skelton, mingled the old fashions with the new classical learning. In his *Bowge of Courte* (Court Entertainment or Dole), and in others of his earlier pieces, he used, like Hawes, Chaucer's seven-lined stanza. But his later poems were mostly written in a verse of his own invention, called after him *Skeltonical*. This was a sort of glorified doggerel, in short, swift, ragged lines, with occasional intermixture of French and Latin.

> Her beautye to augment.
> Dame Nature hath her lent
> A warte upon her cheke,
> Who so lyst to seke
> In her vyságe a skar
> That semyth from afar
> Lyke to the radiant star,
> All with favour fret,
> So properly it is set.
> She is the vyolet,
> The daysy delectáble,
> The columbine commendáble,
> The jelofer [1] amyáble;
> For this most goodly floure,
> This blossom of fressh colóur,
> So Jupiter me succoúr,
> She flourysheth new and new
> In beaute and vertéw;
> *Hac claritate gemina,*
> *O gloriosa femina,* etc.

Skelton was a rude railing rhymer, a singular mixture of a true and original poet with a buffoon; coarse as Rabelais, whimsical, obscure, but always vivacious. He was the rector of Diss, in Norfolk, but his profane and scurrilous wit seems

[1] Gilliflower.

rather out of keeping with his clerical character. His *Tunnyng of Elynoure Rummyng* is a study of very low life, reminding one slightly of Burns's *Jolly Beggars*. His *Phyllyp Sparrowe* is a sportive, pretty, fantastic elegy on the death of a pet bird belonging to Mistress Joanna Scroupe, of Carowe, and has been compared to the Latin poet Catullus's elegy on Lesbia's sparrow. In *Speke, Parrot*, and *Why Come ye not to Courte?* he assailed the powerful Cardinal Wolsey with the most ferocious satire, and was, in consequence, obliged to take sanctuary at Westminster, where he died in 1529. Skelton was a classical scholar, and at one time tutor to Henry VIII. The great humanist, Erasmus, spoke of him as the "one light and ornament of British letters." Caxton asserts that he had read Vergil, Ovid, and Tully, and quaintly adds, "I suppose he hath dronken of Elycon's well."

In refreshing contrast with the artificial court poetry of the 15th and first three quarters of the 16th century, was the folk-poetry, the popular ballad literature which was handed down by oral tradition. The English and Scotch ballads were narrative songs, written in a variety of meters, but chiefly in what is known as the ballad stanza.

> In somer, when the shawes [1] be shene, [2]
>   And leves be large and longe,
> Hit is full merry in feyre forést,
>   To here the foulys song.
>
> To se the dere draw to the dale,
>   And leve the hillës hee, [3]
> And shadow them in the levës grene,
>   Under the grene-wode tree.

It is not possible to assign a definite date to these ballads. They lived on the lips of the people, and were seldom reduced to writing till many years after they were first composed and sung. Meanwhile they underwent repeated

---

[1] Woods.   [2] Bright.   [3] High.

changes, so that we have numerous versions of the same story. They belonged to no particular author, but, like all folk-lore, were handled freely by the unknown poets, minstrels, and ballad reciters, who modernized their language, added to them, or corrupted them, and passed them along. Coming out of an uncertain past, based on some dark legend of heart-break or bloodshed, they bear no poet's name, but are *ferae naturae*, and have the flavor of wild game. In the form in which they are preserved, few of them are older than the 17th or the latter part of the 16th century, though many, in their original shape, are doubtless much older. A very few of the Robin Hood ballads go back to the 15th century, and to the same period is assigned the charming ballad of the *Nut Brown Maid* and the famous border ballad of *Chevy Chase*, which describes a battle between the retainers of the two great houses of Douglas and Percy. It was this song of which Sir Philip Sidney wrote, "I never heard the old song of Percy and Douglas but I found myself more moved than by a trumpet; and yet it is sung but by some blind crouder,[1] with no rougher voice than rude style." But the style of the ballads was not always rude. In their compressed energy of expression, in the impassioned way in which they tell their tale of grief and horror, there reside often a tragic power and art superior to any thing in English poetry between Chaucer and Spenser; superior to any thing in Chaucer and Spenser themselves, in the quality of intensity. The true home of the ballad literature was "the north country," and especially the Scotch border, where the constant forays of moss-troopers and the raids and private warfare of the lords of the marches supplied many traditions of heroism, like those celebrated in the old poem of the *Battle of Otterbourne*, and in the *Hunting of the Cheviot*, or *Chevy Chase*, already mentioned. Some of these are Scotch and others English; the dialect of Lowland

[1] Fiddler.

Scotland did not, in effect, differ much from that of North-
umberland and Yorkshire, both descended alike from the
old Northumbrian of Anglo-Saxon times. Other ballads
were shortened, popular versions of the chivalry romances,
which were passing out of fashion among educated readers in the 16th century and now fell into the hands of
the ballad makers. Others preserved the memory of local
country-side tales, family feuds, and tragic incidents, partly
historical and partly legendary, associated often with particular spots. Such are, for example, *The Dowie Dens of
Yarrow, Fair Helen of Kirkconnell, The Forsaken Bride*,
and *The Twa Corbies*. Others, again, have a coloring of
popular superstition, like the beautiful ballad concerning
Thomas of Ersyldoune, who goes in at Eildon Hill with an
elf queen and spends seven years in fairy land.

But the most popular of all the ballads were those which
cluster about the name of that good outlaw, Robin Hood,
who, with his merry men, hunted the forest of Sher-
wood, where he killed the king's deer and waylaid rich
travelers, but was kind to poor knights and honest workmen.
Robin Hood is the true ballad hero, the darling of the
common people as Arthur was of the nobles. The names of
his confessor, Friar Tuck ; his mistress, Maid Marian ; his
companions, Little John, Scathelock, and Much, the miller's
son, were as familiar as household words. Langland in the
14th century mentions " rimes of Robin Hood," and efforts
have been made to identify him with some actual personage,
as with one of the dispossessed barons who had been adherents
of Simon de Montfort in his war against Henry III. But
there seems to be nothing historical about Robin Hood. He
was a creation of the popular fancy. The game laws under
the Norman kings were very oppressive, and there were,
doubtless, dim memories still cherished among the Saxon
masses of Hereward and Edric the Wild, who had defied the
power of the Conqueror, as well as of later freebooters, who

had taken to the woods and lived by plunder. Robin Hood was a thoroughly national character. He had the English love of fair play, the English readiness to shake hands and make up, and keep no malice when worsted in a square fight. He beat and plundered the fat bishops and abbots, who had more than their share of wealth, but he was generous and hospitable to the distressed, and lived a free and careless life in the good green wood. He was a mighty archer with those national weapons, the long-bow and the cloth-yard shaft. He tricked and baffled legal authority in the person of the proud sheriff of Nottingham, thereby appealing to that secret sympathy with lawless adventure which marked the free-born, vigorous yeomanry of England. And, finally, the scenery of the forest gives a poetic background and a never-failing charm to the exploits of "the old Robin Hood of England" and his merry men.

The ballads came, in time, to have certain tricks of style, such as are apt to characterize a body of anonymous folk-poetry. Such is their use of conventional epithets; "the red, red gold," "the good green wood," "the gray goose wing." Such are certain recurring terms of phrase like,

> But out and spak their stepmother.

Such is, finally, a kind of sing-song repetition, which doubtless helped the ballad singer to memorize his stock, as, for example,

> She had'na pu'd a double rose,
> A rose but only twae.

Or again,

> And mony ane sings o' grass, o' grass,
> And mony ane sings o' corn;
> An mony ane sings o' Robin Hood,
> Kens little whare he was born.
>
> It was na in the ha', the ha',
> Nor in the painted bower;
> But it was in the gude green wood,
> Amang the lily flower.

Copies of some of these old ballads were hawked about in the 16th century, printed in black letter, "broadsides," or single sheets. Wynkyn de Worde printed in 1489 *A Lytell Geste of Robin Hood*, which is a sort of digest of earlier ballads on the subject. In the 17th century a few of the English popular ballads were collected in miscellanies called *Garlands*. Early in the 18th century the Scotch poet, Allan Ramsay, published a number of Scotch ballads in the *Evergreen* and *Tea-Table Miscellany*. But no large and important collection was put forth until Percy's *Reliques* (1765), a book which had a powerful influence upon Wordsworth and Walter Scott. In Scotland some excellent ballads in the ancient manner were written in the 18th century, such as Jane Elliott's *Lament for Flodden*, and the fine ballad of *Sir Patrick Spence*. Walter Scott's *Proud Maisie is in the Wood*, is a perfect reproduction of the pregnant, indirect method of the old ballad makers.

In 1453 Constantinople was taken by the Turks, and many Greek scholars, with their manuscripts, fled into Italy, where they began teaching their language and literature, and especially the philosophy of Plato. There had been little or no knowledge of Greek in western Europe during the Middle Ages, and only a very imperfect knowledge of the Latin classics. Ovid and Statius were widely read, and so was the late Latin poet, Boethius, whose *De Consolatione Philosophiæ* had been translated into English by King Alfred and by Chaucer. Little was known of Vergil at first hand, and he was popularly supposed to have been a mighty wizard, who made sundry works of enchantment at Rome, such as a magic mirror and statue. Caxton's so-called translation of the *Æneid* was in reality nothing but a version of a French romance based on Vergil's epic. Of the Roman historians, orators, and moralists, such as Livy, Tacitus, Cæsar, Cicero, and Seneca, there was almost entire ignorance, as also of poets like Horace, Lucretius, Juvenal, and

Catullus. The gradual rediscovery of the remains of ancient art and literature which took place in the 15th century,
and largely in Italy, worked an immense revolution in the
mind of Europe. Manuscripts were brought out of their
hiding places, edited by scholars, and spread abroad by
means of the printing-press. Statues were dug up and
placed in museums, and men became acquainted with a civilization far more mature than that of the Middle Age, and
with models of perfect workmanship in letters and the fine
arts.

In the latter years of the 15th century a number of Englishmen learned Greek in Italy and brought it back with
them to England. William Grocyn and Thomas Linacre, who
had studied at Florence under the refugee, Demetrius Chal-
condylas, began teaching Greek at Oxford, the former as early
as 1491. A little later John Colet, Dean of St. Paul's and
the founder of St. Paul's School, and his friend, William
Lily, the grammarian, and first master of St. Paul's (1500),
also studied Greek abroad; Colet in Italy, and Lily at
Rhodes and in the city of Rome. Thomas More, afterward
the famous chancellor of Henry VIII., was among the pupils
of Grocyn and Linacre at Oxford. Thither also, in 1497,
came, in search of the new knowledge, the Dutchman,
Erasmus, who became the foremost scholar of his time. From
Oxford the study spread to the sister university, where the
first English Grecian of his day, Sir John Cheke, who
"taught Cambridge and King Edward Greek," became the
incumbent of the new professorship founded about 1540.
Among his pupils was Roger Ascham, already mentioned, in
whose time St. John's College, Cambridge, was the chief
seat of the new learning, of which Thomas Nashe testifies
that it "was an universitie within itself; having more candles
light in it, every winter morning before four of the clock,
than the four of clock bell gave strokes." Greek was not
introduced at the universities without violent opposition from

the conservative element, who were nicknamed Trojans. The opposition came in part from the priests, who feared that that new study would sow seeds of heresy. Yet many of the most devout churchmen were friends of a more liberal culture, among them Thomas More, whose Catholicism was undoubted and who went to the block for his religion. Cardinal Wolsey, whom More succeeded as chancellor, was also a munificent patron of learning, and founded Christ Church College at Oxford. Popular education at once felt the impulse of the new studies, and over twenty endowed grammar schools were established in England in the first twenty years of the 16th century. Greek became a passion even with English ladies. Ascham in his *Schoolmaster*, a treatise on education, published in 1570, says that Queen Elizabeth "readeth here now at Windsor more Greek every day, than some prebendarie of this Church doth read Latin in a whole week." And in the same book he tells how, calling once on Lady Jane Grey, at Brodegate, in Leicestershire, he "found her in her chamber reading *Phædon Platonis* in Greek, and that with as much delite as some gentlemen would read a merry tale in *Bocase*," and when he asked her why she had not gone hunting with the rest, she answered, "I wisse,[1] all their sport in the park is but a shadow to that pleasure that I find in Plato." Ascham's *Schoolmaster*, as well as his earlier book, *Toxophilus*, a Platonic dialogue on archery, bristles with quotations from the Greek and Latin classics, and with that perpetual reference to the authority of antiquity on every topic that he touches, which remained the fashion in all serious prose down to the time of Dryden.

One speedy result of the new learning was fresh translations of the Scriptures into English out of the original tongues. In 1525 William Tyndal printed at Cologne and Worms his version of the New Testament from the Greek.

[1] Surely; a corruption of the Anglo-Saxon *gewis*.

Ten years later Miles Coverdale made, at Zurich, a translation of the whole Bible from the German and Latin. These were the basis of numerous later translations, and the strong beautiful English of Tyndal's Testament is preserved for the most part in our Authorized Version (1611). At first it was not safe to make or distribute these early translations in England. Numbers of copies were brought into the country, however, and did much to promote the cause of the Reformation. After Henry VIII. had broken with the pope the new English Bible circulated freely among the people. Tyndal and Sir Thomas More carried on a vigorous controversy in English upon some of the questions at issue between the Church and the Protestants. Other important contributions to the literature of the Reformation were the homely sermons preached at Westminster and at Paul's Cross by Bishop Hugh Latimer, who was burned at Oxford in the reign of Bloody Mary. The English Book of Common Prayer was compiled in 1549–1552. More was, perhaps, the best representative of a group of scholars who wished to enlighten and reform the Church from the inside, but who refused to follow Henry VIII. in his breach with Rome. Dean Colet and John Fisher, Bishop of Rochester, belonged to the same company, and Fisher was beheaded in the same year (1535) with More, and for the same offense, namely, refusing to take the oath to maintain the act confirming the king's divorce from Catharine of Arragon and his marriage with Anne Boleyn. More's philosophy is best reflected in his *Utopia*, the description of an ideal commonwealth, modeled on Plato's *Republic*, and printed in 1516. The name signifies "no place" (οὐ τόπος), and has furnished an adjective to the language. The *Utopia* was in Latin, but More's *History of Edward V. and Richard III.* written 1513, though not printed till 1557, was in English. It is the first example in the tongue of a history as distinguished from a chronicle; that is, it is a reasoned and artistic

presentation of an historic period, and not a mere chronological narrative of events.

The first three quarters of the 16th century produced no
great original work of literature in England. It was a season of preparation, of education.   The storms of the Reformation interrupted and delayed the literary renascence
through the reigns of Henry VIII., Edward VI., and Queen
Mary. When Elizabeth came to the throne, in 1558, a more
settled order of things began, and a period of great national
prosperity and glory.   Meanwhile the English mind had
been slowly assimilating the new classical culture, which
was extended to all classes of readers by the numerous translations of Greek and Latin authors. A fresh poetic impulse
came from Italy.   In 1557 appeared · *Tottel's Miscellany*,
containing songs and sonnets by a " new company of courtly
makers."   Most of the pieces in the volume had been written
years before by gentlemen of Henry VIII.'s court, and circulated in manuscript. The two chief contributors were Sir
Thomas Wiat, at one time English embassador to Spain, and
that brilliant noble, Henry Howard, the Earl of Surrey, who
was beheaded in 1547 for quartering the king's arms with
his own. Both of them were dead long before their work
was printed.   The verses in *Tottel's Miscellany* show very
clearly the influence of Italian poetry. We have seen that
Chaucer took subjects and something more from Boccaccio
and Petrarch. But the sonnet, which Petrarch had brought
to perfection, was first introduced into England by Wiat.
There was a great revival of sonneteering in Italy in
the 16th century, and a number of Wiat's poems were
adaptations of the sonnets and *canzoni* of Petrarch and
later poets.   Others were imitations of Horace's satires and
epistles. Surrey introduced the Italian blank verse into
English in his translation of two books of the *Æneid*. The
love poetry of *Tottel's Miscellany* is polished and artificial,
like the models which it followed. Dante's Beatrice was a

child, and so was Petrarch's Laura. Following their example, Surrey addressed his love complaints, by way of compliment, to a little girl of the noble Irish family of Geraldine. The Amourists, or love sonneteers, dwelt on the metaphysics of the passion with a tedious minuteness, and the conventional nature of their sighs and complaints may often be guessed by an experienced reader from the titles of their poems: " Description of the restless state of a lover, with suit to his lady to rue on his dying heart; " Hell tormenteth not the damned ghosts so sore as unkindness the lover; " "The lover prayeth not to be disdained, refused, mistrusted nor forsaken," etc. The most genuine utterance of Surrey was his poem written while imprisoned in Windsor—a cage where so many a song-bird has grown vocal. And Wiat's little piece of eight lines, " Of his Return from Spain," is worth reams of his amatory affectations. Nevertheless the writers in *Tottel's Miscellany* were real reformers of English poetry. They introduced new models of style and new metrical forms, and they broke away from the mediæval traditions which had hitherto obtained. The language had undergone some changes since Chaucer's time, which made his scansion obsolete. The accent of many words of French origin, like *natúre, couráge, virtúe, matére*, had shifted to the first syllable, and the *e* of the final syllables *ĕs, ĕn, ĕd,* and *ĕ*, had largely disappeared. But the language of poetry tends to keep up archaisms of this kind, and in Stephen Hawes, who wrote a century after Chaucer, we still find such lines as these:

> But he my strokēs might right well endure,
> He was so great and huge of puissánce.[1]

Hawes's practice is variable in this respect, and so is his contemporary, Skelton's. But in Wiat and Surrey, who wrote only a few years later, the reader first feels sure

[1] Trisyllable—like crĕatúre neighĕboúr, etc., in Chaucer.

3

that he is reading verse pronounced quite in the modern fashion.

But Chaucer's example still continued potent. Spenser revived many of his obsolete words, both in his pastorals and in his *Faerie Queene*, thereby imparting an antique remoteness to his diction, but incurring Ben Jonson's censure, that he "writ no language." A poem that stands midway between Spenser and the late mediæval work of Chaucer's school— such as Hawes's *Passetyme of Pleasure* —was the induction contributed by Thomas Sackville, Lord Buckhurst, in 1563 to a collection of narrative poems called the *Mirrour for Magistrates*. The whole series was the work of many hands, modeled upon Lydgate's *Falls of Princes* (taken from Boccaccio), and was designed as a warning to great men of the fickleness of fortune. The *Induction* is the only noteworthy part of it. It was an allegory, written in Chaucer's seven-lined stanza, and described, with a somber imaginative power, the figure of Sorrow, her abode in the "griesly lake" of Avernus, and her attendants, Remorse, Dread, Old Age, etc. Sackville was the author of the first regular English tragedy *Gorboduc;* and it was at his request that Ascham wrote the *Schoolmaster.*

Italian poetry also fed the genius of Edmund Spenser (1552–1599). While a student at Pembroke Hall, Cambridge, he had translated some of the *Visions of Petrarch*, and the *Visions of Bellay*, a French poet, but it was only in 1579 that the publication of his *Shepheard's Calendar* announced the coming of a great original poet, the first since Chaucer. The *Shepheard's Calendar* was a pastoral in twelve eclogues —one for each month in the year. There had been a revival of pastoral poetry in Italy and France, but, with one or two insignificant exceptions, Spenser's were the first bucolics in English. Two of his eclogues were paraphrases from Clement Marot, a French Protestant poet, whose psalms were greatly in fashion at the court of Francis I. The pas-

toral machinery had been used by Vergil and by his modern
imitators, not merely to portray the loves of Strephon and
Chloe, or the idyllic charms of rustic life; but also as a
vehicle of compliment, elegy, satire, and personal allusion of
many kinds. Spenser, accordingly, alluded to his friends,
Sidney and Harvey, as the shepherds Astrophel and Hob-
binol; paid court to Queen Elizabeth as Cynthia; and introduced, in the form of anagrams, names of the High-Church
Bishop of London, Aylmer, and the Low-Church Archbishop
Grindal. The conventional pastoral is a somewhat delicate
exotic in English poetry, and represents a very unreal Arcadia. Before the end of the 17th century the squeak of the
oaten pipe had become a burden, and the only poem of the
kind which it is easy to read without some impatience is
Milton's wonderful *Lycidas.* The *Shepheard's Calendar,*
however, though it belonged to an artificial order of literature, had the unmistakable stamp of genius in its style.
There was a broad, easy mastery of the resources of language, a grace, fluency, and music which were new to English
poetry. It was written while Spenser was in service with
the Earl of Leicester, and enjoying the friendship of his
nephew, the all-accomplished Sidney and it was, perhaps,
composed at the latter's country seat of Penshurst. In the
following year Spenser went to Ireland as private secretary to
Arthur, Lord Grey of Wilton, who had just been appointed
Lord Deputy of that kingdom. After filling several clerkships in the Irish government, Spenser received a grant of
the castle and estate of Kilcolman, a part of the forfeited
lands of the rebel Earl of Desmond. Here, among landscapes richly wooded, like the scenery of his own fairy land,
"under the cooly shades of the green alders by the Mulla's
shore," Sir Walter Ralcigh found him, in 1589, busy upon
his *Faerie Queene.* In his poem, *Colin Clout's Come Home
Again,* Spenser tells, in pastoral language, how "the shepherd of the ocean" persuaded him to go to London, where

he presented him to the queen, under whose patronage the first three books of his great poem were printed, in 1590. A volume of minor poems, entitled *Complaints*, followed in 1591, and the three remaining books of the *Faerie Queene* in 1596. In 1595–1596 he published also his *Daphnaida, Prothalamion*, and the four hymns on *Love* and *Beauty*, and on *Heavenly Love* and *Heavenly Beauty*. In 1598, in Tyrone's rebellion, Kilcolman Castle was sacked and burned, and Spenser, with his family, fled to London, where he died in January, 1599.

The *Faerie Queene* reflects, perhaps, more fully than any other English work, the many-sided literary influences of the Renascence. It was the blossom of a richly composite culture. Its immediate models were Ariosto's *Orlando Furioso*, the first forty cantos of which were published in 1515, and Tasso's *Gerusalemme Liberata*, printed in 1581. Both of these were, in subject, romances of chivalry, the first based upon the old Charlemagne epos—Orlando being identical with the hero of the French *Chanson de Roland:* the second upon the history of the first crusade, and the recovery of the Holy City from the Saracen. But in both of them there was a splendor of diction and a wealth of coloring quite unknown to the rude mediæval romances. Ariosto and Tasso wrote with the great epics of Homer and Vergil constantly in mind, and all about them was the brilliant light of Italian art, in its early freshness and power. The *Faerie Queene*, too, was a tale of knight-errantry. Its hero was King Arthur, and its pages swarm with the familiar adventures and figures of Gothic romance: distressed ladies and their champions, combats with dragons and giants, enchanted castles, magic rings, charmed wells, forest hermitages, etc. But side by side with these appear the fictions of Greek mythology and the personified abstractions of fashionable allegory. Knights, squires, wizards, hamadryads, satyrs, and river gods, Idleness, Gluttony, and Superstition jostle each other in Spenser's fairy land. Descents to the infernal shades, in the manner of Homer and Vergil, alternate with descriptions of the Palace of Pride in the manner of the *Romaunt of the Rose.* But Spenser's imagination was a powerful spirit, and held all these diverse elements in solution. He removed them to an ideal sphere "apart from place, withholding time," where they seem all alike equally real, the dateless conceptions of the poet's dream.

The poem was to have been "a continued allegory or dark conceit," in twelve books, the hero of each book representing one of the twelve moral virtues. Only six books and the fragment of a seventh were written. By way of complimenting his patrons and securing contemporary interest, Spenser undertook to make his allegory a double one, personal and historical, as well as moral or abstract. Thus Gloriana, the Queen of Faery, stands not only for Glory but for Elizabeth, to whom the poem was dedicated. Prince Arthur is Leicester, as well as Magnificence. Duessa is Falsehood, but also Mary Queen of Scots. Grantorto is Philip II. of Spain. Sir Artegal is Justice, but likewise he is Arthur Grey de Wilton. Other characters shadow forth Sir Walter Raleigh, Sir Philip Sidney, Henry IV. of France, etc.; and such public events as the revolt of the Spanish Netherlands, the Irish rebellion, the execution of Mary Stuart, and the rising of the northern Catholic houses against Elizabeth are told in parable. In this way the poem reflects the spiritual struggle of the time, the warfare of young England against popery and Spain.

The allegory is not always easy to follow. It is kept up most carefully in the first two books, but it sat rather lightly on Spenser's conscience, and is not of the essence of the poem. It is an ornament put on from the outside and detachable at pleasure. The "Spenserian stanza," in which the *Faerie Queene* was written, was adapted from the *ottava rima* of Ariosto. Spenser changed somewhat the order of the rimes in the first eight lines and added a ninth line of twelve syllables, thus affording more space to the copious luxuriance of his style and the long-drawn sweetness of his verse. It was his instinct to dilate and elaborate every image to the utmost, and his similies, especially—each of which usually fills a whole stanza—have the pictorial amplitude of Homer's. Spenser was, in fact, a great painter. His poetry is almost purely sensuous. The personages in the *Faerie Queene* are not characters, but richly colored figures, moving to the accompaniment of delicious music, in an atmosphere of serene remoteness from the earth. Charles Lamb said that he was the poet's poet, that is, he appealed wholly to the artistic sense and to the love of beauty. Not until Keats did another English poet appear so filled with the passion for outward shapes of beauty, so exquisitively alive to all impressions of the senses. Spenser was, in some respects, more an Italian than an English poet. It is said that the Venetian gondoliers still sing the stanzas of Tasso's *Gerusalemme Liberata*. It is not easy to imagine the Thames bargees chanting passages from the *Faerie Queene*. Those English poets who have taken strongest hold upon their public have done so by their profound interpretation of our common life. But Spenser escaped altogether from reality into a region of pure imagination. His aerial creations resemble the blossoms of the epiphytic orchids, which have no root in the soil, but draw their nourishment from the moisture of the air.

> *Their* birth was of the womb of morning dew,
> And *their* conception of the glorious prime.

Among the minor poems of Spenser the most delightful were his *Prothalamion* and *Epithalamion*. The first was a "spousal verse," made for the double wedding of the Ladies Catherine and Elizabeth Somerset, whom the poet figures as two white swans that come swimming down the Thames, the surface of which the nymphs strew with lilies, till it appears "like a bride's chamber-floor."

> Sweet Thames, run softly till I end my song,

is the burden of each stanza. The *Epithalamion* was Spenser's own marriage song, written to crown his series of *Amoretti* or love sonnets, and is the most splendid hymn of triumphant love in the language. Hardly less beautiful than these was *Muiopotmos; or, the Fate of the Butterfly*, an addition to the classical myth of Arachne, the spider. The four hymns in praise of *Love* and *Beauty, Heavenly Love* and *Heavenly Beauty*, are also stately and noble poems, but by reason of their abstractness and the Platonic mysticism which they express, are less generally pleasing than the others mentioned. Allegory and mysticism had no natural affiliation with Spenser's genius. He was a seer of visions, of *images* full, brilliant, and distinct; and not, like Bunyan, Dante, or Hawthorne, a projector into bodily shapes of *ideas*, typical and emblematic; the shadows which haunt the conscience and the mind.

———

1. English Writers. Henry Morley. Cassell & Co., 1887. 4 vols.

2. Skeat's Specimens of English Literature, 1394–1579 (Clarendon Press Series.) Oxford.

3. Morte Darthur. London: Macmillan & Co., 1868. (Globe Edition.)

4. English and Scottish Ballads. Edited by Francis J. Child. Boston: Little, Brown & Co., 1859. 8 vols.

5. Spenser's Poetical Works. Edited by Richard Morris. London: Macmillan & Co., 1877. (Globe Edition.)

6. "A Royal Poet." In Washington Irving's Sketch Book. New York: G. P. Putnam's Sons, 1864.

CHAPTER III.

THE AGE OF SHAKSPERE.

1564-1616.

THE great age of English poetry opened with the publication of Spenser's *Shepheard's Calendar*, in 1579, and closed with the printing of Milton's *Samson Agonistes*, in 1671. Within this period of little less than a century English thought passed through many changes, and there were several successive phases of style in our imaginative literature. Milton, who acknowledged Spenser as his master, and who was a boy of eight years at Shakspere's death, lived long enough to witness the establishment of an entirely new school of poets, in the persons of Dryden and his contemporaries. But, roughly speaking, the dates above given mark the limits of one literary epoch, which may not improperly be called the Elizabethan. In strictness the Elizabethan age ended with the queen's death, in 1603. But the poets of the succeeding reigns inherited much of the glow and splendor which marked the diction of their forerunners ; and "the spacious times of great Elizabeth" have been, by courtesy, prolonged to the year of the Restoration (1660). There is a certain likeness in the intellectual products of the whole period, a largeness of utterance and a high imaginative cast of thought which stamp them all alike with the queen's seal.

Nor is it by any undue stretch of the royal prerogative that the name of the monarch has attached itself to the literature of her reign and of the reigns succeeding hers. The expression "Victorian poetry" has a rather absurd sound when one considers how little Victoria counts for in the literature of her time. But in Elizabethan poetry the maiden queen is really the central figure. She is Cynthia, she is Thetis, great queen of shepherds and of the sea ; she is Spenser's Gloriana, and even Shakspere, the most impersonal of poets, paid tribute to her in *Henry VIII.*, and, in a more delicate and indirect way, in the little allegory introduced into *Midsummer Night's Dream.*

> That very time I saw—but thou could'st not—
> Flying between the cold moon and the earth,
> Cupid all armed. A certain aim he took
> At a fair vestal thronèd by the west,
> And loosed his love-shaft smartly from his bow
> As it should pierce a hundred thousand hearts.
> But I might see young Cupid's fiery shaft
> Quenched in the chaste beams of the watery moon,
> And the imperial votaress passed on
> In maiden meditation, fancy free—

an allusion to Leicester's unsuccessful suit for Elizabeth's hand.

The praises of the queen, which sound through all the poetry of her time, seem somewhat overdone to a modern reader. But they were not merely the insipid language of courtly compliment. England had never before had a female sovereign, except in the instance of the gloomy and bigoted Mary. When she was succeeded by her more brilliant sister the gallantry of a gallant and fantastic age was poured at the latter's feet, the sentiment of chivalry mingling itself with loyalty to the crown. The poets idealized Elizabeth. She was to Spenser, to Sidney, and to Raleigh, not merely a woman and a virgin queen, but the champion of Protestantism, the lady of young England, the heroine of the conflict against popery and Spain. Moreover Elizabeth was a great woman. In spite of the vanity, caprice, and ingratitude which disfigured her character, and the vacillating, tortuous policy which often distinguished her government, she was at bottom a sovereign of large views, strong will, and dauntless courage. Like her father, she "loved a *man*," and she had the magnificent tastes of the Tudors. She was a patron of the arts, passionately fond of shows and spectacles, and sensible to poetic flattery. In her royal progresses through the kingdom, the universities, the nobles, and the cities vied with one another in receiving her with plays, revels, masques, and triumphs, in the mythological taste of the day. "When the queen paraded through a country town," says Warton, the historian of English poetry, "almost every pageant was a pantheon. When she paid a visit at the house of any of her nobility, at entering the hall she was saluted by the *penates*. In the afternoon, when she condescended to walk in the garden, the lake was covered with tritons and nereids; the pages of the family were converted into wood-nymphs, who peeped from every bower; and the footmen gamboled over the lawns in the figure of satyrs. When her majesty hunted in the park she was met by Diana, who, pronouncing our royal prude to be the brightest paragon of unspotted chastity, invited her to groves free from the intrusions of Actæon." The most elaborate of these entertainments of which we have any notice were, perhaps, the games celebrated in her honor by the Earl of Leicester, when she visited him at Kenilworth, in 1575. An account of these was published by a contemporary poet, George Gascoigne, *The Princely Pleasures at the Court of Kenilworth*, and Walter Scott has made them familiar to modern readers in his novel of *Kenilworth*. Sidney was present on this occasion, and, perhaps, Shakspere, then a boy of eleven, and living at Stratford, not far off, may have been taken to see the spectacle; may have seen Neptune riding on the back of a huge dolphin in the castle lake, speaking the copy of verses in which he offered his trident to the empress of the sea; and may have

> heard a mermaid on a dolphin's back
> Uttering such dulcet and harmonious breath
> That the rude sea grew civil at her song.

But in considering the literature of Elizabeth's reign it will be convenient to speak first of the prose. While following up Spenser's career to its close (1599) we have, for the sake of unity of treatment, anticipated somewhat the literary history of the twenty years preceding. In 1579 appeared a book which had a remarkable influence on English prose. This was John Lyly's *Euphues, the Anatomy of Wit.* It was in form a romance, the history of a young Athenian who went to Naples to see the world and get an education; but it is in substance nothing but a series of dialogues on love, friendship, religion, etc., written in language which, from the title of the book, has received the name of *Euphuism.* This new English became very fashionable among the ladies, and "that beauty in court which could not parley Euphuism," says a writer of 1632, "was as little regarded as she which now there speaks not French."

Walter Scott introduced a Euphuist into his novel the *Monastery,* but the peculiar jargon which Sir Piercie Shafton is made to talk is not at all like the real Euphuism. That consisted of antithesis, alliteration, and the profuse illustration of every thought by metaphors borrowed from a kind of fabulous natural history. "Descend into thine own conscience and consider with thyself the great difference between staring and stark-blind, wit and wisdom, love and lust; be merry, but with modesty; be sober, but not too sullen; be valiant, but not too venturous." "I see now that, as the fish *Scolopidus* in the flood *Araxes* at the waxing of the moon is as white as the driven snow, and at the waning as black as the burnt coal; so Euphues, which at the first increasing of our familiarity was very zealous, is now at the last cast become most faithless." Besides the fish *Scolopidus,* the favorite animals of Lyly's menagerie are such as the chameleon, "which though he have most guts draweth least breath;" the bird *Piralis,* "which sitting upon white cloth is white, upon green, green;" and the serpent *Porphirius,* "which, though he be full of poison, yet having no teeth, hurteth none but himself."

Lyly's style was pithy and sententious, and his sentences have the air of proverbs or epigrams. The vice of Euphuism was its monotony. On every page of the book there was something pungent, something quotable; but many pages of such writing became tiresome. Yet it did much to form the hitherto loose structure of English prose, by lending it point and polish. His carefully balanced periods were valuable lessons in rhetoric, and his book became a manual of polite conversation and introduced that fashion of witty repartee, which is evident enough in Shakspere's comic dialogue. In 1580 appeared the second part, *Euphues and his England*, and six editions of the whole work were printed before 1598. Lyly had many imitators. In Stephen Gosson's *School of Abuse*, a tract directed against the stage and published about four months later than the first part of *Euphues*, the language is directly Euphuistic. The dramatist, Robert Greene, published, in 1587, his *Menaphon; Camilla's Alarum to Slumbering Euphues*, and his *Euphues's Censure to Philautus*. His brother dramatist, Thomas Lodge, published, in 1590, *Rosalynde: Euphues's Golden Legacy*, from which Shakspere took the plot of *As You Like It*. Shakspere and Ben Jonson both quote from *Euphues* in their plays, and Shakspere was really writing Euphuism when he wrote such a sentence as "'Tis true, 'tis pity; pity 'tis 'tis true."

That knightly gentleman, Philip Sidney, was a true type of the lofty aspiration and manifold activity of Elizabethan England. He was scholar, poet, courtier, diplomatist, soldier, all in one. Educated at Oxford and then introduced at court by his uncle, the Earl of Leicester, he had been sent to France when a lad of eighteen, with the embassy which went to treat of the queen's proposed marriage to the Duke of Alençon, and was in Paris at the time of the Massacre of

CHAUCER.

SPENSER.

BACON.

MILTON.

St. Bartholomew, in 1572. Afterward he had traveled through Germany, Italy, and the Netherlands, had gone as embassador to the emperor's court, and every-where won golden opinions. In 1580, while visiting his sister Mary, Countess of Pembroke, at Wilton, he wrote, for her pleasure, the *Countess of Pembroke's Arcadia*, which remained in manuscript till 1590. This was a pastoral romance, after the manner of the Italian *Arcadia* of Sanazzaro, and the *Diana Enamorada* of Montemayor, a Portuguese author. It was in prose, but intermixed with songs and sonnets, and Sidney finished only two books and a portion of the third. It describes the adventures of two cousins, Musidorus and Pyrocles, who were wrecked on the coast of Sparta. The plot is very involved and is full of the stock episodes of romance : disguises, surprises, love intrigues, battles, jousts and single combats. Although the insurrection of the Helots against the Spartans forms a part of the story, the Arcadia is not the real Arcadia of the Hellenic Peloponnesus, but the fanciful country of pastoral romance, an unreal clime, like the fairy land of Spenser.

Sidney was our first writer of poetic prose. The poet Drayton says that he

> did first reduce
> Our tongue from Lyly's writing, then in use,
> Talking of stones, stars, plants, of fishes, flies,
> Playing with words and idle similes.

Sidney was certainly no Euphuist, but his style was as "Italianated" as Lyly's, though in a different way. His English was too pretty for prose. His "Sidneian showers of sweet discourse" sowed every page of the *Arcadia* with those flowers of conceit, those sugared fancies which his contemporaries loved, but which the taste of a severer age finds insipid. This splendid vice of the Elizabethan writers appears in Sidney, chiefly in the form of an excessive personification. If he describes a field full of roses, he makes "the roses add such a ruddy show unto it, as though the field were bashful at his own beauty." If he describes ladies bathing in the stream, he makes the water break into twenty bubbles, as "not content to have the picture of their face in large upon him, but he would in each of those bubbles set forth a miniature of them." And even a passage which should be tragic, such as the death of his heroine, Parthenia, he embroiders with conceits like these: "For her exceeding fair eyes having with continued weeping got a little redness about them, her round sweetly swelling lips a little trembling, as though they kissed their neighbor Death; in her cheeks the whiteness striving by little and little to get upon the rosiness of them; her neck, a neck of alabaster, displaying the wound which with most dainty blood labored to drown his own beauties; so as here was a river of purest red, there an island of perfectest white," etc.

The *Arcadia*, like *Euphues*, was a lady's book. It was the favorite court romance of its day, but it surfeits a modern reader with its sweetness, and confuses him with its tangle of adventures. The lady for whom it was written was the mother of that William Herbert, Earl of Pembroke, to whom Shakspere's sonnets are thought to have been dedicated. And she was the subject of Ben Jonson's famous epitaph.

> Underneath this sable herse
> Lies the subject of all verse,
> Sidney's sister, Pembroke's mother;
> Death, ere thou hast slain another
> Learn'd and fair and good as she,
> Time shall throw a dart at thee.

Sidney's *Defense of Poesy* composed in 1581, but not printed till 1595, was written in manlier English than the *Arcadia*, and is one of the very few books of criticism belonging to a creative and uncritical time. He was also the author of a series of love sonnets, *Astrophel and Stella*, in which he paid Platonic court to the Lady Penelope Rich (with whom he was not in love), according to the conventional usage of the amourists.

Sidney died in 1586, from a wound received in a cavalry charge at Zutphen, where he was an officer in the English contingent sent to help the Dutch against Spain. The story has often been told of his giving his cup of water to a wounded soldier with the words, "Thy necessity is yet greater than mine." Sidney was England's darling, and there was hardly a poet in the land from whom his death did not obtain "the meed of some melodious tear." Spenser's *Ruins of Time* were among the number of these funeral songs; but the best of them all was by one Matthew Royden, concerning whom little is known.

Another typical Englishman of Elizabeth's reign was Walter Raleigh, who was even more versatile than Sidney, and more representative of the restless spirit of romantic adventure, mixed with cool, practical enterprise that marked, the times. He fought against the queen's enemies by land and sea in many quarters of the globe; in the Netherlands and in Ireland against Spain, with the Huguenot army against the League in France. Raleigh was from Devonshire, the great nursery of English seamen. He was half-brother to the famous navigator, Sir Humphrey Gilbert, and cousin to another great captain, Sir Richard Grenville. He sailed with Gilbert on one of his voyages against the Spanish treasure fleet, and in 1591 he published a report of the fight, near the Azores, between Grenville's ship, the *Revenge*, and fifteen great ships of Spain, an action, said Francis Bacon, "memorable even beyond credit, and to the height of some heroical fable." Raleigh was active in raising a fleet against the Spanish Armada of 1588. He was present in 1596 at the brilliant action in which the Earl of Essex " singed the Spanish king's beard," in the harbor of Cadiz. The year before he had sailed to Guiana, in search of the fabled El Dorado, destroying on the way the Spanish town of San

José, in the West Indies ; and on his return he published his *Discovery of the Empire of Guiana.* In 1597 he captured the town of Fayal, in the Azores. He took a prominent part in colonizing Virginia, and he introduced tobacco and the potato plant into Europe.

America was still a land of wonder and romance, full of rumors, nightmares, and enchantments. In 1580, when Francis Drake, "the Devonshire Skipper," had dropped anchor in Plymouth Harbor, after his voyage around the world, the enthusiasm of England had been mightily stirred. These narratives of Raleigh, and the similar accounts of the exploits of the bold sailors, Davis, Hawkins, Frobisher, Gilbert, and Drake ; but especially the great cyclopedia of nautical travel, published by Richard Hakluyt in 1589, *The Principal Navigations, Voyages, and Discoveries made by the English Nation*, worked powerfully on the imaginations of the poets. We see the influence of this literature of travel in the *Tempest,* written undoubtedly after Shakspere had been reading the narrative of Sir George Somers's shipwreck on the Bermudas or "Isles of Devils."

Raleigh was not in favor with Elizabeth's successor, James I. He was sentenced to death on a trumped-up charge of high treason. The sentence hung over him until 1618, when it was revived against him and he was beheaded. Meanwhile, during his twelve years' imprisonment in the Tower, he had written his *magnum opus*, the *History of the World.* This is not a history, in the modern sense, but a series of learned dissertations on law, government, theology, magic, war, etc. A chapter with such a caption as the following would hardly be found in a universal history nowadays: "Of their opinion which make Paradise as high as the moon ; and of others which make it higher than the middle regions of the air." The preface and conclusion are noble examples of Elizabethan prose, and the book ends with an oft-quoted apostrophe to Death. " O eloquent, just and mighty Death! Whom none could advise, thou hast persuaded; what none hath dared, thou hast done; and whom all the world hath flattered, thou only hast cast out of the world and despised; thou hast drawn together all the far-fetched greatness, all the pride, cruelty, and ambition of man, and covered it all over with these two narrow words, *hic jacet*."

Although so busy a man, Raleigh found time to be a poet. Spenser calls him "the summer's nightingale," and George Puttenham, in his *Art of English Poesy* (1589), finds his " vein most lofty, insolent, and passionate." Puttenham used *insolent* in its old sense, *uncommon;* but this description is hardly less true, if we accept the word in its modern meaning. Raleigh's most notable verses, *The Lie*, are a challenge to the world, inspired by indignant pride and the weariness of life — the *saeva indignatio* of Swift. The same grave and caustic melancholy, the same disillusion marks his quaint poem, *The Pilgrimage.* It is remarkable how many of the verses among his few poetical remains are asserted in the manuscripts or by tradition to have been " made by Sir Walter Raleigh the night before he was beheaded." Of one such poem the assertion is probably true—namely, the lines " found in his Bible in the gate-house at Westminster."

> Even such is Time, that takes in trust,
>   Our youth, our joys, our all we have,
> And pays us but with earth and dust;
>   Who in the dark and silent grave,
> When we have wandered all our ways,
> Shuts up the story of our days;
> But from this earth, this grave, this dust,
> My God shall raise me up, I trust!

The strictly *literary* prose of the Elizabethan period bore a small proportion to the verse. Many entire departments of prose literature were as yet undeveloped. Fiction was represented — outside of the *Arcadia* and *Euphues* already mentioned — chiefly by tales translated or imitated from Italian *novelle*. George Turberville's *Tragical Tales* (1566) was a collection of such stories, and William Paynter's *Palace of Pleasure* (1576–1577) a similar collection from Boccaccio's *Decameron* and the novels of Bandello. These translations are mainly of interest as having furnished plots to the English dramatists. Lodge's *Rosalind* and Robert Greene's *Pandosto*, the sources respectively of Shakspere's *As You Like It* and *Winter's Tale*, are short pastoral. romances, not without prettiness in their artificial way. The satirical pamphlets of Thomas Nash and his fellows, against "Martin Marprelate," an anonymous writer, or company of writers, who attacked the bishops, are not wanting in wit, but are so cumbered with fantastic whimsicalities, and so bound up with personal quarrels, that oblivion has covered them. The most noteworthy of them were Nash's *Piers Penniless's Supplication to the Devil*, Lyly's *Pap with a Hatchet*, and Greene's *Groat's Worth of Wit*. Of books which were not so much literature as the material of literature, mention may be made of the *Chronicle of England*, published by Ralph Holinshed in 1580. This was Shakspere's English history, and its strong Lancastrian bias influenced Shakspere in his representation of Richard III. and other characters in his historical plays. In his Roman tragedies Shakspere followed closely Sir Thomas North's translation of Plutarch's Lives, made in 1579 from the French version of Jacques Amyot.

Of books belonging to other departments than pure literature, the most important was Richard Hooker's *Ecclesiastical Polity*, the first four books of which appeared in 1594. This was a work on the philosophy of law, and a defense, as against the Presbyterians, of the government of the English Church by bishops. No work of equal dignity and scope had yet been published in English prose. It was written in sonorous, stately, and somewhat involved periods, in a Latin rather than an English idiom, and it influenced strongly the diction of later writers, such as Milton and Sir Thomas Browne. Had the *Ecclesiastical Polity* been written one hundred, or perhaps even fifty, years earlier, it would doubtless have been written in Latin.

The life of Francis Bacon, "the father of inductive philosophy," as he has been called—better, the founder of inductive logic—belongs to English history, and the bulk of his writings, in Latin and English, to the history of English philosophy. But his volume of *Essays* was a contribution to general literature. In their completed form they belong to the year 1625, but the first edition was printed in 1597 and contained only ten short essays, each of them rather a string of pregnant maxims—the text for an essay—than that developed treatment of a subject which we now understand by the word essay. They were, said their author, "as grains of salt, that will rather give you an appetite than offend you with satiety." They were the first essays, so called, in the language. "The word," said Bacon, "is late, but the thing is ancient." The word he took from the French *essais* of Montaigne, the first two books of which had been published in 1592. Bacon testified that his essays were the most popular of his writings because they "came home to men's business and bosoms." Their alternate title explains their character : *Counsels Civil and Moral,* that is, pieces of advice touching the conduct of life, "of a nature whereof men shall find much in experience, little in books." The essays contain the quintessence of Bacon's practical wisdom, his wide knowledge of the world of men. The truth and depth of his sayings, and the extent of ground which they cover, as well as the weighty compactness of his style, have given many of them the currency of proverbs. "Revenge is a kind of wild justice." "He that hath wife and children hath given hostages to fortune." "There is no excellent beauty that hath not some strangeness in the proportion."

Bacon's reason was illuminated by a powerful imagination, and his noble English rises now and then, as in his essay *On Death*, into eloquence—the eloquence of pure thought, touched gravely and afar off by emotion. In general, the atmosphere of his intellect is that *lumen siccum* which he loved to commend, "not drenched or bloodied by the affections." Dr. Johnson said that the wine of Bacon's writings was a dry wine.

A popular class of books in the 17th century were "characters" or "witty descriptions of the properties of sundry persons," such as the Good Schoolmaster, the Clown, the Country Magistrate; much as in some modern *Heads of the People*, where Douglas Jerrold or Leigh Hunt sketches the Medical Student, the Monthly Nurse, etc. A still more modern instance of the kind is George Eliot's *Impressions of Theophrastus Such*, which derives its title from the Greek philosopher, Theophrastus, whose character-sketches were the original models of this kind of literature. The most popular character-book in Europe in the 17th century was La Bruyère's *Caractères*. But this was not published till 1688. In England the fashion had been set in 1614, by the *Characters* of Sir Thomas Overbury, who died by poison the year before his book was printed. One of Overbury's sketches — the *Fair and Happy Milkmaid*—is justly celebrated for its old-world sweetness and quaintness. "Her breath is her own, which scents all the year long of June, like a new-made hay-cock. She makes her hand hard with labor, and her heart soft with pity; and when winter evenings fall early, sitting at her merry wheel, she sings defiance to the giddy wheel of fortune. She bestows her year's wages at next fair, and, in choosing her garments, counts no bravery in the world like decency. The garden and bee-hive are all her physic and surgery, and she lives the longer for it. She dares go alone and unfold sheep in the night, and fears no manner of ill, because she means none; yet to say

truth, she is never alone, but is still accompanied with old
songs, honest thoughts and prayers, but short ones. Thus
lives she, and all her care is she may die in the spring-time,
to have store of flowers stuck upon her winding-sheet."

England was still merry England in the times of good
Queen Bess, and rang with old songs, such as kept this milkmaid company; songs, said Bishop Joseph Hall, which were
"sung to the wheel and sung unto the pail." Shakspere
loved their simple minstrelsy; he put some of them into the
mouth of Ophelia, and scattered snatches of them through
his plays, and wrote others like them himself :

> Now, good Cesario, but that piece of song,
> That old and antique song we heard last night.
> Methinks it did relieve my passion much,
> More than light airs and recollected terms
> Of these most brisk and giddy-paced times.
> Mark it, Cesario, it is old and plain.
> The knitters and the spinners in the sun
> And the free maids that weave their threads with bones
> Do use to chant it; it is silly sooth [1]
> And dallies with the innocence of love
> Like the old age.

Many of these songs, so natural, fresh, and spontaneous,
together with sonnets and other more elaborate forms of
lyrical verse, were printed in miscellanies, such as the *Passionate Pilgrim, England's Helicon,* and Davison's *Poetical
Rhapsody.* Some were anonymous, or were by poets of
whom little more is known than their names. Others were by
well-known writers, and others, again, were strewn through
the plays of Lyly, Shakspere, Jonson, Beaumont, Fletcher,
and other dramatists. Series of love sonnets, like Spenser's
Amoretti and Sidney's *Astrophel and Stella,* were written by
Shakspere, Daniel, Drayton, Drummond, Constable, Watson,
and others, all dedicated to some mistress real or imaginary.
Pastorals, too, were written in great number, such as

---

[1] Simple truth.

William Browne's *Britannia's Pastorals* and *Shepherd's Pipe* (1613–1616) and Marlowe's charmingly rococo little idyl, *The Passionate Shepherd to his Love*, which Shakspere quoted in the *Merry Wives of Windsor*, and to which Sir Walter Raleigh wrote a reply. There were love stories in verse, like Arthur Brooke's *Romeo and Juliet* (the source of Shakspere's tragedy), Marlowe's fragment, *Hero and Leander*, and Shakspere's *Venus and Adonis*, and *Rape of Lucrece*, the first of these on an Italian and the other three on classical subjects, though handled in any thing but a classical manner. Wordsworth said finely of Shakspere, that he "could not have written an epic : he would have died of a plethora of thought." Shakspere's two narrative poems, indeed, are by no means models of their kind. The current of the story is choked at every turn, though it be with golden sand. It is significant of his dramatic habit of mind that dialogue and soliloquy usurp the place of narration, and that, in the *Rape of Lucrece* especially, the poet lingers over the analysis of motives and feelings, instead of hastening on with the action, as Chaucer, or any born story-teller, would have done.

In Marlowe's poem there is the same spendthrift fancy, although not the same subtlety. In the first two divisions of the poem the story does, in some sort, get forward ; but in the continuation, by George Chapman (who wrote the last four "sestiads"),[1] the path is utterly lost, "with woodbine and the gadding vine o'ergrown." One is reminded that modern poetry, if it has lost in richness, has gained in directness, when one compares any passage in Marlowe and Chapman's *Hero and Leander* with Byron's ringing lines :

> The wind is high on Helle's wave,
> As on that night of stormy water,
> When love, who sent, forgot to save
> The young, the beautiful, the brave,
> The lonely hope of Sestos' daughter.

---

[1] From Sestos on the Hellespont, where Hero dwelt.

Marlowe's continuator, Chapman, wrote a number of plays, but he is best remembered by his royal translation of Homer, issued in parts from 1598-1615. This was not so much a literal translation of the Greek, as a great Elizabethan poem, inspired by Homer. It has Homer's fire, but not his simplicity ; the energy of Chapman's fancy kindling him to run beyond his text into all manner of figures and conceits. It was written, as has been said, as Homer would have written if he had been an Englishman of Chapman's time. Keats's fine ode, *On First Looking into Chapman's Homer*, is well known. In his translation of the *Odyssey*, Chapman employed the ten-syllabled heroic line chosen by most of the standard translators ; but for the *Iliad* he used the long "fourteener." Certainly all later versions—Pope's and Cowper's and Lord Derby's and Bryant's—seem pale against the glowing exuberance of Chapman's English, which degenerates easily into sing-song in the hands of a feeble metrist. In Chapman it is often harsh, but seldom tame, and in many passages it reproduces wonderfully the ocean-like roll of Homer's hexameters.

> From his bright helm and shield did burn a most unwearied fire,
> Like rich Autumnus' golden lamp, whose brightness men admire
> Past all the other host of stars when, with his cheerful face
> Fresh washed in lofty ocean waves, he doth the sky enchase.

The national pride in the achievements of Englishmen, by land and sea, found expression, not only in prose chronicles and in books, like Stow's *Survey of London*, and Harrison's *Description of England* (prefixed to Holinshed's *Chronicle*), but in long historical and descriptive poems, like William Warner's *Albion's England*, 1586 ; Samuel Daniel's *History of the Civil Wars*, 1595-1602; Michael Drayton's *Barons' Wars*, 1596, *England's Heroical Epistles*, 1598, and *Polyolbion*, 1613. The very plan of these works was fatal to their success. It is not easy to digest history and geography into poetry. Drayton was the most considerable poet of the three, but his *Polyolbion* was nothing more than a "gazeteer in rime," a topographical survey of England and Wales, with tedious personifications of rivers, mountains, and valleys, in thirty books and nearly one hundred thousand lines. It was Drayton who said of Marlowe, that he "had in him those brave translunary things that the first poets had ; " and there are brave things in Drayton, but they are only occasional passages, oases among dreary wastes of sand. His *Agincourt* is a spirited war-song, and his *Nymphidia; or, Court of Faery*, is not unworthy of comparison with Drake's *Culprit Fay*, and is interesting as bringing in Oberon and Robin Goodfellow, and the popular fairy lore of Shakspere's *Midsummer Night's Dream*.

The "well-languaged Daniel," of whom Ben Jonson said that he was "a good honest man, but no poet," wrote, however, one fine meditative piece, his *Epistle to the Countess of Cumberland*, a sermon apparently on the text of the Roman poet Lucretius's famous passage in praise of philosophy,

> Suave, mari magno, turbantibus æquora ventis,
> E terra magnum alterius spectare laborem.

But the Elizabethan genius found its fullest and truest expression in the drama. It is a common phenomenon in the history of literature that some old literary form or mold will run along for centuries without having any thing poured into it worth keeping, until the moment comes when the genius of the time seizes it and makes it the vehicle of immortal thought and passion. Such was in England the fortune of the stage play. At a time when Chaucer was writing character-sketches that were really dramatic, the formal drama consisted of rude miracle plays that had no literary quality whatever. These were taken from the Bible, and acted at first by the priests as illustrations of Scripture history and additions to the church service on feasts and saints' days. Afterward the town guilds, or incorporated trades, took hold of them, and produced them annually on scaffolds in the open air. In some English cities, as Coventry and Chester, they continued to be performed almost to the close of the 16th century. And in the celebrated Passion Play at Oberammergau, in Bavaria, we have an instance of a miracle play that has survived to our own day. These were followed by the moral plays, in which allegorical characters, such as Clergy, Lusty Juventus, Riches, Folly, and Good Demeanaunce were the persons of the drama. The comic character in the miracle plays had been the Devil, and he was retained in some of the moralities side by side with the abstract vice, who became the clown or fool of Shaksperian comedy. The "formal Vice, Iniquity," as Shakspere calls him, had it for his business to belabor the roaring Devil with his wooden sword :

> . . . with his dagger of lath
> In his rage and his wrath
> Cries 'Aha!' to the Devil,
> 'Pare your nails, Goodman Evil!'

He survives also in the harlequin of the pantomimes, and in Mr. Punch, of the puppet shows, who kills the Devil and carries him off on his back, when the latter is sent to fetch him to hell for his crimes.

Masques and interludes—the latter a species of short farce—were popular at the court of Henry VIII. Elizabeth was often entertained at the universities or at the inns of court with Latin plays, or with translations from Seneca, Euripides, and Ariosto. Original comedies and tragedies began to be written, modeled upon Terence and Seneca, and chronicle histories founded on the annals of English kings. There was a master of the revels at court, whose duty it was to select plays to be performed before the queen, and these were acted by the children of the Royal Chapel, or by the choir boys of St. Paul's Cathedral. These early plays are of inter-

est to students of the history of the drama, and throw much
light upon the construction of later plays, like Shakspere's ;
but they are rude and inartistic, and without any literary
value.

There were also private companies of actors maintained
by wealthy noblemen, like the Earl of Leicester, and bands
of strolling players, who acted in inn-yards and bear-gardens.
It was not until stationary theaters were built and stock companies of actors regularly licensed and established, that any
plays were produced which deserve the name of literature.
In 1576 the first London play-houses, known as the Theater
and the Curtain, were erected in the suburb of Shoreditch, outside the city walls.   Later the Rose, the Hope, the Globe, and
the Swan were built on the Bankside, across the Thames, and
play-goers resorting to them were accustomed to "take boat."
These locations were chosen in order to get outside the jurisdic-
tion of the mayor and corporation, who were Puritans, and
determined in their opposition to the stage.   For the same
reason the Blackfriars, belonging to the company that owned
the Globe—the company in which Shakspere was a stockholder—was built, about 1596, within the "liberties" of the
dissolved monastery of the Blackfriars.

These early theaters were of the rudest construction.   The
six-penny spectators, or "groundlings," stood in the yard or
pit, which had neither floor nor roof.   The shilling spectators
sat on the stage, where they were accommodated with stools
and tobacco pipes, and whence they chaffed the actors or the
"opposed rascality" in the yard.   There was no scenery,
and the female parts were taken by boys.   Plays were acted
in the afternoon.   A placard, with the letters "Venice," or
"Rome," or whatever, indicated the place of the action.
With such rude appliances must Shakspere bring before his
audience the midnight battlements of Elsinore and the moon-
lit garden of the Capulets.   The dramatists had to throw
themselves upon the imagination of their public, and it says

much for the imaginative temper of the public of that day, that it responded to the appeal. It suffered the poet to transport it over wide intervals of space and time, and " with aid of some few foot and half-foot words, fight over York and Lancaster's long jars." Pedantry undertook, even at the very beginnings of the Elizabethan drama, to shackle it with the so-called rules of Aristotle, or classical unities of time and place, to make it keep violent action off the stage and comedy distinct from tragedy. But the playwrights appealed from the critics to the truer sympathies of the audience, and they decided for feedom and action, rather than restraint and recitation. Hence our national drama is of Shakspere and not of Racine. By 1603 there were twelve play-houses in London in full blast, although the city then numbered only one hundred and fifty thousand inhabitants.

Fresh plays were produced every year. The theater was more to the Englishmen of that time than it has ever been before or since. It was his club, his novel, his newspaper, all in one. No great drama has ever flourished apart from a living stage, and it was fortunate that the Elizabethan dramatists were, almost all of them, actors, and familiar with stage effect. Even the few exceptions, like Beaumont and Fletcher, who were young men of good birth and fortune, and not dependent on their pens, were probably intimate with the actors, lived in a theatrical atmosphere, and knew practically how plays should be put on.

It had now become possible to earn a livelihood as an actor and playwright. Richard Burbage and Edward Alleyn, the leading actors of their generation, made large fortunes. Shakspere himself made enough from his share in the profits of the Globe to retire with a competence, some seven years before his death, and purchase a handsome property in his native Stratford. Accordingly, shortly after 1580, a number of men of real talent began to write for the stage as a career. These were young graduates of the universities,

Marlowe, Greene, Peele, Kyd, Lyly, Lodge, and others, who came up to town and led a bohemian life as actors and playwrights. Most of them were wild and dissipated and ended in wretchedness. Peele died of a disease brought on by his evil courses; Greene, in extreme destitution, from a surfeit of Rhenish wine and pickled herring, and Marlowe was stabbed in a tavern brawl.

The Euphuist Lyly produced eight plays between 1584 and 1601. They were written for court entertainments, mostly in prose and on mythological subjects. They have little dramatic power, but the dialogue is brisk and vivacious, and there are several pretty songs in them. All the characters talk Ephuism. The best of these was *Alexander and Campaspe*, the plot of which is briefly as follows. Alexander has fallen in love with his beautiful captive, Campaspe, and employs the artist Apelles to paint her portrait. During the sittings Apelles becomes enamored of his subject and declares his passion, which is returned. Alexander discovers their secret, but magnanimously forgives the treason and joins the lovers' hands. The situation is a good one, and capable of strong treatment in the hands of a real dramatist. But Lyly slips smoothly over the crisis of the action and, in place of passionate scenes, gives us clever discourses and soliloquies, or, at best, a light interchange of question and answer, full of conceits, repartees, and double meanings. For example :

"*Apel.* Whom do you love best in the world?

"*Camp.* He that made me last in the world.

"*Apel.* That was God.

"*Camp.* I had thought it had been a man," etc.

Lyly's service to the drama consisted in his introduction of an easy and sparkling prose as the language of high comedy, and Shakspere's indebtedness to the fashion thus set is seen in such passages as the wit combats between Benedict and Beatrice in *Much Ado about Nothing*, greatly superior as they are to any thing of the kind in Lyly.

The most important of the dramatists who were Shakspere's forerunners, or early contemporaries, was Christopher or—as he was familiarly called—Kit Marlowe. Born in the same year with Shakspere (1564), he died in 1593, at which date his great successor is thought to have written no original plays, except the *Comedy of Errors* and *Love's Labour's Lost.* Marlowe first popularized blank verse as the language of tragedy in his *Tamburlaine,* written before 1587, and in subsequent plays he brought it to a degree of strength and flexibility which left little for Shakspere to do but to take it as he found it. *Tamburlaine* was a crude, violent piece, full of exaggeration and bombast, but with passages here and there of splendid declamation, justifying Ben Jonson's phrase, "Marlowe's mighty line." Jonson, however, ridiculed, in his *Discoveries,* the "scenical strutting and furious vociferation" of Marlowe's hero; and Shakspere put a quotation from *Tamburlaine* into the mouth of his ranting Pistol. Marlowe's *Edward II.* was the most regularly constructed and evenly written of his plays. It was the best historical drama on the stage before Shakspere, and not undeserving of the comparison which it has provoked with the latter's *Richard II.* But the most interesting of Marlowe's plays, to a modern reader, is the *Tragical History of Doctor Faustus.* The subject is the same as in Goethe's *Faust,* and Goethe, who knew the English play, spoke of it as greatly planned. The opening of Marlowe's *Faustus* is very similar to Goethe's. His hero, wearied with unprofitable studies, and filled with a mighty lust for knowledge and the enjoyment of life, sells his soul to the Devil in return for a few years of supernatural power. The tragic irony of the story might seem to lie in the frivolous use which Faustus makes of his dearly bought power, wasting it in practical jokes and feats of legerdermain; but of this Marlowe was probably unconscious. The love story of Margaret, which is the central point of Goethe's drama, is entirely wanting in Marlowe's, and so is the subtle conception of Goethe's Mephistophiles. Marlowe's handling of the supernatural is materialistic and downright, as befitted an age which believed in witchcraft. The greatest part of the English *Faustus* is the last scene, in which the agony and terror of suspense with which the magician awaits the stroke of the clock that signals his doom are powerfully drawn.

> *O, lente, lente currite, noctis equi !*
> The stars move still, time runs, the clock will strike. . . .
> O soul, be changed into little water-drops,
> And fall into the ocean, ne'er be found !

Marlowe's genius was passionate and irregular. He had no humor, and the comic portions of *Faustus* are scenes of low buffoonery.

George Peele's masterpiece, *David and Bethsabe*, was also, in many respects, a fine play, though its beauties were poetic rather than dramatic, consisting not in the characterization —which is feeble—but in the Eastern luxuriance of the imagery. There is one noble chorus—

> O proud revolt of a presumptuous man,

which reminds one of passages in Milton's *Samson Agonistes*, and occasionally Peele rises to such high Æschylean audacities as this:

> At him the thunder shall discharge his bolt,
> And his fair spouse, with bright and fiery wings,
> Sit ever burning on his hateful bones.

Robert Greene was a very unequal writer. His plays are slovenly and careless in construction, and he puts classical allusions into the mouths of milkmaids and serving boys, with the grotesque pedantry and want of keeping common among the playwrights of the early stage. He has, notwithstanding, in his comedy parts, more natural lightness and grace than either Marlowe or Peele. In his *Friar Bacon and Friar Bungay*, there is a fresh breath, as of the green

English country, in such passages as the description of Oxford, the scene at Harleston Fair, and the picture of the dairy in the keeper's lodge at merry Fressingfield.

In all these ante-Shaksperian dramatists there was a defect of art proper to the first comers in a new literary departure. As compared not only with Shakspere, but with later writers, who had the inestimable advantage of his example, their work was full of imperfection, hesitation, experiment. Marlowe was probably, in native genius, the equal at least of Fletcher or Webster, but his plays, as a whole, are certainly not equal to theirs. They wrote in a more developed state of the art. But the work of this early school settled the shape which the English drama was to take. It fixed the practice and traditions of the national theater. It decided that the drama was to deal with the whole of life, the real and the ideal, tragedy and comedy, prose and verse, in the same play, without limitations of time, place, and action. It decided that the English play was to be an action, and not a dialogue, bringing boldly upon the mimic scene feasts, dances, processions, hangings, riots, plays within plays, drunken revels, beatings, battle, murder, and sudden death. It established blank verse, with occasional riming couplets at the close of a scene or of a long speech, as the language of the tragedy and high comedy parts, and prose as the language of the low comedy and "business" parts. And it introduced songs, a feature of which Shakspere made exquisite use. Shakspere, indeed, like all great poets, invented no new form of literature, but touched old forms to finer purposes, refining every thing, discarding nothing. Even the old chorus and dumb show he employed, though sparingly, as also the old jig, or comic song, which the clown used to give between the acts.

Of the life of William Shakspere, the greatest dramatic poet of the world, so little is known that it has been possible for ingenious persons to construct a theory—and support it

with some show of reason—that the plays which pass under
his name were really written by Bacon or some one else.
There is no danger of this paradox ever making serious head-
way, for the historical evidence that Shakspere wrote Shakspere's plays, though not overwhelming, is sufficient. But it
is startling to think that the greatest creative genius of his
day, or perhaps of all time, was suffered to slip out of life so
quietly that his title to his own works could even be ques-
tioned only two hundred and fifty years after the event.
That the single authorship of the Homeric poems should be
doubted is not so strange, for Homer is almost prehistoric.
But Shakspere was a modern Englishman, and at the time of
his death the first English colony in America was already
nine years old. The important known facts of his life can
be told almost in a sentence. He was born at Stratford-on-
Avon in 1564, married when he was eighteen, went to London probably in 1587, and became an actor, playwriter, and
stockholder in the company which owned the Blackfriars
and the Globe theaters. He seemingly prospered, and retired about 1609 to Stratford, where he lived in the house
that he had bought some years before, and where he died in
1616. His *Venus and Adonis* was printed in 1593, his *Rape
of Lucrece* in 1594, and his *Sonnets* in 1609. So far as is
known, only eighteen of the thirty-seven plays generally attributed to Shakspere were printed during his life-time. These
were printed singly, in quarto shape, and were little more than
stage books, or librettos. The first collected edition of his works
was the so-called "First Folio" of 1623, published by his
fellow-actors, Heming and Condell. No contemporary of
Shakspere thought it worth while to write a life of the
stage-player. There is a number of references to him in the
literature of the time; some generous, as in Ben Jonson's
well-known verses; others singularly unappreciative, like
Webster's mention, of "the right happy and copious industry
of Master Shakspere." But all these together do not begin

to amount to the sum of what was said about Spenser, or Sidney, or Raleigh, or Ben Jonson. There is, indeed, nothing to show that his contemporaries understood what a man they had among them in the person of "Our English Terence, Mr. Will Shakespeare." The age, for the rest, was not a self-conscious one, nor greatly given to review writing and literary biography. Nor is there enough of self-revelation in Shakspere's plays to aid the reader in forming a notion of the man. He lost his identity completely in the characters of his plays, as it is the duty of a dramatic writer to do. His sonnets have been examined carefully in search of internal evidence as to his character and life, but the speculations founded upon them have been more ingenious than convincing.

Shakspere probably began by touching up old plays. *Henry VI.* and the bloody tragedy of *Titus Andronicus*, if Shakspere's at all, are doubtless only his revision of pieces already on the stage. The *Taming of the Shrew* seems to be an old play worked over by Shakspere and some other dramatist, and traces of another hand are thought to be visible in parts of *Henry VIII., Pericles*, and *Timon of Athens*. Such partnerships were common among the Elizabethan dramatists, the most illustrious example being the long association of Beaumont and Fletcher. The plays in the First Folio were divided into histories, comedies, and tragedies, and it will be convenient to notice them briefly in that order.

It was a stirring time when the young adventurer came to London to try his fortune. Elizabeth had finally thrown down the gage of battle to Catholic Europe, by the execution of Mary Stuart, in 1587. The following year saw the destruction of the colossal Armada, which Spain had sent to revenge Mary's death; and hard upon these events followed the gallant exploits of Grenville, Essex, and Raleigh.

That Shakspere shared the exultant patriotism of the times, and the sense of their aloofness from the continent of

Europe, which was now born in the breasts of Englishmen, is evident from many a passage in his plays.

> This happy breed of men, this little world,
> This precious stone set in a silver sea,
> This blessed plot, this earth, this realm, this England,
> This land of such dear souls, this dear, dear land,
> England, bound in with the triumphant sea!

His English histories are ten in number. Of these *King John* and *Henry VIII.* are isolated plays. The others form a consecutive series, in the following order: *Richard II.* the two parts of *Henry IV., Henry V.*, the three parts of *Henry VI.*, and *Richard III.* This series may be divided into two, each forming a tetralogy, or group of four plays. In the first the subject is the rise of the house of Lancaster. But the power of the Red Rose was founded in usurpation. In the second group, accordingly, comes the Nemesis, in the civil wars of the Roses, reaching their catastrophe in the downfall of both Lancaster and York, and the tyranny of Gloucester. The happy conclusion is finally reached in the last play of the series, when this new usurper is overthrown in turn, and Henry VII., the first Tudor sovereign, ascends the throne and restores the Lancastrian inheritance, purified, by bloody atonement, from the stain of Richard II.'s murder. These eight plays are, as it were, the eight acts of one great drama; and, if such a thing were possible, they should be represented on successive nights, like the parts of a Greek trilogy. In order of composition the second group came first. *Henry VI.* is strikingly inferior to the others. *Richard III.* is a good acting play, and its popularity has been sustained by a series of great tragedians, who have taken the part of the king. But, in a literary sense, it is unequal to *Richard II.*, or the two parts of *Henry IV.* The latter is unquestionably Shakspere's greatest historical tragedy, and it contains his master-creation in the region of low comedy, the immortal Falstaff.

The constructive art with which Shakspere shaped history into drama is well seen in comparing his *King John* with the two plays on that subject which were already on the stage. These, like all the other old "Chronicle histories," such as *Thomas Lord Cromwell* and the *Famous Victories of Henry V.*, follow a merely chronological, or biographical, order, giving events loosely, as they occurred, without any unity of effect, or any reference to their bearing on the catastrophe. Shakspere's order was logical. He compressed and selected, disregarding the fact of history oftentimes, in favor of the higher truth of fiction; bringing together a crime and its punishment as cause and effect, even though they had no such relation in the chronicle, and were separated, perhaps, by many years.

Shakspere's first two comedies were experiments. *Love's Labour's Lost* was a play of manners, with hardly any plot. It brought together a number of *humors*, that is, oddities and affectations of various sorts, and played them off on one another, as Ben Jonson afterward did in his comedies of humor. Shakspere never returned to this type of play, unless, perhaps, in the *Taming of the Shrew*. There the story turned on a single "humor," Katharine's bad temper, just as the story in Jonson's *Silent Woman* turned on Morose's hatred of noise. The *Taming of the Shrew* is, therefore, one of the least Shaksperian of Shakspere's plays; a *bourgeois* domestic comedy, with a very narrow interest. It belongs to the school of French comedy, like Molière's *Malade Imaginaire*, not to the romantic comedy of Shakspere and Fletcher.

The *Comedy of Errors* was an experiment of an exactly opposite kind. It was a play purely of incident; a farce, in which the main improbability being granted, namely, that the twin Antipholi and twin Dromios are so alike that they cannot be distinguished, all the amusing complications follow naturally enough. There is little character-drawing in the

play.   Any, two pairs of twins, in the same predicament,
would be equally droll.   The fun lies in the situation.   This
was a comedy of the Latin school, and resembled the *Men-
naechmi* of Plautus.   Shakspere never returned to this type
of play, though there is an element of "errors" in *Midsummer Night's Dream*.   In the *Two Gentlemen of Verona* he
finally hit upon that species of romantic comedy which he
may be said to have invented or created out of the scattered
materials at hand in the works of his predecessors.   In this
play, as in the *Merchant of Venice, Midsummer Night's
Dream, Much Ado about Nothing, As You Like It, Twelfth
Night, Winter's Tale, All's Well that Ends Well, Measure
for Measure*, and the *Tempest*, the plan of construction is
as follows.   There is one main intrigue carried out by the
high comedy characters, and a secondary intrigue, or under-
plot, by the low comedy characters.   The former is by no
means purely comic, but admits the presentation of the
noblest motives, the strongest passions, and the most delicate
graces of romantic poetry.   In some of the plays it has a
prevailing lightness and gayety, as in *As You Like It* and
Twelfth Night.   In others, like *Measure for Measure*, it is
barely saved from becoming tragedy by the happy close.
Shylock certainly remains a tragic figure, even to the end, and
a play like *Winter's Tale*, in which the painful situation is prolonged for years, is only technically a comedy.   Such dramas,
indeed, were called, on many of the title-pages of the time,
"tragi-comedies."   The low comedy interlude, on the other
hand, was broadly comic.   It was cunningly interwoven with
the texture of the play, sometimes loosely, and by way of
variety or relief, as in the episode of Touchstone and Audrey,
in *As You Like It;* sometimes closely, as in the case of Dogberry and Verges, in *Much Ado about Nothing*, where the
blundering of the watch is made to bring about the denouement of the main action.   The *Merry Wives of Windsor* is
an exception to this plan of construction.   It is Shakspere's

only play of contemporary, middle-class English life, and, is written almost throughout in prose. It is his only pure comedy, except the *Taming of the Shrew.*

Shakspere did not abandon comedy when writing tragedy, though he turned it to a new account. The two species graded into one another. Thus *Cymbeline* is, in its fortunate ending, really as much of a comedy as *Winter's Tale*— to which its plot bears a resemblance—and is only technically a tragedy because it contains a violent death. In some of the tragedies, as in *Macbeth* and *Julius Cæsar*, the comedy element is reduced to a minimum. But in others, as *Romeo and Juliet*, and *Hamlet*, it heightens the tragic feeling by the irony of contrast. Akin to this is the use to which Shakspere put the old Vice, or Clown, of the moralities. The Fool in Lear, Touchstone in *As You Like It*, and Thersites in *Troilus and Cressida*, are a sort of parody of the function of the Greek chorus, commenting the action of the drama with scraps of bitter, or half-crazy, philosophy, and wonderful gleams of insight into the depths of man's nature.

The earliest of Shakspere's tragedies, unless *Titus Andronicus* be his, was, doubtless, *Romeo and Juliet*, which is full of the passion and poetry of youth and of first love. It contains a large proportion of riming lines, which is usually a sign in Shakspere of early work. He dropped rime more and more in his later plays, and his blank verse grew freer and more varied in its pauses and the number of its feet. *Romeo and Juliet* is also unique, among his tragedies, in this respect, that the catastrophe is brought about by a fatality, as in the Greek drama. It was Shakspere's habit to work out his tragic conclusions from within, through character, rather than through external chances. This is true of all the great tragedies of his middle life, *Hamlet, Othello, Lear, Macbeth*, in every one of which the catastrophe is involved in the character and actions of the hero. This is so, in a special sense, in *Hamlet*, the subtlest of all Shakspere's plays, and, if

not his masterpiece, at any rate the one which has most attracted and puzzled the greatest minds. It is observable
that in Shakspere's comedies there is no one central figure,
but that, in passing into tragedy, he intensified and concentrated the attention upon a single character. This difference is seen even in the naming of the plays; the tragedies always take their titles from their heroes, the comedies
never.

Somewhat later, probably, than the tragedies already mentioned were the three Roman plays, *Julius Cœsar*, *Coriolanus*, and *Anthony and Cleopatra*. It is characteristic of
Shakspere that he invented the plot of none of his plays, but
took material that he found at hand. In these Roman tragedies he followed Plutarch closely, and yet, even in so doing,
gave, if possible, a greater evidence of real creative power
than when he borrowed a mere outline of a story from some
Italian novelist. It is most instructive to compare *Julius
Cœsar* with Ben Jonson's *Catiline* and *Sejanus*. Jonson was
careful not to go beyond his text. In *Catiline* he translates
almost literally the whole of Cicero's first oration against
Catiline. *Sejanus* is a mosaic of passages from Tacitus and
Suetonius. There is none of this dead learning in Shakspere's play. Having grasped the conceptions of the characters of Brutus, Cassius, and Mark Anthony, as Plutarch gave
them, he pushed them out into their consequences in every
word and act, so independently of his original, and yet so
harmoniously with it, that the reader knows that he is reading history, and needs no further warrant for it than Shakspere's own. *Timon of Athens* is the least agreeable and
most monotonous of Shakspere's undoubted tragedies, and
Troilus and Cressida, said Coleridge, is the hardest to characterize. The figures of the old Homeric world fare but
hardly under the glaring light of modern standards of morality
which Shakspere turns upon them. Ajax becomes a stupid
bully, Ulysses a crafty politician, and swift-footed Achilles

a vain and sulky chief of faction. In losing their ideal remoteness the heroes of the *Iliad* lose their poetic quality, and the lover of Homer experiences an unpleasant disenchantment.

It was customary in the 18th century to speak of Shakspere as a rude though prodigious genius. Even Milton could describe him as" warbling his native wood-notes wild." But a truer criticism, beginning in England with Coleridge, has shown that he was also a profound artist. It is true that he wrote for his audiences, and that his art is not every-where and at all points perfect. But a great artist will contrive, as Shakspere did, to reconcile practical exigencies, like those of the public stage, with the finer requirements of his art. Strained interpretations have been put upon this or that item in Shakspere's plays ; and yet it is generally true that some deeper reason can be assigned for his method in a given case than that "the audience liked puns," or, "the audience liked ghosts." Compare, for example, his delicate management of the supernatural with Marlowe's procedure in *Faustus*. Shakspere's age believed in witches, elves, and apparitions; and yet there is always something shadowy or allegorical in his use of such machinery. The ghost in *Hamlet* is merely an embodied suspicion. Banquo's wraith, which is invisible to all but Macbeth, is the haunting of an evil conscience. The witches in the same play are but the promptings of ambition, thrown into a human shape, so as to become actors in the drama. In the same way, the fairies in *Midsummer Night's Dream* are the personified caprices of the lovers, and they are unseen by the human characters, whose likes and dislikes they control, save in the instance where Bottom is " translated " (that is, becomes mad) and has sight of the invisible world. So in the *Tempest*, Ariel is the spirit of the air and Caliban of the earth, ministering, with more or less of unwillingness, to man's necessities.

Shakspere is the most universal of writers. He touches

more men at more points than Homer, or Dante, or Goethe.
The deepest wisdom, the sweetest poetry, the widest range
of character, are combined in his plays. He made the English language an organ of expression unexcelled in the history
of literature. Yet he is not an English poet simply, but a
world-poet. Germany has made him her own, and the Latin
races, though at first hindered in a true appreciation of him
by the canons of classical taste, have at length learned to
know him. An ever-growing mass of Shaksperian literature,
in the way of comment and interpretation, critical, textual,
historical, or illustrative, testifies to the durability and
growth of his fame. Above all, his plays still keep, and
probably always will keep, the stage. It is common to speak
of Shakspere and the other Elizabethan dramatists as if
they stood, in some sense, on a level. But in truth there
is an almost measureless distance between him and all
his contemporaries. The rest shared with him in the
mighty influences of the age. Their plays are touched here
and there with the power and splendor of which they
were all joint heirs. But, as a whole, they are obsolete.
They live in books, but not in the hearts and on the tongues
of men.

The most remarkable of the dramatists contemporary with
Shakspere was Ben Jonson, whose robust figure is in striking contrast with the other's gracious impersonality. Jonson
was nine years younger than Shakspere. He was educated
at Westminster School, served as a soldier in the low countries, became an actor in Henslowe's company, and was
twice imprisoned—once for killing a fellow-actor in a duel,
and once for his part in the comedy of *Eastward Hoe*, which
gave offense to King James. He lived down to the time
of Charles I. (1635), and became the acknowledged arbiter
of English letters and the center of convivial wit combats at the Mermaid, the Devil, and other famous London
taverns.

What things have we seen ·
Done at the Mermaid; heard words that have been
So nimble and so full of subtle flame,
As if that every one from whom they came
Had meant to put his whole wit in a jest,
And had resolved to live a fool the rest
Of his dull life.[1]

The inscription on his tomb in Westminster Abbey is simply

O rare Ben Jonson!

Jonson's comedies were modeled upon the *vetus comœdia* of Aristophanes, which was satirical in purpose, and they belonged to an entirely different school from Shakspere's. They were classical and not romantic, and were pure comedies, admitting no admixture of tragic motives. There is hardly one lovely or beautiful character in the entire range of his dramatic creations. They were comedies not of character, in the high sense of the word, but of manners or humors. His design was to lash the follies and vices of the day, and his *dramatis personœ* consisted for the most part of gulls, impostors, fops, cowards, swaggering braggarts, and "Pauls men." In his first play, *Every Man in his Humor* (acted in 1598), in *Every Man Out of his Humor*, *Bartholomew Fair*, and, indeed, in all of his comedies, his subject was the fashionable affectations, the whims, oddities, and eccentric developments of London life. His procedure was to bring together a number of these fantastic humorists, and "squeeze out the humor of such spongy souls," by playing them off upon each other, involving them in all manner of comical misadventures, and rendering them utterly ridiculous and contemptible. There was thus a perishable element in his art, for manners change; and, however effective this exposure of contemporary affectations may have been before an audience of Jonson's day, it is as hard for a modern reader to detect his points as it will be for a reader two hundred

[1] Francis Beaumont. *Letter to Ben Jonson.*

years hence to understand the satire upon the æsthetic craze
in such pieces of the present day as *Patience*, or the *Colonel*.
Nevertheless, a patient reader, with the help of copious foot-
notes, can gradually put together for himself an image of
that world of obsolete humors in which Jonson's comedy
dwells, and can admire the dramatist's solid good sense, his
great learning, his skill in construction, and the astonishing
fertility of his invention. His characters are not revealed
from within, like Shakspere's, but built up painfully from
outside by a succession of minute, laborious particulars.
The difference will be plainly manifest if such a character
as Slender, in the *Merry Wives of Windsor*, be compared
with any one of the inexhaustible variety of idiots in Jonson's plays ; with Master Stephen, for example, in *Every
Man in his Humor;* or, if Falstaff be put side by side with
Captain Bobadil, in the same comedy, perhaps Jonson's masterpiece in the way of comic caricature. *Cynthia's Revels*
was a satire on the courtiers and the *Poetaster* on Jonson's
literary enemies. The *Alchemist* was an exposure of quack-
ery, and is one of his best comedies, but somewhat over-
weighted with learning. *Volpone* is the most powerful of
all his dramas, but is a harsh and disagreeable piece ; and
the state of society which it depicts is too revolting for
comedy. The *Silent Woman* is, perhaps, the easiest of all
Jonson's plays for a modern reader to follow and appreciate.
There is a distinct plot to it, the situation is extremely ludicrous, and the emphasis is laid upon a single humor or eccen-
tricity, as in some of Molière's lighter comedies, like *Le
Malade Imaginaire*, or *Le Médecin malgré lui*.

In spite of his heaviness in drama, Jonson had a light
enough touch in lyric poetry. His songs have not the careless sweetness of Shakspere's, but they have a grace of their
own. Such pieces as his *Love's Triumph, Hymn to Diana*,
the adaptation from Philostratus,

Drink to me only with thine eyes,

and many others entitle their author to rank among the first of English lyrists. Some of these occur in his two collections of miscellaneous verse, the *Forest* and *Underwoods;* others in the numerous masques which he composed. These were a species of entertainment, very popular at the court of James I., combining dialogue with music, intricate dances, and costly scenery. Jonson left an unfinished pastoral drama, the *Sad Shepherd,* which contains passages of great beauty; one, especially, descriptive of the shepherdess

> Earine,
> Who had her very being and her name
> With the first buds and breathings of the spring,
> Born with the primrose and the violet
> And earliest roses blown.

———

1. A History of Elizabethan Literature. George Saintsbury. London: Macmillan & Co., 1877.

2. Palgrave's Golden Treasury of Songs and Lyrics. London: Macmillan & Co., 1877.

3. The Courtly Poets from Raleigh to Montrose. Edited by J. Hannah. London: Bell & Daldy, 1870.

4. The Countess of Pembroke's Arcadia. London : Sampson Low, Son & Marston, 1867.

5. Bacon's Essays. Edited by W. Aldis Wright. Macmillan & Co. (Golden Treasury Series.)

6. The Cambridge Shakspere. (Clark & Wright.)

7. Charles Lamb's Specimens of English Dramatic Poets.

8. Ben Jonson's Volpone and Silent Woman. Cunningham's Edition. London: J. C. Hotten, (3 vols.)

CHAPTER IV.

THE AGE OF MILTON.

1608–1674.

THE Elizabethan age proper closed with the death of the queen, and the accession of James I., in 1603, but the literature of the fifty years following was quite as rich as that of the half-century that had passed since she came to the throne, in 1557. The same qualities of thought and style which had marked the writers of her reign prolonged themselves in their successors, through the reigns of the first two Stuart kings and the Commonwealth. Yet there was a change in spirit. Literature is only one of the many forms in which the national mind expresses itself. In periods of political revolution, literature, leaving the serene air of fine art, partakes the violent agitation of the times. There were seeds of civil and religious discord in Elizabethan England. As between the two parties in the Church there was a compromise and a truce rather than a final settlement. The Anglican doctrine was partly Calvinistic and partly Arminian. The form of government was Episcopal, but there was a large body of Presbyterians in the Church who desired a change. In the ritual and ceremonies many "rags of popery" had been retained, which the extreme reformers wished to tear away. But Elizabeth was a worldly-minded woman, impatient of theological disputes. Though circumstances had made her the champion of Protestantism in Europe she kept many Catholic notions; disapproved, for example, of the marriage of priests, and hated sermons. She was jealous of her prerogative in the State, and in the Church she enforced uniformity. The authors of the *Martin Marprelate* pamphlets against the bishops were punished by death or imprisonment. While the queen lived things were kept well together and England was at one in face of the common foe. Admiral Howard, who commanded the English naval forces against the Armada, was a Catholic.

But during the reign of James I. (1603–1625) and Charles I. (1625–1649) Puritanism grew stronger through repression. "England," says the historian Green, "became the people of a book, and that book the Bible." The power of the king was used to impose the power of the bishops upon the English and Scotch Churches until religious discontent became also political discontent, and finally overthrew the throne. The writers of this period divided more and more into two hostile camps. On the side of Church and king was the bulk of the learning and genius of the time. But on the side of free religion and the Parliament were the stern conviction, the fiery zeal, the exalted imagination of English Puritanism. The spokesman of this movement was Milton, whose great figure dominates the literary history of his generation, as Shakspere does of the generation preceding.

The drama went on in the course marked out for it by Shakspere's example until the theaters were closed by Parliament, in 1642. Of the Stuart dramatists the most important were Beaumont and Fletcher, all of whose plays were produced during the reign of James I. These were fifty-three in number, but only thirteen of them were joint productions. Francis Beaumont was twenty years younger than Shakspere, and died a few years before him. He was the son of a judge of the Common Pleas. His collaborator, John Fletcher, a son of the bishop of London, was five years older than Beaumont, and survived him nine years. He was much the more prolific of the two and wrote alone some forty plays. Although the life of one of these partners was conterminous with Shakspere's, their works exhibit a later phase

of the dramatic art. The Stuart dramatists followed the lead
of Shakspere rather than of Ben Jonson. Their plays, like
the former's, belong to the romantic drama. They present
a poetic and idealized version of life, deal with the highest
passions and the wildest buffoonery, and introduce a great
variety of those daring situations and incidents which we
agree to call romantic. But, while Shakspere seldom or
never overstepped the modesty of nature, his successors ran
into every license. They sought to stimulate the jaded
appetite of their audience by exhibiting monstrosities of
character, unnatural lusts, subtleties of crime, virtues and
vices both in excess.

Beaumont and Fletcher's plays are much easier and more
agreeable reading than Ben Jonson's. Though often loose
in their plots and without that consistency in the development of their characters which distinguished Jonson's more
conscientious workmanship, they are full of graceful dialogue
and beautiful poetry. Dryden said that after the Restoration two of their plays were acted for one of Shakspere's
or Jonson's throughout the year, and he added that they
"understood and imitated the conversation of gentlemen
much better, whose wild debaucheries and quickness of wit
in repartees no poet can ever paint as they have done."
Wild debauchery was certainly not the mark of a gentleman
in Shakspere, nor was it altogether so in Beaumont and
Fletcher. Their gentlemen are gallant and passionate lovers,
gay cavaliers, generous, courageous, courteous—according
to the fashion of their times—and sensitive on the point of
honor. They are far superior to the cold-blooded rakes of
Dryden and the Restoration comedy. Still the manners and
language in Beaumont and Fletcher's plays are extremely
licentious, and it is not hard to sympathize with the objec-
tions to the theater expressed by the Puritan writer, William
Prynne, who, after denouncing the long hair of the cavaliers
in his tract, *The Unloveliness of Lovelocks*, attacked the

stage, in 1633, with *Histrio-mastix: the Player's Scourge;* an offense for which he was fined, imprisoned, pilloried, and had his ears cropped. Coleridge said that Shakspere was coarse, but never gross. He had the healthy coarseness of nature herself. But Beaumont and Fletcher's pages are corrupt. Even their chaste women are immodest in language and thought. They use not merely that frankness of speech which was a fashion of the times, but a profusion of obscene imagery which could not proceed from a pure mind. Chastity with them is rather a bodily accident than a virtue of the heart, says Coleridge.

Among the best of their light comedies are *The Chances, The Scornful Lady, The Spanish Curate,* and *Rule a Wife and Have a Wife.* But far superior to these are their tragedies and tragi-comedies, *The Maid's Tragedy, Philaster, A King and No King*—all written jointly—and *Valentinian* and *Thierry and Theodoret,* written by Fletcher alone, but perhaps, in part, sketched out by Beaumont. The tragic masterpiece of Beaumont and Fletcher is *The Maid's Tragedy,* a powerful but repulsive play, which sheds a singular light not only upon its authors' dramatic methods, but also upon the attitude toward royalty favored by the doctrine of the divine right of kings, which grew up under the Stuarts. The heroine, Evadne, has been in secret a mistress of the king, who marries her to Amintor, a gentleman of his court, because, as she explains to her bridegroom, on the wedding night,

> I must have one
> To father children, and to bear the name
> Of husband to me, that my sin may be
> More honorable.

This scene is, perhaps, the most affecting and impressive in the whole range of Beaumont and Fletcher's drama. Yet when Evadne names the king as her paramour, Amintor exclaims :

O thou hast named a word that wipes away
All thoughts revengeful. In that sacred name
"The king" there lies a terror. What frail man
Dares lift his hand against it? Let the gods
Speak to him when they please; till when, let us
Suffer and wait.

And the play ends with the words

On lustful kings,
Unlooked-for sudden deaths from heaven are sent,
But cursed is he that is their instrument.

Aspatia, in this tragedy, is a good instance of Beaumont
and Fletcher's pathetic characters. She is troth-plight wife to
Amintor, and after he, by the king's command, has forsaken
her for Evadne, she disguises herself as a man, provokes her
unfaithful lover to a duel, and dies under his sword, blessing
the hand that killed her. This is a common type in Beaumont and Fletcher, and was drawn originally from Shakspere's Ophelia. All their good women have the instinctive
fidelity of a dog, and a superhuman patience and devotion,
a "gentle forlornness" under wrongs, which is painted with
an almost feminine tenderness. In *Philaster, or Love Lies
Bleeding*, Euphrasia, conceiving a hopeless passion for
Philaster—who is in love with Arethusa—puts on the dress
of a page and enters his service. He employs her to carry
messages to his lady-love, just as Viola, in *Twelfth Night*, is
sent by the duke to Olivia. Philaster is persuaded by
slanderers that his page and his lady have been unfaithful to
him, and in his jealous fury he wounds Euphrasia with his
sword. Afterward, convinced of the boy's fidelity, he asks
forgiveness, whereto Euphrasia replies,

Alas, my lord, my life is not a thing
Worthy your noble thoughts. 'Tis not a life,
'Tis but a piece of childhood thrown away.

Beaumont and Fletcher's love-lorn maids wear the willow very sweetly, but in all their piteous passages there is

nothing equal to the natural pathos—the pathos which arises from the deep springs of character—of that one brief question and answer in *King Lear*.

Lear. So young and so untender?

Cordelia.   So young, my lord, and true.

The disguise of a woman in man's apparel is a common incident. in the romantic drama ; and the fact that on the Elizabethan stage the female parts were taken by boys made the deception easier. Viola's situation in *Twelfth Night* is precisely similiar to Euphrasia's, but there is a difference in the handling of the device which is characteristic of a distinction between Shakspere's art and that of his contemporaries. The audience in *Twelfth Night* is taken into confidence and made aware of Viola's real nature from the start, while Euphrasia's *incognito* is preserved till the fifth act, and then disclosed by an accident. This kind of mystification and surprise was a trick below Shakspere. In this instance, moreover, it involved a departure from dramatic probability. Euphrasia could, at any moment, by revealing her identity, have averted the greatest sufferings and dangers from Philaster, Arethusa, and herself, and the only motive for her keeping silence is represented to have been a feeling of maidenly shame at her position. Such strained and fantastic motives are too often made the pivot of the action in Beaumont and Fletcher's tragi-comedies. Their characters have not the depth and truth of Shakspere's, nor are they drawn so sharply. One reads their plays with pleasure, and remembers here and there a passage of fine poetry, or a noble or lovely trait, but their characters, as wholes, leave a fading impression. Who, even after a single reading or representation, ever forgets Falstaff, or Shylock, or King Lear?

The moral inferiority of Beaumont and Fletcher is well seen in such a play as *A King and No King*. Here Arbaces falls in love with his sister, and, after a furious conflict in his own mind, finally succumbs to his guilty passion. He is rescued from the consequences of his weakness by the discovery that Panthea is not, in fact, his sister. But this is to cut the knot and not to untie it. It leaves the denouement to chance, and not to those moral forces through which Shakspere always wrought his conclusions. Arbaces has failed, and the piece of luck which keeps his failure innocent is rejected by every right-feeling spectator. In one of John Ford's tragedies the situation which in *A King and No King* is only apparent becomes real, and incest is boldly made the subject of the play. Ford pushed the morbid and unnatural in character and passion into even wilder extremes than Beaumont and Fletcher. His best play, the *Broken Heart*, is a prolonged and unrelieved torture of the feelings.

Fletcher's *Faithful Shepherdess* is the best English pastoral drama with the exception of Jonson's fragment, the *Sad Shepherd*. Its choral songs are richly and sweetly modulated, and the influence of the whole poem upon Milton is very apparent in his *Comus*. The *Knight of the Burning Pestle*, written by Beaumont and Fletcher jointly, was the first burlesque comedy in the language, and is excellent fooling. Beaumont and Fletcher's blank verse is musical, but less masculine than Marlowe's or Shakspere's, by reason of their excessive use of extra syllables and feminine endings.

In John Webster the fondness for abnormal and sensational themes, which beset the Stuart stage, showed itself in the exaggeration of the terrible into the horrible. Fear, in Shakspere—as in the great murder scene in *Macbeth*—is a pure passion ; but in Webster it is mingled with something physically repulsive. Thus his *Duchess of Malfi* is presented in the dark with a dead man's hand, and is told that it is the hand of her murdered husband. She is shown a dance of mad-men and, "behind a traverse, the artificial figures of her

children, appearing as if dead." Treated in this elaborate
fashion, that "terror," which Aristotle said it was one of the
objects of tragedy to move, loses half its dignity. Webster's
images have the smell of the charnel house about them:

> She would not after the report keep fresh
> As long as flowers on graves.

> We are only like dead walls or vaulted graves,
> That, ruined, yield no echo.
>   O this gloomy world!
> In what a shadow or deep pit of darkness
> Doth womanish and fearful mankind live!

Webster had an intense and somber genius. In diction he
was the most Shaksperian of the Elizabethan dramatists, and
there are sudden gleams of beauty among his dark horrors
which light up a whole scene with some abrupt touch of
feeling.

> Cover her face: mine eyes dazzle: she died young,

says the brother of the Duchess, when he has procured her
murder and stands before the corpse. *Vittoria Corombona*
is described in the old editions as "a night-piece," and it
should, indeed, be acted by the shuddering light of torches,
and with the cry of the screech-owl to punctuate the speeches.
The scene of Webster's two best tragedies was laid, like
many of Ford's, Cyril Tourneur's, and Beaumont and
Fletcher's, in Italy—the wicked and splendid Italy of the
Renaissance, which had such a fascination for the Elizabethan imagination. It was to them the land of the Borgias
and the Cenci; of families of proud nobles, luxurious, cultivated, but full of revenge and ferocious cunning; subtle
poisoners, who killed with a perfumed glove or fan; parri-
cides, atheists, committers of unnamable crimes, and inventors
of strange and delicate varieties of sin.

But a very few have here been mentioned of the great
host of dramatists who kept the theaters busy through the

reigns of Elizabeth, James I., and Charles I. The last of
the race was James Shirley, who died in 1666, and whose
thirty-eight plays were written during the reign of Charles
I. and the Commonwealth.

In the miscellaneous prose and poetry of this period
there is lacking the free, exulting, creative impulse of the
elder generation, but there are a soberer feeling and a
certain scholarly choiceness which commend themselves to
readers of bookish tastes. Even that quaintness of thought
which is a mark of the Commonwealth writers is not without its attraction for a nice literary palate. Prose became
now of greater relative importance than ever before. Almost every distinguished writer lent his pen to one or the
other party in the great theological and political controversy
of the time. There were famous theologians, like Hales,
Chillingworth, and Baxter ; historians and antiquaries, like
Selden, Knolles, and Cotton ; philosophers, such as Hobbes,
Lord Herbert of Cherbury, and More, the Platonist; and
writers in natural science—which now entered upon its modern, experimental phase, under the stimulus of Bacon's writings—among whom may be mentioned Wallis, the mathe-
matician ; Boyle, the chemist ; and Harvey, the discoverer
of the circulation of the blood. These are outside of our
subject, but in the strictly literary prose of the time, the
same spirit of roused inquiry is manifest, and the same disposition to a thorough and exhausive treatment of a subject, which is proper to the scientific attitude of mind. The
line between true and false science, however, had not yet
been drawn. The age was pedantic, and appealed too much
to the authority of antiquity. Hence we have such monuments of perverse and curious erudition as Robert Burton's
Anatomy of Melancholy, 1621; and Sir Thomas Browne's
*Pseudodoxia Epidemica, or Inquiries into Vulgar and Com-
mon Errors*, 1646. The former of these was the work of an
Oxford scholar, an astrologer, who cast his own horoscope,

and a victim himself of the atrabilious humor, from which
he sought relief in listening to the ribaldry of bargemen,
and in compiling this *Anatomy*, in which the causes, symptoms, prognostics, and cures of melancholy are considered
in numerous partitions, sections, members, and subsections.
The work is a mosaic of quotations. All literature is ransacked for anecdotes and instances, and the book has thus
become a mine of out-of-the-way learning in which later
writers have dug. Lawrence Sterne helped himself freely
to Burton's treasures, and Dr. Johnson said that the *Anatomy* was the only book that ever took him out of bed two
hours sooner than he wished to rise.

The vulgar and common errors which Sir Thomas Browne
set himself to refute were such as these: That dolphins
are crooked, that Jews stink, that a man hath one rib less
than a woman, that Xerxes's army drank up rivers, that
cicades are bred out of cuckoo-spittle, that Hannibal split
Alps with vinegar, together with many similar fallacies
touching Pope Joan, the Wandering Jew, the decuman or
tenth wave, the blackness of negroes, Friar Bacon's brazen
head, etc. Another book in which great learning and ingenuity were applied to trifling ends was the same author's
*Garden of Cyrus ; or, the Quincuncial Lozenge or Network
Plantations of the Ancients*, in which a mystical meaning
is sought in the occurrence throughout nature and art of the
figure of the quincunx or lozenge. Browne was a physician
of Norwich, where his library, museum, aviary, and botanic
garden were thought worthy of a special visit by the Royal
Society. He was an antiquary and a naturalist, and deeply
read in the school-men and the Christian Fathers. He was
a mystic, and a writer of a rich and peculiar imagination,
whose thoughts have impressed themselves upon many kindred minds, like Coleridge, De Quincey, and Emerson. Two
of his books belong to literature, *Religio Medici*, published
in 1642, and *Hydriotaphia; or, Urn Burial*, 1658, a discourse

upon rites of burial and incremation, suggested by some
Roman funeral urns dug up in Norfolk. Browne's style,
though too highly latinized, is a good example of Commonwealth prose; that stately, cumbrous, brocaded prose which
had something of the flow and measure of verse, rather
than the quicker, colloquial movement of modern writing.
Browne stood aloof from the disputes of his time, and in
his very subjects there is a calm and meditative remoteness
from the daily interests of men. His *Religio Medici* is full
of a wise tolerance and a singular elevation of feeling.
"At the sight of a cross, or crucifix, I can dispense with
my hat, but scarce with the thought or memory of my Sav-
iour." "They only had the advantage of a bold and noble
faith who lived before his coming." "They go the fairest
way to heaven that would serve God without a hell." "All
things are artificial, for nature is the art of God." The last
chapter of the *Urn Burial* is an almost rhythmical descant
on mortality and oblivion. The style kindles slowly into a
somber eloquence. It is the most impressive and extraordinary passage in the prose literature of the time. Browne,
like Hamlet, loved to "consider too curiously." His subtlety led him to "pose his apprehension with those involved
enigmas and riddles of the Trinity—with incarnation and
resurrection;" and to start odd inquiries: "what song the
Syrens sang, or what name Achilles assumed when he hid
himself among women;" or whether, after Lazarus was
raised from the dead, "his heir might lawfully detain his
inheritance." The quaintness of his phrase appears at every
turn. "Charles the Fifth can never hope to live within two
Methuselahs of Hector." "Generations pass while some
trees stand, and old families survive not three oaks."
"Mummy is become merchandise; Mizraim cures wounds,
and Pharaoh is sold for balsams."

One of the pleasantest of old English humorists is Thomas
Fuller, who was a chaplain in the royal army during the civil

war, and wrote, among other things, a *Church History of Britain;* a book of religious meditations, *Good Thoughts in Bad Times;* and a "character" book, *The Holy and Profane State.* His most important work, the *Worthies of England,* was published in 1662, the year after his death. This was a description of every English county ; its natural commodities, manufactures, wonders, proverbs, etc., with brief biographies of its memorable persons. Fuller had a well-stored memory, sound piety, and excellent common sense. Wit was his leading intellectual trait, and the quaintness which he shared with his contemporaries appears in his writings in a fondness for puns, droll turns of expression and bits of eccentric suggestion. His prose, unlike Browne's, Milton's, and Jeremy Taylor's, is brief, simple, and pithy. His dry vein of humor was imitated by the American Cotton Mather, in his *Magnalia,* and by many of the English and New England divines of the 17th century.

Jeremy Taylor was also a chaplain in the king's army, was several times imprisoned for his opinions, and was afterward made, by Charles II., bishop of Down and Connor. He is a devotional rather than a theological writer, and his *Holy Living* and *Holy Dying* are religious classics. Taylor, like Sidney was a "warbler of poetic prose." He has been called the prose Spenser, and his English has the opulence, the gentle elaboration, the "linked sweetness long drawn out" of the poet of the *Faerie Queene.* In fullness and resonance Taylor's diction resembles that of the great orators, though it lacks their nervous energy. His pathos is exquisitely tender, and his numerous similes have Spenser's pictorial amplitude. Some of them have become commonplaces for admiration, notably his description of the flight of the skylark, and the sentence in which he compares the gradual awakening of the human faculties to the sunrise, which " first opens a little eye of heaven, and sends away the spirits of darkness, and gives light to a cock, and calls up the lark to

matins, and by and by gilds the fringes of a cloud, and
peeps over the eastern hills." Perhaps the most impressive
single passage of Taylor's is the opening chapter in *Holy
Dying.* From the midst of the sickening paraphernalia of
death which he there accumulates rises that delicate image
of the fading rose, one of the most perfect things in its
wording in all our prose literature. " But so have I seen
a rose newly springing from the clefts of its hood, and at
first it was as fair as the morning, and full with the dew of
heaven as a lamb's fleece ; but when a ruder breath had
forced open its virgin modesty, and dismantled its too youthful and unripe retirements, it began to put on darkness and
to decline to softness and the symptoms of a sickly age ; it
bowed the head and broke its stock; and at night, having
lost some of its leaves and all its beauty, it fell into the
portion of weeds and outworn faces."

With the progress of knowledge and discussion many
kinds of prose literature, which were not absolutely new,
now began to receive wider extension. Of this sort are the
Letters from Italy, and other miscellanies included in the
Reliquiæ Wottonianæ, or remains of Sir Henry Wotton,
English embassador at Venice in the reign of James I., and
subsequently Provost of Eton College. Also the *Table Talk*
—full of incisive remarks—left by John Selden, whom Milton pronounced the first scholar of his age, and who was a
distinguished authority in legal antiquities and international
law, furnished notes to Drayton's *Polyolbion,* and wrote upon
Eastern religions, and upon the Arundel marbles. Literary
biography was represented by the charming little *Lives* of
good old Izaak Walton, the first edition of whose *Compleat
Angler* was printed in 1653. The lives were five in number; of Hooker, Wotton, Donne, Herbert, and Sanderson.
Several of these were personal friends of the author, and
Sir Henry Wotton was a brother of the angle. The *Compleat Angler,* though not the first piece of sporting literature

in English, is unquestionably the most popular, and still remains a favorite with "all that are lovers of virtue, and dare trust in Providence, and be quiet, and go a-angling." As in Ascham's *Toxophilus*, the instruction is conveyed in dialogue form, but the technical part of the book is relieved by many delightful digressions. Piscator and his friend Venator pursue their talk under a honeysuckle hedge or a sycamore-tree during a passing shower. They repair, after the day's fishing, to some honest ale-house, with lavender in the window and a score of ballads stuck about the wall, where they sing catches—"old-fashioned poetry but choicely good"—composed by the author or his friends, drink barley wine, and eat their trout or chub. They encounter milk-maids, who sing to them and give them a draft of the red cow's milk and they never cease their praises of the angler's life, of rural contentment among the cowslip meadows, and the quiet streams of Thames, or Lea, or Shawford Brook.

The decay of a great literary school is usually signalized by the exaggeration of its characteristic traits. The manner of the Elizabethan poets was pushed into mannerism by their successors. That manner, at its best, was hardly a simple one, but in the Stuart and Commonwealth writers it became mere extravagance. Thus Phineas Fletcher — a cousin of the dramatist — composed a long Spenserian allegory, the *Purple Island*, descriptive of the human body. George Herbert and others made anagrams, and verses shaped like an altar, a cross, or a pair of Easter wings. This group of poets was named, by Dr. Johnson, in his life of Cowley, the metaphysical school. Other critics have preferred to call them the fantastic or conceited school, the later Euphuists or the English Marinists and Gongorists, after the poets Marino and Gongora, who brought this fashion to its extreme in Italy and in Spain. The English *conceptistas* were mainly clergymen of the established church: Donne, Herbert, Vaughan, Quarles, and Herrick. But Crashaw was

a Roman Catholic, and Cowley—the latest of them—a
layman.

The one who set the fashion was Dr. John Donne, Dean
of St. Paul's, whom Dryden pronounced a great wit, but not
a great poet, and whom Ben Jonson esteemed the best poet
in the world for some things, but likely to be forgotten for
want of being understood. Besides satires and epistles in
verse, he composed amatory poems in his youth, and divine
poems in his age, both kinds distinguished by such subtle
obscurity, and far-fetched ingenuities, that they read like a
series of puzzles. When this poet has occasion to write a
valediction to his mistress upon going into France, he compares their temporary separation to that of a pair of
compasses :

> Such wilt thou be to me, who must,
>   Like the other foot obliquely run;
> Thy firmness makes my circle just,
>   And makes me end where I begun.

If he would persuade her to marriage he calls her attention
to a flea—

> Me it sucked first and now sucks thee,
> And in this flea our two bloods mingled be.

He says that the flea is their marriage-temple, and bids her
forbear to kill it lest she thereby commit murder, suicide and
sacrilege all in one. Donne's figures are scholastic and smell
of the lamp. He ransacked cosmography, astrology, alchemy,
optics, the canon law, and the divinity of the school-men for
ink-horn terms and similes. He was in verse what Browne
was in prose. He loved to play with distinctions, hyper-
boles, parodoxes, the very casuistry and dialectics of love or
devotion.

> Thou canst not every day give me my heart:
> If thou canst give it then thou never gav'st it:
> Love's riddles are that though thy heart depart
> It stays at home, and thou with losing sav'st it.

Donne's verse is usually as uncouth as his thought. But there is a real passion slumbering under these ashy heaps of conceit, and occasionally a pure flame darts up, as in the justly admired lines :

> Her pure and eloquent blood
> Spoke in her cheek, and so divinely wrought
> That one might almost say her body thought.

This description of Donne is true, with modifications, of all the metaphysical poets. They had the same forced and unnatural style. The ordinary laws of the association of ideas were reversed with them. It was not the nearest, but the remotest, association that was called up. "Their attempts," said Johnson, "were always analytic : they broke every image into fragments." The finest spirit among them was "holy George Herbert," whose *Temple* was published in 1633. The titles in this volume were such as the following : Christmas, Easter, Good Friday, Holy Baptism, The Cross, The Church Porch, Church Music, The Holy Scriptures, Redemption, Faith, Doomsday. Never since, except, perhaps, in Keble's *Christian Year*, have the ecclesiastic ideals of the Anglican Church—the "beauty of holiness"— found such sweet expression in poetry. The verses entitled *Virtue*—

> Sweet day, so cool, so calm, so bright,

are known to most readers, as well as the line,

> Who sweeps a room as for thy laws makes that and the action fine.

The quaintly named pieces, the *Elixir*, the *Collar*, and the *Pulley*, are full of deep thought and spiritual feeling. But Herbert's poetry is constantly disfigured by bad taste. Take this passage from *Whitsunday*,

> Listen, sweet dove, unto my song,
>   And spread thy golden wings on me,
> Hatching my tender heart so long,
>   Till it get wing and fly away with thee,

which is almost as ludicrous as the epitaph written by his
contemporary, Carew, on the daughter of Sir Thomas Went-
worth, whose soul

> . . . grew so fast within
> It broke the outward shell of sin,
> And so was hatched a cherubin.

Another of these church poets was Henry Vaughan, "the
Silurist," or Welshman, whose fine piece, the *Retreat*, has
been often compared with Wordsworth's *Ode on the Intimations of Immortality*. Frances Quarles's *Divine Emblems*
long remained a favorite book with religious readers both in
old and New England. Emblem books, in which engravings
of a figurative design were accompanied with explanatory
letterpress in verse, were a popular class of literature in the
17th century. The most famous of them all were Jacob
Catt's Dutch emblems.

One of the most delightful of the English lyric poets is
Robert Herrick, whose *Hesperides*, 1648, has lately received
such sympathetic illustration from the pencil of an American
artist, Mr. E. A. Abbey. Herrick was a clergyman of the
English Church and was expelled by the Puritans from his
living, the vicarage of Dean Prior, in Devonshire. The
most quoted of his religious poems is, *How to Keep a True
Lent*. But it may be doubted whether his tastes were pre-
vailingly clerical ; his poetry certainly was not. He was a
disciple of Ben Jonson, and his boon companion at

> . . . those lyric feasts
> Made at the Sun,
> The Dog, the Triple Tun;
> Where we such clusters had
> As made us nobly wild, not mad.
> And yet each verse of thine,
> Outdid the meat, outdid the frolic wine.

Herrick's *Noble Numbers* seldom rises above the expression
of a cheerful gratitude and contentment. He had not the

subtlety and elevation of Herbert, but he surpassed him in the
grace, melody, sensuous beauty, and fresh lyrical impulse of
his verse.   The conceits of the metaphysical school appear
in Herrick only in the form of an occasional pretty quaintness.   He is the poet of English parish festivals and of English
flowers, the primrose, the whitethorn, the daffodil.   He sang
the praises of the country life, love songs to "Julia," and
hymns of thanksgiving for simple blessings.   He has been
called the English Catullus, but he strikes rather the Horatian note of *Carpe diem* and regret at the shortness of life
and youth in many of his best-known poems, such as *Gather
ye Rose-buds while ye may*, and *To Corinna, To Go a
Maying*.

Richard Crashaw was a Cambridge scholar who was turned
out of his fellowship at Peterhouse by the Puritans in 1644,
for refusing to subscribe the Solemn League and Covenant ;
became a Roman Catholic, and died in 1650 as a canon of
the Virgin's Chapel at Loretto.   He is best known to the
general reader by his *Wishes for his Unknown Mistress*,

> That not impossible she

which is included in most of the anthologies.   His religious
poetry expresses a rapt and mystical piety, fed on the ecstatic
visions of St. Theresa, "undaunted daughter of desires," who
is the subject of a splendid apostrophe in his poem, *The
Flaming Heart*.   Crashaw is, in fact, a poet of passages and
of single lines, his work being exceedingly uneven and disfigured by tasteless conceits.   In one of his Latin epigrams
occurs the celebrated line upon the miracle at Cana :

> Vidit et erubuit nympha pudica Deum:

as englished by Dryden,

> The conscious water saw its Lord and blushed.

Abraham Cowley is now less remembered for his poetry
than for his pleasant volume of essays, published after the

Restoration; but he was thought in his own time a better poet than Milton. His collection of love songs—the *Mistress* —is a mass of cold conceits, in the metaphysical manner; but his elegies on Crashaw and Harvey have much dignity and natural feeling. He introduced the Pindaric ode into English, and wrote an epic poem on a biblical subject—the *Davideis*—now quite unreadable. Cowley was a royalist, and followed the exiled court to France.

Side by side with the church poets were the cavaliers— Carew, Waller, Lovelace, Suckling, L'Estrange, and others— gallant courtiers and officers in the royal army, who mingled love and loyalty in their strains. Colonel Richard Lovelace, who lost every thing in the king's service, and was several times imprisoned, wrote two famous songs—*To Lucasta on going to the Wars*—in which occur the lines,

I could not love thee, dear, so much,
Loved I not honor more—

and to *Althœa from Prison*, in which he sings "the sweetness, mercy, majesty, and glories" of his king, and declares that "stone-walls do not a prison make, nor iron bars a cage." Another of the cavaliers was Sir John Suckling, who formed a plot to rescue the Earl of Strafford, raised a troop of horse for Charles I., was impeached by the Parliament and fled to France. He was a man of wit and pleasure, who penned a number of gay trifles, but has been saved from oblivion chiefly by his exquisite *Ballad upon a Wedding*. Thomas Carew and Edmund Waller were poets of the same stamp —graceful and easy, but shallow in feeling. Carew, however, showed a nicer sense of form than most of the fantastic school. Some of his love songs are written with delicate art. There are noble lines in his elegy on Donne and in one passage of his masque *Cœlum Britannicum*. In his poem entitled *The Rapture* great splendor of language and imagery is devoted to the service of an unbridled sensuality. Waller, who followed the court to Paris, was the author of two songs,

which are still favorites, *Go, Lovely Rose,* and *On a Girdle,*
and he first introduced the smooth, correct manner of writing
in couplets, which Dryden and Pope carried to perfection.
Gallantry rather than love was the inspiration of these courtly
singers. In such verses as Carew's *Encouragements to a Lover,*
and George Wither's *The Manly Heart,*

> If she be not so to me,
> What care I how fair she be ?—

we see the revolt against the high, passionate, Sidneian love
of the Elizabethan sonneteers, and the note of *persiflage* that
was to mark the lyrical verse of the Restoration. But the
poetry of the cavaliers reached its high-water mark in one
fiery-hearted song by the noble and unfortunate James
Graham, Marquis of Montrose, who invaded Scotland in the
interest of Charles II., and was taken prisoner and put to
death at Edinburgh in 1650.

> My dear and only love, I pray
> That little world of thee
> Be governed by no other sway
> Than purest monarchy.

In language borrowed from the politics of the time, he cau-
tions his mistress against *synods* or *committees* in her heart ;
swears to make her glorious by his pen and famous by his
sword ; and, with that fine recklessness which distinguished
the dashing troopers of Prince Rupert, he adds, in words
that have been often quoted,

> He either fears his fate too much,
> Or his deserts are small,
> That dares not put it to the touch
> To gain or lose it all.

John Milton, the greatest English poet except Shakspere,
was born in London in 1608. His father was a scrivener, an
educated man, and a musical composer of some merit. At
his home Milton was surrounded with all the inflences of a

refined and well-ordered Puritan household of the better class.   He inherited his father's musical tastes, and during the latter part of his life he spent a part of every afternoon in playing the organ.   No poet has written more beautifully of music than Milton.   One of his sonnets was addressed to Henry Lawes, the composer, who wrote the airs to the songs in *Comus*.   Milton's education was most careful and thorough. He spent seven years at Cambridge, where, from his personal beauty and fastidious habits, he was called "The lady of Christ's."   At Horton, in Buckinghamshire, where his father had a country seat, he passed five years more, perfecting himself in his studies, and then traveled for fifteen months, mainly in Italy, visiting Naples and Rome, but residing at Florence.   Here he saw Galileo, a prisoner of the Inquisition "for thinking otherwise in astronomy than his Dominican and Franciscan licensers thought."   Milton was the most scholarly and the most truly classical of English poets.   His Latin verse, for elegance and correctness, ranks with Addison's ; and his Italian poems were the admiration of the Tuscan scholars.   But his learning appears in his poetry only in the form of a fine and chastened result, and not in laborious allusion and pedantic citation, as too often in Ben Jonson, for instance.   "My father," he wrote, "destined me, while yet a little child, for the study of humane letters."   He was also destined for the ministry, but, "coming to some maturity of years and perceiving what tyrany had invaded the Church, . . . I thought it better to prefer a blameless silence, before the sacred office of speaking, bought and begun with servitude and forswearing."   Other hands than a bishop's were laid upon his head.   "He who would not be frustrate of his hope to write well hereafter," he says, "ought himself to be a true poem."   And he adds that his "natural haughtiness" saved him from all impurity of living.   Milton had a sublime self-respect.   The dignity and earnestness of the Puritan gentleman blended in his training with the culture of the Renaissance. Born into an age of spiritual conflict, he dedicated his gift to the service of Heaven, and he became, like Heine, a valiant soldier in the war for liberation. He was the poet of a cause, and his song was keyed to

> the Dorian mood
> Of flutes and soft recorders such as raised
> To height of noblest temper, heroes old
> Arming to battle.

On comparing Milton with Shakspere, with his universal sympathies and receptive imagination, one perceives a loss in breadth, but a gain in intense personal conviction. He introduced a new note into English poetry: the passion for truth and the feeling of religious sublimity. Milton's was an heroic age, and its song must be lyric rather than dramatic ; its singer must be in the fight and of it.

Of the verses which he wrote at Cambridge the most important was his splendid ode *On the Morning of Christ's Nativity.* At Horton he wrote, among other things, the companion pieces, *L'Allegro* and *Il Penseroso*, of a kind quite new in English, giving to the landscape an expression in harmony with the two contrasted moods. *Comus*, which belongs to the same period, was the perfection of the Elizabethan court masque, and was presented at Ludlow Castle in 1634, on the occasion of the installation of the Earl of Bridgewater as Lord President of Wales. Under the guise of a skillful addition to the Homeric allegory of Circe, with her cup of enchantment, it was a Puritan song in praise of chastity and temperance. *Lycidas*, in like manner, was the perfection of the Elizabethan pastoral elegy. It was contributed to a volume of memorial verses on the death of Edward King, a Cambridge friend of Milton's, who was drowned in the Irish Channel in 1637. In one stern strain, which is put into the mouth of St. Peter, the author "foretells the ruin of our corrupted clergy, then at their height."

> But that two-handed engine at the door
> Stands ready to smite once and smite no more.

This was Milton's last utterance in English verse before the outbreak of the civil war, and it sounds the alarm of the impending struggle.   In technical quality *Lycidas* is the most wonderful of all Milton's poems.   The cunningly intricate harmony of the verse, the pressed and packed language, with its fullness of meaning and allusion, make it worthy of the minutest study.   In these early poems, Milton, merely as a poet, is at his best.   Something of the Elizabethan style still clings to them; but their grave sweetness, their choice wording, their originality in epithet, name, and phrase, were novelties of Milton's own.   His English masters were Spenser, Fletcher, and Sylvester, the translator of Du Bartas's *La Semaine*, but nothing of Spenser's prolixity, or Fletcher's effeminacy, or Sylvester's quaintness is found in Milton's pure, energetic diction.   He inherited their beauties, but his taste had been tempered to a finer edge by his studies in Greek and Hebrew poetry.   He was the last of the Elizabethans, and his style was at once the crown of the old and a departure into the new.   In masque, elegy, and sonnet he set the seal to the Elizabethan poetry, said the last word, and closed one great literary era.

In 1639 the breach between Charles I. and his Parliament brought Milton back from Italy.   "I thought it base to be traveling at my ease for amusement, while my fellow-countrymen at home were fighting for liberty."   For the next twenty years he threw himself into the contest, and poured forth a succession of tracts, in English and Latin, upon the various public questions at issue.   As a political thinker, Milton had what Bacon calls "the humor of a scholar."   In a country of endowed grammar schools and universities hardly emerged from a mediæval discipline and curriculum, he wanted to set up Greek gymnasia and philosophical schools, after the fashion of the Porch and the Academy.   He would have imposed an Athenian democracy upon a people trained in the traditions of monarchy and episcopacy. At the very moment when England had grown tired of the Protectorate and was preparing to welcome back the Stuarts, he was writing *An Easy and Ready Way to Establish a Free Commonwealth.* Milton acknowledged that in prose he had the use of his left hand only. There are passages of fervid eloquence, where the style swells into a kind of lofty chant, with a rhythmical rise and fall to it, as in parts of the English Book of Common Prayer. But in general his sentences are long and involved, full of inversions and latinized constructions. Controversy at that day was conducted on scholastic lines. Each disputant, instead of appealing at once to the arguments of expediency and common sense, began with a formidable display of learning, ransacking Greek and Latin authors and the Fathers of the Church for opinions in support of his own position. These authorities he deployed at tedious length, and followed them up with heavy scurrilities and "excusations," by way of attack and defense. The dispute between Milton and Salmasius over the execution of Charles I. was like a duel between two knights in full armor striking at each other with ponderous maces. The very titles of these pamphlets are enough to frighten off a modern reader: *A Confutation of the Animadversions upon a Defense of a Humble Remonstrance against a Treatise, entitled Of Reformation.* The most interesting of Milton's prose tracts is his *Areopagitica : A Speech for the Liberty of Unlicensed Printing,* 1644. The arguments in this are of permanent force; but if the reader will compare it, or Jeremy Taylor's *Liberty of Prophesying,* with Locke's *Letters on Toleration,* he will see how much clearer and more convincing is the modern method of discussion, introduced by writers like Hobbes and Locke and Dryden. Under the Protectorate Milton was appointed Latin Secretary to the Council of State. In the diplomatic correspondence which was his official duty, and in the composition of his tract, *Defensio pro Popululo Anglicano,* he over-

taxed his eyes, and in 1654 became totally blind. The only
poetry of Milton's belonging to the years 1640–1660 are a
few sonnets of the pure Italian form, mainly called forth by
public occasions.   By the Elizabethans the sonnets had been
used mainly in love poetry.   In Milton's hands, said Wordsworth, " the thing became a trumpet."   Some of his were
addressed to political leaders, like Fairfax, Cromwell, and Sir
Henry Vane; and of these the best is, perhaps, the sonnet
written on the massacre of the Vaudois Protestants—" a collect in verse," it has been called—which has the fire of a
Hebrew prophet invoking the divine wrath upon the op-
pressors of Israel.   Two were on his own blindness, and in
these there is not one selfish repining, but only a regret that
the value of his service is impaired—

> Will God exact day labor, light denied ?

After the restoration of the Stuarts, in 1660, Milton was
for a while in peril, by reason of the part that he had taken
against the king.   But

> On evil days though fallen, and evil tongues,
> In darkness and with dangers compassed round
> And solitude,

he bated no jot of heart or hope.   Henceforth he becomes
the most heroic and affecting figure in English literary history.   Years before he had planned an epic poem on the subject of King Arthur, and again a sacred tragedy on man's
fall and redemption.   These experiments finally took shape
in *Paradise Lost*, which was given to the world in 1667.
This is the epic of English Puritanism and of Protestant
Christianity.   It was Milton's purpose to

> assert eternal Providence
> And justify the ways of God to men,

or, in other words, to embody his theological system in
verse.   This gives a doctrinal rigidity and even dryness to
parts of the *Paradise Lost*, which injure its effect as a poem.

His " God the father turns a school divine: " his Christ, as
has been wittily said, is " God's good boy:" the discourses of
Raphael to Adam are scholastic lectures: Adam himself is
too sophisticated for the state of innocence, and Eve is somewhat insipid. The real protagonist of the poem is Satan, upon
whose mighty figure Milton unconsciously bestowed something of his own nature, and whose words of defiance might
almost have come from some Republican leader when the
Good Old Cause went down.

> What though the field be lost ?
> All is not lost; the unconquerable will
> And study of revenge, immortal hate,
> And courage never to submit or yield.

But when all has been said that can be said in disparagement
or qualification, *Paradise Lost* remains the foremost of English poems and the sublimest of all epics. Even in those
parts where theology encroaches most upon poetry, the diction, though often heavy, is never languid. Milton's blank
verse in itself is enough to bear up the most prosaic theme,
and so is his epic English, a style more massive and splendid
than Shakspere's, and comparable, like Tertullian's Latin, to
a river of molten gold. Of the countless single beauties that
sow his page

> Thick as autumnal leaves that strew the brooks
> In Valombrosa,

there is no room to speak, nor of the astonishing fullness of
substance and multitude of thoughts which have caused the
Paradise Lost to be called the book of universal knowledge.
" The heat of Milton's mind," said Dr. Johnson, " might be
said to sublimate his learning and throw off into his work the
spirit of science, unmingled with its grosser parts." The
truth of this remark is clearly seen upon a comparison of
Milton's description of the creation, for example, with cor-
responding passages in Sylvester's *Divine Weeks and Works*

(translated from the Huguenot poet, Du Bartas), which was, in some sense, his original. But the most heroic thing in Milton's heroic poem is Milton. There are no strains in *Paradise Lost* so absorbing as those in which the poet breaks the strict epic bounds and speaks directly of himself, as in the majestic lament over his own blindness, and in the invocation to Urania, which open the third and seventh books. Every-where, too, one reads between the lines. We think of the dissolute cavaliers, as Milton himself undoubtedly was thinking of them, when we read of "the sons of Belial flown with insolence and wine," or when the Puritan turns among the sweet landscapes of Eden, to denounce

> court amours
> Mixed dance, or wanton mask, or midnight ball,
> Or serenade which the starved lover sings
> To his proud fair, best quitted with disdain.

And we think of Milton among the triumphant royalists when we read of the Seraph Abdiel "faithful found among the faithless."

> Nor number nor example with him wrought
> To swerve from truth or change his constant mind,
> Though single. From amidst them forth he passed,
> Long way through hostile scorn, which he sustained
> Superior, nor of violence feared aught:
> And with retorted scorn his back he turned
> On those proud towers to swift destruction doomed.

Paradise Regained and *Samson Agonistes* were published in 1671. The first of these treated in four books Christ's temptation in the wilderness, a subject that had already been handled in the Spenserian allegorical manner by Giles Fletcher, a brother of the Purple Islander, in his *Christ's Victory and Triumph*, 1610. The superiority of *Paradise Lost* to its sequel is not without significance. The Puritans were Old Testament men. Their God was the Hebrew Jehovah, whose single divinity the Catholic mythology had overlaid with the figures of the Son, the Virgin Mary, and the saints. They identified themselves in thought with his chosen people, with the militant theocracy of the Jews. Their sword was the sword of the Lord and of Gideon. "To your tents, O Israel," was the cry of the London mob when the bishops were committed to the Tower. And when the fog lifted, on the morning of the battle of Dunbar, Cromwell exclaimed, "Let God arise and let his enemies be scattered: like as the sun riseth, so shalt thou drive them away."

Samson Agonistes, though Hebrew in theme and spirit, was in form a Greek tragedy. It has chorus and semi-chorus, and preserved the so-called dramatic unities; that is, the scene was unchanged, and there were no intervals of time between the acts. In accordance with the rules of the Greek theater, but two speakers appeared upon the stage at once, and there was no violent action. The death of Samson is related by a messenger. Milton's reason for the choice of this subject is obvious. He himself was Samson, shorn of his strength, blind, and alone among enemies; given over

> to the unjust tribunals, under change of times,
> And condemnation of the ungrateful multitude.

As Milton grew older he discarded more and more the graces of poetry, and relied purely upon the structure and the thought. In *Paradise Lost*, although there is little resemblance to Elizabethan work—such as one notices in *Comus* and the Christmas hymn—yet the style is rich, especially in the earlier books. But in *Paradise Regained* it is severe to bareness, and in *Samson*, even to ruggedness. Like Michelangelo, with whose genius he had much in common, Milton became impatient of finish or of mere beauty. He blocked out his work in masses, left rough places and surfaces not filled in, and inclined to express his meaning by a symbol, rather than work it out in detail. It was a part of his austerity, his increasing preference for structural over

decorative methods, to give up rime for blank verse. His
latest poem, *Samson Agonistes*, is a metrical study of the
highest interest.

Milton was not quite alone among the poets of his time in
espousing the popular cause.   Andrew Marvell, who was his
assistant in the Latin secretaryship and sat in Parliament for
Hull, after the Restoration, was a good Republican, and
wrote a fine *Horatian Ode upon Cromwell's Return from
Ireland.* There is also a rare imaginative quality in his *Song
of the Exiles in Bermuda, Thoughts in a Garden,* and *The
Girl Describes her Fawn.* George Wither, who was imprisoned for his satires, also took the side of the Parliament, but
there is little that is distinctively Puritan in his poetry.

---

1. Milton's Poetical Works.   Edited by David Masson.
London: Macmillan & Co., 1882. 3 vols.

2. Selections from Milton's Prose.   Edited by F. D. Myers.
New York : D. Appleton & Co., 1883.   (Parchment Series.)

3. England's Antiphon.   By George Macdonald.   London:
Macmillan & Co., 1868.

4. Robert Herrick's Hesperides.   London: George Rout-
ledge & Sons, 1885.   (Morley's Universal Library).

5. Sir Thomas Browne's Religio Medici and Hydriotaphia.
Edited by Willis Bund.   Sampson Low & Co., 1873.

6. Thomas Fuller's Good Thoughts in Bad Times.   Boston: Ticknor & Fields, 1863.

7. Walton's Complete Angler.   Edited by Sir Harris
Nicolas.   London: Chatto & Windus, 1875.

CHAPTER V.

FROM THE RESTORATION TO THE DEATH OF POPE.

1660-1744.

THE Stuart Restoration was a period of descent from poetry to prose, from passion and imagination to wit and the understanding. The serious, exalted mood of the civil war and Commonwealth had spent itself and issued in disillusion. There followed a generation of wits, logical, skeptical, and prosaic, without earnestness, as without principle. The characteristic literature of such a time is criticism, satire, and burlesque, and such, indeed, continued to be the course of English literary history for a century after the return of the Stuarts. The age was not a stupid one, but one of active inquiry. The Royal Society, for the cultivation of the natural sciences, was founded in 1662. There were able divines in the pulpit and at the universities—Barrow, Tillotson, Stillingfleet, South, and others: scholars, like Bentley; historians, like Clarendon and Burnet; scientists, like Boyle and Newton; philosophers, like Hobbes and Locke. But of poetry, in any high sense of the word, there was little between the time of Milton and the time of Goldsmith and Gray.

The English writers of this period were strongly influenced by the contemporary literature of France, by the comedies of Molière, the tragedies of Corneille and Racine, and the satires, epistles, and versified essays of Boileau. Many of the Restoration writers—Waller, Cowley, Davenant, Wycherley, Villiers, and others—had been in France during the exile, and brought back with them French tastes. John

Dryden (1631–1700), who is the great literary figure of his generation, has been called the first of the moderns. From the reign of Charles II., indeed, we may date the beginnings of modern English life. What we call "society" was forming, the town, the London world. "Coffee, which makes the politician wise," had just been introduced, and the ordinaries of Ben Jonson's time gave way to coffee-houses, like Will's and Button's, which became the head-quarters of literary and political gossip. The two great English parties, as we know them to-day, were organized: the words Whig and Tory date from this reign. French etiquette and fashions came in, and French phrases of convenience—such as *coup de grace, bel esprit,* etc.—began to appear in English prose. Literature became intensely urban and partisan. It reflected city life, the disputes of faction, and the personal quarrels of authors. The politics of the great rebellion had been of heroic proportions, and found fitting expression in song. But in the Revolution of 1688 the issues were constitutional and to be settled by the arguments of lawyers. Measures were in question rather than principles, and there was little inspiration to the poet in Exclusion Bills and Acts of Settlement.

Court and society, in the reign of Charles II. and James II., were shockingly dissolute, and in literature, as in life, the reaction against Puritanism went to great extremes. The social life of the time is faithfully reflected in the diary of Samuel Pepys. He was a simple-minded man, the son of a London tailor, and became, himself, secretary to the admiralty. His diary was kept in cipher, and published only in 1825. Being written for his own eye, it is singularly outspoken; and its *naïve,* gossipy, confidential tone makes it a most diverting book, as it is, historically, a most valuable one.

Perhaps the most popular book of its time was Samuel Butler's *Hudibras* (1663–1664), a burlesque romance in ridicule of the Puritans. The king carried a copy of it in his pocket, and Pepys testifies that it was quoted and praised on all sides. Ridicule of the Puritans was nothing new. Zeal-of-the-land Busy, in Ben Jônson's *Bartholomew Fair*, is an early instance of the kind. There was nothing laughable about the earnestness of men like Cromwell, Milton, Algernon Sidney, and Sir Henry Vane. But even the French Revolution had its humors; and as the English Puritan Revolution gathered head and the extremer sectaries pressed to the front —Quakers, New Lights, Fifth Monarchy Men, Ranters, etc., —its grotesque sides came uppermost. Butler's hero is a Presbyterian justice of the peace who sallies forth with his secretary, Ralpho—an Independent and Anabaptist—like Don Quixote with Sancho Panza, to suppress May games and bear-baitings. (Macaulay, it will be remembered, said that the Puritans disapproved of bear-baiting, not because it gave pain to the bear, but because it gave pleasure to the spectators.) The humor of *Hudibras* is not of the finest. The knight and the squire are discomfited in broadly comic adventures, hardly removed from the rough physical drolleries of a pantomime or circus. The deep heart-laughter of Cervantes, the pathos on which his humor rests, is, of course, not to be looked for in Butler. But he had wit of a sharp, logical kind, and his style surprises with all manner of verbal antics. He is almost as great a phrase-master as Pope, though in a coarser kind. His verse is a smart doggerel, and his poem has furnished many stock sayings, as for example,

> 'Tis strange what difference there can be
> 'Twixt tweedle-dum and tweedle-dee.

Hudibras has had many imitators, not the least successful of whom was the American John Trumbull, in his revolutionary satire, *M'Fingal*, some couplets of which arc generally quoted as Butler's, as, for example,

> No man e'er felt the halter draw
> With good opinion of the law.

The rebound against Puritanism is seen no less plainly in the drama of the Restoration, and the stage now took vengeance for its enforced silence under the Protectorate. Two theaters were opened under the patronage, respectively. of the king and of his brother, the Duke of York. The manager of the latter, Sir William Davenant—who had fought on the king's side, been knighted for his services, escaped to France, and was afterward captured and imprisoned in England for two years—had managed to evade the law against stage plays as early as 1656, by presenting his *Siege of Rhodes* as an "opera," with instrumental music and dialogue in recitative, after a fashion newly sprung up in Italy. This he brought out again in 1661, with the dialogue recast into riming couplets in the French fashion. Movable painted scenery was now introduced from France, and actresses took the female parts formerly played by boys. This last innovation was said to be at the request of the king, one of whose mistresses, the famous Nell Gwynne, was the favorite actress at the King's Theater.

Upon the stage, thus reconstructed, the so-called "classical" rules of the French theater were followed, at least in theory. The Louis XIV. writers were not purely creative, like Shakspere or his contemporaries in England, but critical and self-conscious. The Academy had been formed in 1636 for the preservation of the purity of the French language, and discussion abounded on the principles and methods of literary art. Corneille not only wrote tragedies, but essays on tragedy, and one in particular on the *Three Unities*. Dryden followed his example in his *Essay of Dramatic Poesie* (1667), in which he treated of the unities, and argued for the use of rime in tragedy in preference to blank verse. His own practice varied. Most of his tragedies were written in rime, but in the best of them, *All for Love*, founded on Shakspere's *Antony and Cleopatra*, he returned to blank verse. One of the principles of the classical school was to

keep comedy and tragedy distinct.   The tragic dramatists of
the Restoration, Dryden, Howard, Settle, Crowne, Lee, and
others, composed what they called "heroic plays," such as
the *Indian Emperor*, the *Conquest of Granada*, the *Duke of
Lerma*, the *Empress of Morocco*, the *Destruction of Jerusalem*, *Nero*, and the *Rival Queens*.   The titles of these pieces
indicate their character.   Their heroes were great historic
personages.   Subject and treatment were alike remote from
nature and real life.   The diction was stilted and artificial,
and pompous declamation took the place of action and genuine passion.   The tragedies of Racine seem chill to an
Englishman brought up on Shakspere, but to see how great
an artist Racine was, in his own somewhat narrow way, one
has but to compare his *Phedre*, or *Iphigenie*, with Dryden's
ranting tragedy of *Tyrannic Love*.   These bombastic heroic
plays were made the subject of a capital burlesque, the
Rehearsal, by George Villiers, Duke of Buckingham, acted
in 1671 at the King's Theater.   The indebtedness of the
English stage to the French did not stop with a general
adoption of its dramatic methods, but extended to direct
imitation and translation.   Dryden's comedy, *An Evening's
Love*, was adapted from Thomas Corneille's *Le Feint Astro-
logue*, and his *Sir Martin Mar-all*, from Molière's *L'Etourdi*.
Shadwell borrowed his *Miser* from Molière, and Otway made
versions of Racine's *Bèrènice* and Molière's *Fourberies de
Scapin*.   Wycherley's *Country Wife* and *Plain Dealer*
although not translations, were based, in a sense, upon Molière's *Ecole des Femmes* and *Le Misanthrope*.   The only one
of the tragic dramatists of the Restoration who prolonged the
traditions of the Elizabethan stage was Otway, whose *Venice Preserved*, written in blank verse, still keeps the boards.
There are fine passages in Dryden's heroic plays, passages
weighty in thought and nobly sonorous in language.   There
is one great scene (between Antony and Ventidius) in his *All
for Love*.   And one, at least, of his comedies, the *Spanish*

Friar, is skillfully constructed. But his nature was not pliable enough for the drama, and he acknowledged that, in writing for the stage, he "forced his genius."

In sharp contrast with these heroic plays was the comic drama of the Restoration, the plays of Wycherley, Killigrew, Etherege, Farquhar, Van Brugh, Congreve, and others ; plays like the *Country Wife*, the *Parson's Wedding*, *She Would if She Could,* the *Beaux' Stratagem*, the *Relapse*, and the *Way of the World.* These were in prose, and represented the gay world and the surface of fashionable life. Amorous intrigue was their constantly recurring theme. Some of them were written expressly in ridicule of the Puritans. Such was the *Committee* of Dryden's brother-in-law, Sir Robert Howard, the hero of which is a distressed gentleman, and the villain a London cit, and president of the committee appointed by Parliament to sit upon the sequestration of the estates of royalists. Such were also the *Roundheads* and the *Banished Cavaliers* of Mrs. Aphra Behn, who was a female spy in the service of Charles II., at Antwerp, and one of the coarsest of the Restoration comedians. The profession of piety had become so disagreeable that a shameless cynicism was now considered the mark of a gentleman. The ideal hero of Wycherley or Etherege was the witty young profligate, who had seen life, and learned to disbelieve in virtue. His highest qualities were a contempt for cant, physical courage, a sort of spendthrift generosity, and a good-natured readiness to back up a friend in a quarrel, or an amour. Virtue was *bourgeois*—reserved for London trades-people. A man must be either a rake or a hypocrite. The gentlemen were rakes, the city people were hypocrites. Their wives, however, were all in love with the gentlemen, and it was the proper thing to seduce them, and to borrow their husbands' money. For the first and last time, perhaps, in the history of the English drama, the sympathy of the audience was deliberately sought

for the seducer and the rogue, and the laugh turned against
the dishonored husband and the honest man. (Contrast this
with Shakspere's *Merry Wives of Windsor*.) The women
were represented as worse than the men—scheming, igno-
rant, and corrupt. The dialogue in the best of these plays
was easy, lively, and witty the situations in some of them
audacious almost beyond belief. Under a thin varnish
of good breeding, the sentiments and manners were really
brutal. The loosest gallants of Beaumont and Fletcher's
theater retain a fineness of feeling and that *politesse de cœur*
which marks the gentleman. They are poetic creatures,
and own a capacity for romantic passion. But the Manlys
and Horners of the Restoration comedy have a prosaic,
cold-blooded profligacy that disgusts.

Charles Lamb, in his ingenious essay on "The Artificial
Comedy of the Last Century," apologized for the Restoration stage, on the ground that it represented a world of whim
and unreality in which the ordinary laws of morality had no
application. But Macaulay answered truly, that at no time
has the stage been closer in its imitation of real life. The
theater of Wycherley and Etherege was but the counterpart
of that social condition which we read of in Pepys's *Diary*,
and in the *Memoirs* of the Chevalier de Grammont. This
prose comedy of manners was not, indeed, "artificial" at all,
in the sense in which the contemporary tragedy—the
"heroic play"—was artificial. It was, on the contrary, far
more natural, and, intellectually, of much higher value. In
1698 Jeremy Collier, a non-juring Jacobite clergyman, published his *Short View of the Immorality and Profaneness of
the English Stage*, which did much toward reforming the
practice of the dramatists. The formal characteristics, without the immorality, of the Restoration comedy re-appeared
briefly in Goldsmith's *She Stoops to Conquer*, 1772, and
Sheridan's *Rivals, School for Scandal*, and *Critic*, 1775–9; our
last strictly "classical" comedies. None of this school of

English comedians approached their model, Molière. He
excelled his imitators not only in his French urbanity—the
polished wit and delicate grace of his style—but in the dex-
terous unfolding of his plot, and in the wisdom and truth of
his criticism of life, and his insight into character. It is a
symptom of the false taste of the age that Shakspere's plays
were rewritten for the Restoration stage. Davenant made
new versions of *Macbeth* and *Julius Cæsar*, substituting rime
for blank verse. In conjunction with Dryden, he altered
the *Tempest*, complicating the intrigue by the introduction
of a male counterpart to Miranda — a youth who had never
seen a woman. Shadwell "improved" *Timon of Athens*,
and Nahum Tate furnished a new fifth act to *King Lear*,
which turned the play into a comedy ! In the prologue to
his doctored version of *Troilus and Cressida*, Dryden made
the ghost of Shakspere speak of himself as

> Untaught, unpracticed in a barbarous age.

Thomas Rymer, whom Pope pronounced a good critic, was
very severe upon Shakspere in his *Remarks on the Tragedies of the Last Age ;* and in his *Short View of Tragedy*,
1693, he said, "In the neighing of a horse or in the growling
of a mastiff, there is more humanity than, many times,
in the tragical flights of Shakspere." "To Deptford by
water," writes Pepys, in his diary for August 20, 1666,
"reading *Othello, Moor of Venice ;* which I ever here-
tofore esteemed a mighty good play ; but, having so
lately read the *Adventures of Five Hours*, it seems a mean
thing."

In undramatic poetry the new school, both in England and
in France, took its point of departure in a reform against
the extravagances of the Marinists, or conceited poets,
specially represented in England by Donne and Cowley.
The new poets, both in their theory and practice, insisted
upon correctness, clearness, polish, moderation, and good

sense. Boileau's *L'Art Poétique*, 1673, inspired by Horace's *Ars Poetica*, was a treatise in verse upon the rules of correct composition, and it gave the law in criticism for over a century, not only in France, but in Germany and England. It gave English poetry a didactic turn and started the fashion of writing critical essays in riming couplets. The Earl of Mulgrave published two "poems" of this kind, an *Essay on Satire*, and an *Essay on Poetry*. The Earl of Roscommon — who, said Addison, "makes even rules a noble poetry"—made a metrical version of Horace's *Ars Poetica*, and wrote an original *Essay on Translated Verse*. Of the same kind were Addison's epistle to Sacheverel, entitled *An Account of the Greatest English Poets*, and Pope's *Essay on Criticism*, 1711, which was nothing more than versified maxims of rhetoric, put with Pope's usual point and brilliancy. The classicism of the 18th century, it has been said, was a classicism in red heels and a periwig. It was Latin rather than Greek ; it turned to the least imaginative side of Latin literature and found its models, not in Vergil, Catullus, and Lucretius, but in the satires, epistles, and didactic pieces of Juvenal, Horace, and Persius.

The chosen medium of the new poetry was the heroic couplet. This had, of course, been used before by English poets as far back as Chaucer. The greater part of the *Canterbury Tales* was written in heroic couplets. But now a new strength and precision were given to the familiar measure by imprisoning the sense within the limit of the couplet, and by treating each line as also a unit in itself. Edmund Waller had written verse of this kind as early as the reign of Charles I. He, said Dryden, "first showed us to conclude the sense most commonly in distichs, which, in the verse of those before him, runs on for so many lines together that the reader is out of breath to overtake it." Sir John Denham, also, in his *Cooper's Hill*, 1643, had written such verse as this :

> O, could I flow like thee, and make thy stream
> My great example as it is my theme!
> Though deep yet clear, though gentle yet not dull,
> Strong without rage, without o'erflowing full.

Here we have the regular flow, and the nice balance between
the first and second member of each couplet, and the first
and second part of each line, which characterized the verse
of Dryden and Pope.

> Waller was smooth, but Dryden taught to join
> The varying verse, the full resounding line,
> The long resounding march and energy divine.

Thus wrote Pope, using for the nonce the triplet and alex-
andrine by which Dryden frequently varied the couplet.
Pope himself added a greater neatness and polish to Dryden's verse and brought the system to such monotonous perfection that he "made poetry a mere mechanic art."

The lyrical poetry of this generation was almost entirely
worthless. The dissolute wits of Charles the Second's court,
Sedley, Rochester, Sackville, and the "mob of gentlemen
who wrote with ease," threw off a few amatory trifles; but
the age was not spontaneous or sincere enough for genuine
song. Cowley introduced the Pindaric ode, a highly artificial form of the lyric, in which the language was tortured
into a kind of spurious grandeur, and the meter teased into a
sound and fury, signifying nothing. Cowley's Pindarics
were filled with something which passed for fire, but has now
utterly gone out. Nevertheless, the fashion spread, and "he
who could do nothing else," said Dr. Johnson, "could write
like Pindar." The best of these odes was Dryden's famous
Alexander's Feast, written for a celebration of St. Cecilia's
day by a musical club. To this same fashion, also, we owe
Gray's two fine odes, the *Progress of Poesy* and the *Bard*.
written a half-century later.

Dryden was not so much a great poet as a solid thinker,
with a splendid mastery of expression, who used his ener-

getic verse as a vehicle for political argument and satire. His first noteworthy poem, *Annus Mirabilis*, 1667, was a narrative of the public events of the year 1666; namely, the Dutch war and the great fire of London.   The subject of *Absalom and Ahitophel*—the first part of which appeared in 1681 — was the alleged plot of the Whig leader, the Earl of Shaftesbury, to defeat the succession of the Duke of York, afterward James II., by securing the throne to Monmouth, a natural son of Charles II.   The parallel afforded by the story of Absalom's revolt against David was wrought out by Dryden with admirable ingenuity and keeping.   He was at his best in satirical character-sketches, such as the brilliant portraits in this poem of Shaftesbury, as the false counselor Ahitophel, and of the Duke of Buckingham as Zimri.   The latter was Dryden's reply to the *Rehearsal.*.   *Absalom and Ahitophel* was followed by the *Medal*, a continuation of the same subject, and *Mac Flecknoe*, a personal onslaught on the "true blue Protestant poet" Thomas Shadwell, a political and literary foe of Dryden.   Flecknoe, an obscure Irish poetaster, being about to retire from the throne of duncedom, resolved to settle the succession upon his son, Shadwell, whose claims to the inheritance are vigorously asserted.

> The rest to some faint meaning make pretense,
> But Shadwell never deviates into sense. . . .
> The midwife laid her hand on his thick skull
> With this prophetic blessing—*Be thou dull.*

Dryden is our first great satirist.   The formal satire had been written in the reign of Elizabeth by Donne, and by Joseph Hall, Bishop of Exeter, and subsequently by Marston, the dramatist, by Wither, Marvell, and others ; but all of these failed through an over violence of language, and a purpose too pronouncedly moral.   They had no lightness of touch, no irony and mischief.   They bore down too hard, imitated Juvenal, and lashed English society in terms befitting the corruption of imperial Rome.   They denounced, instructed, preached, did every thing but satirize. The satirist must raise a laugh. Donne and Hall abused men in classes; priests were worldly, lawyers greedy, courtiers obsequious, etc. But the easy scorn of Dryden and the delightful malice of Pope gave a pungent personal interest to their sarcasm, infinitely more effective than these commonplaces of satire. Dryden was as happy in controversy as in satire, and is unexcelled in the power to reason in verse. His *Religo Laici*, 1682, was a poem in defense of the English Church. But when James II. came to the throne Dryden turned Catholic and wrote the *Hind and Panther*, 1687, to vindicate his new belief. Dryden had the misfortune to be dependent upon royal patronage and upon a corrupt stage. He sold his pen to the court, and in his comedies he was heavily and deliberately lewd, a sin which he afterward acknowledged and regretted. Milton's "soul was like a star and dwelt apart," but Dryden wrote for the trampling multitude. He had a coarseness of moral fiber, but was not malignant in his satire, being of a large, careless, and forgetting nature. He had that masculine, enduring cast of mind which gathers heat and clearness from motion, and grows better with age. His *Fables*—modernizations from Chaucer and translations from Boccaccio, written the year before he died—are among his best works.

Dryden is also our first critic of any importance. His critical essays were mostly written as prefaces or dedications to his poems and plays. But his *Essay of Dramatic Poesie*, which Dr. Johnson called our "first regular and valuable treatise on the art of writing," was in the shape of a Platonic dialogue. When not misled by the French classicism of his day, Dryden was an admirable critic, full of penetration and sound sense. He was the earliest writer, too, of modern literary prose. If the imitation of French models was an injury to poetry it was a benefit to prose. The best modern prose is French, and it was the essayists of the gallicised Restoration age—Cowley, Sir William Temple, and above all, Dryden—who gave modern English prose that simplicity, directness, and colloquial air which marks it off from the more artificial diction of Milton, Taylor and Browne.

A few books whose shaping influences lay in the past belong by their date to this period. John Bunyan, a poor tinker, whose reading was almost wholly in the Bible and Fox's *Book of Martyrs*, imprisoned for twelve years in Bedford jail for preaching at conventicles, wrote and, in 1678, published his *Pilgrim's Progress*, the greatest of religious allegories. Bunyan's spiritual experiences were so real to him that they took visible concrete shape in his imagination as men, women, cities, landscapes. It is the simplest, the most transparent of allegories. Unlike the *Faerie Queene*, the story of *Pilgrim's Progress* has no reason for existing apart from its inner meaning, and yet its reality is so vivid that children read of Vanity Fair and the Slough of Despond and Doubting Castle and the Valley of the Shadow of Death with the same belief with which they read of Crusoe's cave or Aladdin's palace.

It is a long step from the Bedford tinker to the cultivated poet of *Paradise Lost*. They represent the poles of the Puritan party. Yet it may admit of a doubt whether the Puritan epic is, in essentials, as vital and original a work as the Puritan allegory. They both came out quietly and made little noise at first. But the *Pilgrim's Progress* got at once into circulation, and hardly a single copy of the first edition remains. Milton, too—who received ten pounds for the copyright of *Paradise Lost*—seemingly found that "fit audience though few" for which he prayed, as his poem reached its second impression in five years (1672). Dryden visited him in his retirement and asked leave to turn it into rime and put it on the stage as an opera. "Ay," said Milton, good humoredly, "you may tag my verses." And accordingly they appeared, duly tagged, in Dryden's operatic masque, the *State of Innocence*. In this startling conjunction we have the two ages in a nutshell: the Commonwealth was an epic, the Restoration an opera.

The literary period covered by the life of Pope, 1688–1744, is marked off by no distinct line from the generation before it.   Taste continued to be governed by the precepts of Boileau and the French classical school. Poetry remained chiefly didactic and satirical, and satire in Pope's hands was more personal even than in Dryden's, and addressed itself less to public issues.   The literature of the "Augustan age" of Queen Anne (1702–1714) was still more a literature of the town and of fashionable society than that of the Restoration had been.   It was also closely involved with party struggles of Whig and Tory, and the ablest pens on either side were taken into alliance by the political leaders. Swift was in high favor with the Tory ministers, Oxford and Bolingbroke, and his pamphlets, the *Public Spirit of the Whigs* and the *Conduct of the Allies*, were rewarded with the deanery of St. Patrick's, Dublin.   Addison became secretary of state under a Whig government.   Prior was in the diplomatic service. Daniel De Foe, the author of *Robinson Crusoe*, 1719, was a prolific political writer, conducted his *Review* in the interest of the Whigs, and was imprisoned and pilloried for his ironical pamphlet, *The Shortest Way with the Dissenters*.   Steele, who was a violent writer on the Whig side, held various public offices, such as Commissioner of Stamps, and Commissioner for Forfeited Estates, and sat in Parliament. After the Revolution of 1688 the manners and morals of English society were somewhat on the mend.   The court of William and Mary, and of their successor, Queen Anne, set no such example of open profligacy as that of Charles II. But there was much hard drinking, gambling, dueling, and intrigue in London, and vice was fashionable till Addison partly preached and partly laughed it down in the *Spectator*. The women were mostly frivolous and uneducated, and not unfrequently fast.   They are spoken of with systematic disrespect by nearly every writer of the time, except Steele. "Every woman," wrote Pope, "is at heart a rake." The reading public had now become large enough to make letters a profession.   Dr. Johnson said that Pope was the first writer in whose case the book-seller took the place of the patron.   His translation of Homer, published by subscription, brought him between eight and nine thousand pounds and made him independent. But the activity of the press produced a swarm of poorly-paid hack-writers, penny-a-liners, who lived from hand to mouth and did small literary jobs to order.   Many of these inhabited Grub Street, and their lampoons against Pope and others of their more successful rivals called out Pope's *Dunciad*, or epic of the dunces, by way of retaliation.   The politics of the time were sordid, and consisted mainly of an ignoble scramble for office.   The Whigs were fighting to maintain the Act of Succession in favor of the House of Hanover, and the Tories were secretly intriguing with the exiled Stuarts.   Many of the leaders, such as the great Whig champion, John Churchill, Duke of Marlborough, were without political principle or even personal honesty.   The Church, too, was in a condition of spiritual deadness.   Bishoprics and livings were sold, and given to political favorites.   Clergymen, like Swift and Lawrence Sterne, were worldly in their lives and immoral in their writings, and were practically unbelievers.   The growing religious skepticism appeared in the Deist controversy. Numbers of men in high position were Deists ; the Earl of Shaftesbury, for example, and Pope's brilliant friend, Henry St. John, Lord Bolingbroke, the head of the Tory ministry, whose political writings had much influence upon his young French acquaintance, Voltaire.   Pope was a Roman Catholic, though there was little to show it in his writings, and the underlying thought of his famous *Essay on Man* was furnished him by Bolingbroke.   The letters of the cold-hearted Chesterfield to his son were accepted as a manual of

conduct, and La Rochefoucauld's cynical maxims were
quoted as authority on life and human nature. Said Swift:

> As Rochefoucauld his maxims drew
> From nature, I believe them true.
> They argue no corrupted mind
> In him; the fault is in mankind.

The succession which Dryden had willed to Congreve was
taken up by Alexander Pope. He was a man quite unlike
Dryden—sickly, deformed, morbidly precocious, and spiteful;
nevertheless he joined on to and continued Dryden. He was
more careful in his literary workmanship than his great forerunner, and in his *Moral Essays* and *Satires* he brought the
Horatian epistle in verse, the formal satire and that species
of didactic poem of which Boileau had given the first example, to an exquisite perfection of finish and verbal art. Dryden had translated Vergil, and so Pope translated Homer.
The throne of the dunces, which Dryden had conferred upon
Shadwell, Pope, in his *Dunciad*, passed on to two of his own
literary foes, Theobald and Colley Cibber. There is a great
waste of strength in this elaborate squib, and most of the
petty writers, whose names it has preserved, as has been said,
like flies in amber, are now quite unknown. But, although
we have to read it with notes, to get the point of its allusions, it is easy to see what execution it must have done at
the time, and it is impossible to withhold admiration from
the wit, the wickedness, the triumphant mischief of the thing.
In the *Epistle to Dr. Arbuthnot*, the satirical sketch of Addison—who had offended Pope by praising a rival translation
of Homer—is as brilliant as any thing of the kind in Dryden.
Pope's very malignity made his sting sharper than Dryden's.
He secreted venom, and worked out his revenges deliberately,
bringing all the resources of his art to bear upon the question
of how to give the most pain most cleverly.

Pope's masterpiece is, perhaps, the *Rape of the Lock*, a
mock heroic poem, a "dwarf *Iliad*," recounting, in five

cantos, a society quarrel, which arose from Lord Petre's cutting a lock of hair from the head of Mrs. Arabella Fermor.   Boileau, in his *Lutrin*, had treated with the same epic dignity a dispute over the placing of the reading-desk in a parish church.   Pope was the Homer of the drawing-room, the boudoir, the tea-urn, the ombre-party, the sedan-chair, the parrot cage, and the lap-dogs.   This poem, in its sparkle and airy grace, is the topmost blossom of a highly artificial society, the quintessence of whatever poetry was possible in those

> Tea-cup times of hood and hoop,
> And when the patch was worn,

with whose decorative features, at least, the recent Queen Anne revival has made this generation familiar.   It may be said of it, as Thackery said of Gay's pastorals : "It is to poetry what charming little Dresden china figures are to sculpture, graceful, minikin, fantastic, with a certain beauty always accompanying them."   The *Rape of the Lock*, perhaps, stops short of beauty, but it attains elegance and prettiness in a supreme degree.   In imitation of the gods and goddesses in the *Iliad*, who intermeddle for or against the human characters, Pope introduced the Sylphs of the Rosicrucian philosophy.   We may measure the distance between imagination and fancy, if we will compare these little filagree creatures with Shakspere's elves, whose occupation it was

> To tread the ooze of the salt deep,
> Or run upon the sharp wind of the north, . . .
> Or on the beached margent of the sea
> To dance their ringlets to the whispering wind.

Very different are the offices of Pope's fays :

> Our humble province is to tend the fair ;
> Not a less pleasing, though less glorious, care ;
> To save the powder from too rude a gale,
> Nor let the imprisoned essences exhale. . . .
> Nay oft in dreams invention we bestow
> To change a flounce or add a furbelow.

Pope was not a great poet; it has been doubted whether he was a poet at all. He does not touch the heart, or stimulate the imagination, as the true poet always does. In the poetry of nature, and the poetry of passion, he was altogether impotent. His *Windsor Forest* and his *Pastorals* are artificial and false, not written with "the eye upon the object." His epistle of *Eloisa to Abelard* is declamatory and academic, and leaves the reader cold. The only one of his poems which is at all possessed with feeling is his pathetic *Elegy to the Memory of an Unfortunate Lady*. But he was a great literary artist. Within the cramped and starched regularity of the heroic couplet, which the fashion of the time and his own habit of mind imposed upon him, he secured the largest variety of modulation and emphasis of which that verse was capable. He used antithesis, periphrasis, and climax with great skill. His example dominated English poetry for nearly a century, and even now, when a poet like Dr. Holmes, for example, would write satire or humorous verse of a dignified kind, he turns instinctively to the measure and manner of Pope. He was not a consecutive thinker, like Dryden, and cared less about the truth of his thought than about the pointedness of its expression. His language was closer-grained than Dryden's. His great art was the art of putting things. He is more quoted than any other English poet but Shakspere. He struck the average intelligence, the common sense of English readers, and furnished it with neat, portable formulas, so that it no longer needed to "vent its observation in mangled terms," but could pour itself out compactly, artistically in little ready-made molds. But this high-wrought brilliancy, this unceasing point, soon fatigue. His poems read like a series of epigrams; and every line has a hit or an effect.

From the reign of Queen Anne date the beginnings of the periodical essay. Newspapers had been published since the time of the civil war; at first irregularly, and then regularly. But no literature of permanent value appeared in periodical form until Richard Steele started the *Tatler*, in 1709.   In this he was soon joined by his friend, Joseph Addison ; and in its successor, the *Spectator*, the first number of which was issued March 1, 1711, Addison's contributions outnumbered Steele's. The *Tatler* was published on three, the *Spectator* on six, days of the week.   The *Tatler* gave political news, but each number of the *Spectator* consisted of a single essay.   The object of these periodicals was to reflect the passing humors of the time, and to satirize the follies and minor immoralities of the town. "I shall endeavor," wrote Addison, in the tenth paper of the *Spectator*, "to enliven morality with wit, and to temper wit with morality. . . . It was said of Socrates that he brought Philosophy down from Heaven to inhabit among men ; and I shall be ambitious to have it said of me that I have brought Philosophy out of closets and libraries, schools and colleges, to dwell in clubs and assemblies, at tea-tables and in coffee-houses."   Addison's satire was never personal.   He was a moderate man, and did what he could to restrain Steele's intemperate party zeal.   His character was dignified and pure, and his strongest emotion seems to have been his religious feeling.   One of his contemporaries called him "a parson in a tie wig," and he wrote several excellent hymns.   His mission was that of censor of the public taste.   Sometimes he lectured and sometimes he preached, and in his Saturday papers he brought his wide reading and nice scholarship into service for the instruction of his readers.   Such was the series of essays in which he gave an elaborate review of *Paradise Lost*.   Such also was his famous paper, the *Vision of Mirza*, an oriental allegory of human life.   The adoption of this slightly pedagogic tone was justified by the prevalent ignorance and frivolity of the age.   But the lighter portions of the *Spectator* are those which have worn the best.   Their style is at once correct and easy, and it is as a humorist, a sly observer of manners, and, above all, a delightful talker, that Addison is best known to posterity.   In the personal sketches of the mem-

bers of the Spectator Club, of Will. Honeycomb, Captain
Sentry, Sir Andrew Freeport, and, above all, Sir Roger de
Coverley, the quaint and honest country gentleman, may be
found the nucleus of the modern prose fiction of character.
Addison's humor is always a trifle grave. There is no whimsy,
no frolic in it, as in Sterne or Lamb. "He thinks justly," said
Dr. Johnson, "but he thinks faintly." The *Spectator* had a
host of followers, from the somewhat heavy *Rambler* and
Idler of Johnson, down to the *Salmagundi* papers of our own
Irving, who was, perhaps, Addison's latest and best literary
descendant. In his own age Addison made some figure as a
poet and dramatist. His *Campaign*, celebrating the victory of
Blenheim, had one much admired couplet, in which Marlborough was likened to the angel of tempest, who,

> Pleased the Almighty's orders to perform,
> Rides in the whirlwind and directs the storm.

His stately, classical tragedy, *Cato*, which was acted at Drury
Lane Theater in 1712, with immense applause, was pronounced by Dr. Johnson "unquestionably the noblest production of Addison's genius." Is is, notwithstanding, cold
and tedious, as a whole, though it has some fine declamatory passages—in particular the soliloquy of Cato in the
fifth act—

> It must be so: Plato, thou reasonest well, etc.

The greatest of the Queen Anne wits, and one of the most
savage and powerful satirists that ever lived, was Jonathan
Swift. As secretary in the family of Sir William Temple,
and domestic chaplain to the Earl of Berkeley, he had known
in youth the bitterness of poverty and dependence. Afterward
he wrote himself into influence with the Tory ministry, and
was promised a bishopric, but was put off with the deanery
of St. Patrick's, and retired to Ireland to "die like a poisoned
rat in a hole." His life was made tragical by the forecast of
the madness which finally overtook him. "The stage dark-

ened," said Scott, "ere the curtain fell." Insanity deepened into idiocy and a hideous silence, and for three years before his death he spoke hardly ever a word. He had directed that his tombstone should bear the inscription, *Ubi saeva indignatio cor ulterius lacerare nequit.* "So great a man he seems to me," wrote Thackeray, "that thinking of him is like thinking of an empire falling." Swift's first noteworthy publication was his *Tale of a Tub,* 1704, a satire on religious differences. But his great work was *Gulliver's Travels,* 1726, the book in which his hate and scorn of mankind, and the long rage of mortified pride and thwarted ambition found their fullest expression. Children read the voyages to Lilliput and Brobdingnag, to the flying island of Laputa and the country of the Houyhnhnms, as they read *Robinson Crusoe,* as stories of wonderful adventure. Swift had all of De Foe's realism, his power of giving veri-similitude to his narrative by the invention of a vast number of small, exact, consistent details. But underneath its fairy tales *Gulliver's Travels* is a satire, far more radical than any of Dryden's or Pope's, because directed, not against particular parties or persons, but against human nature. In his account of Lilliput and Brobdingnag, Swift tries to show that human greatness, goodness, beauty disappear if the scale be altered a little. If men were six inches high instead of six feet, their wars, governments, science, religion—all their institutions, in fine, and all the courage, wisdom, and virtue by which these have been built up, would appear laughable. On the other hand, if they were sixty feet high instead of six, they would become disgusting. The complexion of the finest ladies would show blotches, hairs, excrescences, and an overpowering effluvium would breathe from the pores of the skin. Finally, in his loathsome caricature of mankind, as Yahoos, he contrasts them, to their shame, with the beasts, and sets instinct above reason.

The method of Swift's satire was grave irony. Among his minor writings in this kind are his *Argument against*

Abolishing Christianity, his *Modest Proposal* for utilizing
the surplus population of Ireland by eating the babies of the
poor, and his *Predictions of Isaac Bickerstaff*. In the last
he predicted the death of one Partridge, an almanac maker,
at a certain day and hour. When the time set was past, he
published a minute account of Partridge's last moments; and
when the subject of this excellent fooling printed an indignant denial of his own death, Swift answered very temper-
ately, proving that he was dead and remonstrating with
him on the violence of his language. "To call a man a fool
and villain, an impudent fellow, only for differing from him
in a point merely speculative, is, in my humble opinion, a
very improper style for a person of his education." Swift
wrote verses as well as prose, but their motive was the
reverse of poetical. His gross and cynical humor vul-
garized whatever it touched. He leaves us no illusions, and
not only strips his subject, but flays it and shows the raw
muscles beneath the skin. He delighted to dwell upon the
lowest bodily functions of human nature. "He saw blood-
shot," said Thackeray.

———

1. History of Eighteenth Century Literature (1660–1780).
Edmund Gosse. London: Macmillan & Co., 1889.

2. Macaulay's Essay, The Comic Dramatists of the Restoration.

3. The Poetical Works of John Dryden. Macmillan &
Co., 1873. (Globe Edition.)

4. Thackeray's English Humorists of the last Century.

5. Sir Roger de Coverley. New York: Harpers, 1878.

6. Swift's Tale of a Tub, Gulliver's Travels, Directions to
Servants, Polite Conversation, The Great Question Debated,
Verses on the Death of Dean Swift.

7. The Poetical Works of Alexander Pope. London:
Macmillan & Co., 1869. (Globe Edition.)

CHAPTER VI.

FROM THE DEATH OF POPE TO THE FRENCH REVOLUTION.

1744–1789.

Pope's example continued potent for fifty years after his death. Especially was this so in satiric and didactic poetry. Not only Dr. Johnson's adaptations from Juvenal, *London*, 1738, and the *Vanity of Human Wishes*, 1749, but Gifford's *Baviad*, 1791, and *Maeviad*, 1795, and Byron's *English Bards and Scotch Reviewers*, 1809, were in the verse and the manner of Pope. In Johnson's *Lives of the Poets*, 1781, Dryden and Pope are treated as the two greatest English poets. But long before this a revolution in literary taste had begun, a movement which is variously described as the Return to Nature or the Rise of the New Romantic School.

For nearly a hundred years poetry had dealt with manners and the life of towns—the gay, prosaic life of Congreve or of Pope. The sole concession to the life of nature was the old pastoral, which, in the hands of cockneys like Pope and Ambrose Philips, who merely repeated stock descriptions at second or third hand, became even more artificial than a *Beggar's Opera* or a *Rape of the Lock*. These at least were true to their environment, and were natural just because they were artificial. But the *Seasons* of James Thomson, published in installments from 1726–1730, had opened a new field. Their theme was the English landscape, as varied by the changes of the year, and they were written by a true lover and observer of nature. Mark Akenside's *Pleasures of Imagination*, 1744, published the year of Pope's death, was written, like the *Seasons*, in blank verse ;

and although its language had the formal, didactic cast of
the Queen Anne poets, it pointed unmistakably in the new
direction. Thomson had painted the soft beauties of a
highly cultivated land — lawns, gardens, forest-preserves,
orchards, and sheep-walks. But now a fresh note was struck
in the literature, not of England alone, but of Germany
and France—romanticism, the chief element in which was a
love of the wild. Poets turned from the tameness of
modern existence to savage nature and the heroic simplicity
of life among primitive tribes. In France, Rousseau introduced the idea of the natural man, following his instincts in
disregard of social conventions. In Germany Bodmer published, in 1753, the first edition of the old German epic, the
Nibelungen Lied. Works of a similar tendency in England
were the odes of William Collins and Thomas Gray, published between 1747 and 1757; especially Collins's *Ode on
the Superstitions of the Highlands,* and Gray's *Bard,* a Pindaric in which the last survivor of the Welsh bards invokes
vengeance on Edward I., the destroyer of his guild. Gray
and Mason, his friend and editor, made translations from the
ancient Welsh and Norse poetry. Thomas Percy's *Reliques
of Ancient English Poetry,* 1765, aroused the taste for old
ballads. Richard Hurd's *Letters on Chivalry and Romance,*
Thomas Warton's *History of English Poetry.* 1774-1778,
Tyrwhitt's critical edition of Chaucer, and Horace Walpole's
Gothic romance, the *Castle of Otranto,* 1765, stimulated this
awakened interest in the picturesque aspects of feudal life, and
contributed to the fondness for supernatural and mediæval
subjects. James Beattie's *Minstrel,* 1771, described the edu-
cating influence of Scottish mountain scenery upon the genius
of a young poet. But the most remarkable instances of this
passion for wild nature and the romantic past were the *Poems
of Ossian* and Thomas Chatterton's literary forgeries.

In 1762 James Macpherson published the first installment
of what professed to be a translation of the poems of Ossian,

a Gaelic bard, whom tradition placed in the 3d century. Macpherson said that he made his version—including two complete epics, *Fingal* and *Temora*—from Gaelic MSS., which he had collected in the Scottish Highlands. A fierce controversy at once sprang up over the genuineness of these remains. Macpherson was challenged to produce his originals, and when, many years after, he published the Gaelic text, it was asserted that this was nothing but a translation of his own English into modern Gaelic. Of the MSS. which he professed to have found not a scrap remained : the Gaelic text was printed from transcriptions in Macpherson's handwriting or in that of his secretaries.

But whether these poems were the work of Ossian or of Macpherson, they made a deep impression at the time. Napoleon admired them greatly, and Goethe inserted passages from the "Songs of Selma" in his *Sorrows of Werther*. Macpherson composed—or translated—them in an abrupt, rhapsodical prose, resembling the English version of Job or of the prophecies of Isaiah. They filled the minds of their readers with images of vague sublimity and desolation ; the mountain torrent, the mist on the hills, the ghosts of heroes half seen by the setting moon, the thistle in the ruined courts of chieftains, the grass whistling on the windy heath, the gray rock by the blue stream of Lutha, and the cliffs of sea-surrounded Gormal.

"A tale of the times of old ! "

"Why, thou wanderer unseen ! Thou bender of the thistle of Lora ; why, thou breeze of the valley, hast thou left mine ear ? I hear no distant roar of streams ! No sound of the harp from the rock ! Come, thou huntress of Lutha, Malvina, call back his soul to the bard. I look forward to Lochlin of lakes, to the dark billowy bay of U-thorno, where Fingal decends from Ocean, from the roar of winds. Few are the heroes of Morven in a land unknown."

Thomas Chatterton, who died by his own hand in 1770, at the age of seventeen, is one of the most wonderful examples of precocity in the history of literature. His father had been sexton of the ancient Church of St. Mary Redcliff, in Bristol, and the boy's sensitive imagination took the stamp of his surroundings. He taught himself to read from a black-letter Bible. He drew charcoal sketches of churches, castles, knightly tombs, and heraldic blazonry. When only eleven years old, he began the fabrication of documents in prose and verse, which he ascribed to a fictitious Thomas Rowley, a secular priest at Bristol in the 15th century. Chatterton pretended to have found these among the contents of an old chest in the muniment room of St. Mary Redcliff's. The Rowley poems included two tragedies, *Aella* and *Goddwyn*, two cantos of a long poem on the *Battle of Hastings*, and a number of ballads and minor pieces. Chatterton had no precise knowledge of early English, or even of Chaucer. His method of working was as follows. He made himself a manuscript glossary of the words marked as archaic in Bailey's and Kersey's English dictionaries, composed his poems first in modern language, and then turned them into ancient spelling, and substituted here and there the old words in his glossary for their modern equivalents. Naturally he made many mistakes, and though Horace Walpole, to whom he sent some of his pieces, was unable to detect the forgery, his friends, Gray and Mason, to whom he submitted them, at once pronounced them spurious. Nevertheless there was a controversy over Rowley hardly less obstinate than that over Ossian, a controversy made possible only by the then almost universal ignorance of the forms, scansion, and vocabulary of early English poetry. Chatterton's poems are of little value in themselves, but they are the record of an industry and imitative quickness marvelous in a mere child, and they show how, with the instinct of genius, he threw himself into the main literary current of his time. Discarding the couplet of Pope, the poets now went back for models to the Elizabethan writers. Thomas Warton published in 1753 his *Observations on the Faerie Queene.* Beattie's *Minstrel,* Thomson's *Castle of Indolence.* and William Shenstone's *Schoolmistress* were all written in the Spenserian stanza. Shenstone gave a partly humorous effect to his poem by imitating Spenser's archaisms, and Thomson reproduced in many passages the copious harmony and luxuriant imagery of the *Faerie Queene.* John Dyer's *Fleece* was a poem in blank verse on English wool-growing, after the fashion of Vergil's *Georgics.* The subject was unfortunate, for, as Dr. Johnson said, it is impossible to make poetry out of serges and druggets. Dyer's *Grongar Hill,* which mingles reflection with natural description in the manner of Gray's *Elegy written in a Country Churchyard,* was composed in the octosyllabic verse of Milton's *L'Allegro* and *Il Penseroso.* Milton's minor poems, which had hitherto been neglected, exercised a great influence on Collins and Gray. Collins's *Ode to Simplicity* was written in the stanza of Milton's *Nativity,* and his exquisite unrimed *Ode to Evening* was a study in versification, after Milton's translation of Horace's *Ode to Pyrrha,* in the original meters. Shakspere began to be studied more reverently : numerous critical editions of his plays were issued, and Garrick restored his pure text to the stage. Collins was an enthusiastic student of Shakspere, and one of his sweetest poems, the *Dirge in Cymbeline,* was inspired by the tragedy of *Cymbeline.* The verse of Gray, Collins, and the Warton brothers abounds in verbal reminiscences of Shakspere ; but their genius was not allied to his, being exclusively lyrical and not at all dramatic. The Muse of this romantic school was Fancy rather than Passion. A thoughtful melancholy, a gentle, scholarly pensiveness, the spirit of Milton's *Il Penseroso,* pervades their poetry. Gray was a fastidious scholar, who produced very little, but that little of the finest quality. His famous

Elegy, expressing a meditative mood in language of the choicest perfection, is the representative poem of the second half of the 18th century, as the *Rape of the Lock* is of the first. The romanticists were quietists, and their scenery is characteristic. They loved solitude and evening, the twilight vale, the mossy hermitage, ruins, glens, and caves. Their style was elegant and academic, retaining a little of the stilted poetic diction of their classical forerunners. Personification and periphrasis were their favorite mannerisms : Collins's Odes were largely addressed to abstractions, such as Fear, Pity, Liberty, Mercy and Simplicity. A poet in their dialect was always a "bard ;" a countryman was "the untutored swain," and a woman was a "nymph" or "the fair," just as in Dryden and Pope. Thomson is perpetually mindful of Vergil, and afraid to speak simply. He uses too many Latin epithets, like *amusive* and *precipitant*, and calls a fish-line

The floating line snatched from the hoary steed.

They left much for Cowper and Wordsworth to do in the way of infusing the new blood of a strong, racy English into our exhausted poetic diction. Their poetry is impersonal, bookish, literary. It lacks emotional force, except now and then in Gray's immortal *Elegy*, in his *Ode on a Distant Prospect of Eton College*, in Collins's lines, *On the Death of Thomson*, and his little ode beginning, "How sleep the brave."

The new school did not lack critical expounders of its principles and practice. Joseph Warton published, in 1756, the first volume of his *Essay on the Genius and Writings of Pope*, an elaborate review of Pope's writings *seriatim*, doing him certainly full justice, but ranking him below Shakspere, Spenser, and Milton. "Wit and satire," wrote Warton, "are transitory and perishable, but nature and passion are eternal. . . . He stuck to describing modern manners; but those manners, because they are familiar, artificial, and polished, are, in their very nature, unfit for any lofty effort of the Muse. Whatever poetical enthusiasm he actually possessed he withheld and stifled. Surely it is no narrow and niggardly encomium to say, he is the great Poet of Reason, the first of Ethical authors in verse." Warton illustrated his critical positions by quoting freely not only from Spenser and Milton, but from recent poets, like Thomson, Gray, Collins, and Dyer. He testified that the *Seasons* had "been very instrumental in diffusing a general taste for the beauties of nature and landscape." It was symptomatic of the change in literary taste that the natural or English school of landscape gardening now began to displace the French and Dutch fashion of clipped hedges, and regular parterres, and that Gothic architecture came into repute. Horace Walpole was a virtuoso in Gothic art, and in his castle at Strawberry Hill he made a collection of ancient armor, illuminated manuscripts, and bric-a-brac of all kinds. Gray had been Walpole's traveling companion in France and Italy, and the two had quarreled and separated, but were afterward reconciled. From Walpole's private printing-press at Strawberry Hill Gray's two "sister odes," the *Bard*, and the *Progress of Poesy*, were first issued in 1757. Both Gray and Walpole were good correspondents, and their printed letters are among the most delightful literature of the kind.

The central figure among the English men of letters of that generation was Samuel Johnson (1709–1784), whose memory has been preserved less by his own writings than by James Boswell's famous *Life of Johnson*, published in 1791. Boswell was a Scotch laird and advocate, who first met Johnson in London, when the latter was fifty-four years old. Boswell was not a very wise or witty person, but he reverenced the worth and intellect which shone through his subject's uncouth exterior. He followed him about, note-book in hand, bore all his snubbings patiently, and made the best biography ever written. It is related that the doctor once said that if he thought Boswell meant to write his life, he should prevent it by taking Boswell's. And yet Johnson's own writings and this biography of him have changed places in relative importance so completely that Carlyle predicted that the former would soon be reduced to notes on the latter; and Macaulay said that the man who was known to his contemporaries as a great writer was known to posterity as an agreeable companion.

Johnson was one of those rugged, eccentric, self-developed characters so common among the English. He was the son of a Lichfield book-seller, and after a course at Oxford, which was cut short by poverty, and an unsuccessful career as a school-master, he had come up to London, in 1737, where he supported himself for many years as a book-seller's hack. Gradually his great learning and abilities, his ready social wit and powers as a talker, caused his company to be sought at the tables of those whom he called "the great." He was a clubbable man, and he drew about him at the tavern a group of the most distinguished intellects of the time: Edmund Burke, the orator and statesman ; Oliver Goldsmith, Sir Joshua Reynolds, the portrait painter, and David Garrick, the great actor, who had been a pupil in Johnson's school, near Lichfield. Johnson was the typical John Bull of the last century. His oddities, virtues, and prejudices were thoroughly English. He hated Frenchmen, Scotchmen, and Americans, and had a cockneyish attachment to London. He was a high Tory, and an orthodox churchman; he loved a lord in the abstract, and yet he asserted a sturdy independence against any lord in particular. He was deeply religious, but had an abiding fear of death. He was burly in person, and slovenly in dress, his shirt-frill always covered with snuff. He was a great diner out, an inordinate tea-drinker, and a voracious and untidy feeder. An inherited scrofula, which often took the form of hypochondria and threatened to affect his brain, deprived him of control over the muscles of his face. Boswell describes how his features worked, how he snorted, grunted, whistled, and rolled about in his chair when getting ready to speak. He records his minutest traits, such as his habit of pocketing the orange peels at the club, and his superstitious way of touching all the posts between his house and the Mitre Tavern, going back to do it, if he skipped one by chance. Though bearish in his manners and arrogant in dispute, especially when talking "for victory," Johnson had a large and tender heart. He loved his ugly, old wife—twenty-one years his senior—and he had his house full of unfortunates—a blind woman, an invalid surgeon, a destitute widow, a negro servant—whom he supported for many years, and bore with all their ill-humors patiently.

Among Johnson's numerous writings the ones best entitled to remembrance are, perhaps, his *Dictionary of the English Language*, 1755; his moral tale, *Rasselas*, 1759; the introduction to his edition of Shakspere, 1765, and his *Lives of the Poets*, 1781. Johnson wrote a sonorous, cadenced prose, full of big Latin words and balanced clauses. Here is a sentence, for example, from his *Visit to the Hebrides*: "We were now treading that illustrious island which was once the luminary of the Caledonian regions, whence savage clans and roving barbarians derived the benefits of knowledge and the blessings of religion. To abstract the mind from all local emotion would be impossible, if it were endeavored, and would be foolish, if it were possible." The difference between his colloquial style and his book style is well illustrated in the instance cited by Macaulay. Speaking of Villiers's *Rehearsal*, Johnson said, "It has not wit enough to keep it sweet;" then paused and added—translating English into Johnsonese—"it has not vitality sufficient to preserve it from putrefaction." There is more of this in Johnson's *Rambler* and *Idler* papers than in his latest work, the *Lives of the Poets*. In this he showed himself a sound and judicious

critic, though with decided limitations. His understanding
was solid, but he was a thorough classicist, and his taste in
poetry was formed on Pope. He was unjust to Milton and
to his own contemporaries, Gray, Collins, Shenstone, and
Dyer. He had no sense of the higher and subtler graces of
romantic poetry, and he had a comical indifference to the
"beauties of nature." When Boswell once ventured to remark that poor Scotland had, at least, some "noble wild
prospects," the doctor replied that the noblest prospect a
Scotchman ever saw was the road that led to London.

The English novel of real life had its origin at this time.
Books like De Foe's *Robinson Crusoe, Captain Singleton,
Journal of the Plague*, etc., were tales of incident and adventure rather than novels. The novel deals primarily with
character and with the interaction of characters upon one
another, as developed by a regular plot. The first English
novelist, in the modern sense of the word, was Samuel Richardson, a printer, who began authorship in his fiftieth year
with his *Pamela*, 1740, the story of a young servant girl who
resisted the seductions of her master, and finally, as the reward of her virtue, became his wife. *Clarissa Harlowe*, 1748,
was the tragical history of a high-spirited young lady who,
being driven from her home by her family because she
refused to marry the suitor selected for her, fell into the
toils of Lovelace, an accomplished rake. After struggling
heroically against every form of artifice and violence, she was
at last drugged and ruined. She died of a broken heart, and
Lovelace, borne down by remorse, was killed in a duel by a
cousin of Clarissa. *Sir Charles Grandison*, 1753, was Richardson's portrait of an ideal fine gentleman, whose stately
doings fill eight volumes, but who seems to the modern reader
a bore and a prig. All these novels were written in the form
of letters passing between the characters, a method which
fitted Richardson's subjective cast of mind. He knew little
of life, but he identified himself intensely with his principal

character and produced a strong effect by minute, accumulated touches. *Clarissa Harlowe* is his masterpiece, though even in that the situation is painfully prolonged, the heroine's virtue is self-conscious and rhetorical, and there is something almost ludicrously unnatural in the copiousness with which she pours herself out in gushing epistles to her female correspondent at the very moment when she is beset with dangers, persecuted, agonized, and driven nearly mad. In Richardson's novels appears, for the first time, that sentimentalism which now began to infect European literature. *Pamela* was translated into French and German, and fell in with the current of popular feeling which found fullest expression in Rousseau's *Nouvelle Heloise*, 1759, and Goethe's *Leiden des Jungen Werther*, which set all the world a-weeping in 1774.

Coleridge said that to pass from Richardson's books to those of Henry Fielding was like going into the fresh air from a close room heated by stoves. Richardson, it has been affirmed, knew *man*, but Fielding knew *men*. The latter's first novel, *Joseph Andrews*, 1742, was begun as a travesty of *Pamela*. The hero, a brother of Pamela, was a young footman in the employ of Lady Booby, from whom his virtue suffered a like assault to that made upon Pamela's by her master. This reversal of the natural situation was in itself full of laughable possibilities, had the book gone on simply as a burlesque. But the exuberance of Fielding's genius led him beyond his original design. His hero, leaving Lady Booby's service, goes traveling with good Parson Adams, and is soon engaged in a series of comical and rather boisterous adventures.

Fielding had seen life, and his characters were painted from the life with a bold, free hand. He was a gentleman by birth, and had made acquaintance with society and the town in 1727, when he was a handsome, stalwart young fellow, with high animal spirits and a great appetite for pleasure. He soon ran himself into debt and began writing for the stage; married, and spent his wife's fortune, living for a while in much splendor as a country gentleman, and afterward in a reduced condition as a rural justice with a salary of five hundred pounds of "the dirtiest money on earth." Fielding's masterpiece was *Tom Jones*, 1749, and it remains one of the best of English novels. Its hero is very much after Fielding's own heart, wild, spendthrift, warm-hearted, forgiving, and greatly in need of forgiveness. The same type of character, with the lines deepened, re-appears in Captain Booth, in *Amelia*, 1751, the heroine of which is a portrait of Fielding's wife. With Tom Jones is contrasted Blifil, the embodiment of meanness, hypocrisy, and cowardice. Sophia Western, the heroine, is one of Fielding's most admirable creations. For the regulated morality of Richardson, with its somewhat old-grannified air, Fielding substituted instinct. His virtuous characters are virtuous by impulse only, and his ideal of character is manliness. In *Jonathan Wild* the hero is a highwayman. This novel is ironical, a sort of prose mock-heroic, and is one of the strongest, though certainly the least pleasing, of Fielding's writings.

Tobias Smollett was an inferior Fielding with a difference. He was a Scotch ship-surgeon, and had spent some time in the West Indies. He introduced into fiction the now familiar figure of the British tar, in the persons of Tom Bowling and Commodore Trunnion, as Fielding had introduced, in Squire Western, the equally national type of the hard-swearing, deep-drinking, fox-hunting Tory squire. Both Fielding and Smollett were of the hearty British "beef-and-beer" school; their novels are downright, energetic, coarse, and high-blooded; low life, physical life, runs riot through their pages —tavern brawls, the breaking of pates, and the off-hand courtship of country wenches. Smollett's books, such as *Roderick Random*, 1748; *Peregrine Pickle*, 1751, and *Ferdinand Count Fathom*, 1752, were more purely stories of broadly comic adventure than Fielding's. The latter's view of life was by no means idyllic ; but with Smollett this English realism ran into vulgarity and a hard Scotch literalness, and character was pushed to caricature. "The generous wine of Fielding," says Taine, "in Smollett's hands becomes brandy of the dram-shop." A partial exception to this is to be found in his last and best novel, *Humphrey Clinker*, 1770. The influence of Cervantes and of the French novelist, Le Sage, who finished his *Adventures of Gil Blas* in 1735, are very perceptible in Smollett.

A genius of much finer mold was Lawrence Sterne, the author of *Tristram Shandy*, 1759–1767, and the *Sentimental Journey*, 1768. *Tristram Shandy* is hardly a novel: the story merely serves to hold together a number of characters, such as Uncle Toby and Corporal Trim, conceived with rare subtlety and originality. Sterne's chosen province was the whimsical, and his great model was Rabelais. His books are full of digressions, breaks, surprises, innuendoes, double meanings, mystifications, and all manner of odd turns. Coleridge and Carlyle unite in pronouncing him a great humorist. Thackeray says that he was only a great jester. Humor is the laughter of the heart, and Sterne's pathos is closely interwoven with his humor. He was the foremost of English sentimentalists, and he had that taint of insincerity which distinguishes sentimentalism from genuine sentiment, like Goldsmith's, for example. Sterne, in life, was selfish, heartless, and untrue. A clergyman, his worldliness and vanity and the indecency of his writings were a scandal to the Church, though his sermons were both witty and affecting. He enjoyed the titillation of his own emotions, and he had practiced so long at detecting the latent pathos that lies in the expression of dumb things and of poor, patient animals, that he could summon the tear of sensibility at the thought of a discarded postchaise, a dead donkey, a starling in a cage, or of Uncle Toby putting a house fly out of the window, and saying, "There is room enough in the world for

thee and me." It is a high proof of his cleverness that he
generally succeeds in raising the desired feeling in his readers even from such trivial occasions. He was a minute philosopher, his philosophy was kindly, and he taught the delicate
art of making much out of little. Less coarse than Fielding,
he is far more corrupt. Fielding goes bluntly to the point ;
Sterne lingers among the temptations and suspends the expectation to tease and excite it. Forbidden fruit had a relish
for him, and his pages seduce. He is full of good sayings
both tender and witty. It was Sterne, for example, who
wrote, "God tempers the wind to the shorn lamb."

A very different writer was Oliver Goldsmith, whose
Vicar of Wakefield, 1766, was the earliest, and is still one of
the best, novels of domestic and rural life. The book, like
its author, was thoroughly Irish, full of bulls and inconsist-
encies. Very improbable things happened in it with a cheerful defiance of logic. But its characters are true to nature,
drawn with an idyllic sweetness and purity, and with touches
of a most loving humor. Its hero, Dr. Primrose, was painted
after Goldsmith's father, a poor clergyman of the English
Church in Ireland, and the original, likewise, of the country
parson in Goldsmith's *Deserted Village*, 1770, who was "passing rich on forty pounds a year." This poem, though written in the fashionable couplet of Pope, and even containing
a few verses contributed by Dr. Johnson—so that it was not
at all in line with the work of the romanticists—did, perhaps,
as much as any thing of Gray or of Collins to recall English
poetry to the simplicity and freshness of country life.

Except for the comedies of Sheridan and Goldsmith, and,
perhaps, a few other plays, the stage had now utterly declined.
The novel, which is dramatic in essence, though not in form,
began to take its place, and to represent life, though less intensely, yet more minutely than the theater could do. In the
novelists of the 18th century, the life of the people, as distinguished from " society " or the upper classes, began to invade

JOHNSON.

GOLDSMITH.

COWPER.

BURNS.

literature. Richardson was distinctly a *bourgeois* writer, and his contemporaries — Fielding, Smollett, Sterne, and Goldsmith—ranged over a wide variety of ranks and conditions. This is one thing which distinguishes the literature of the second half of the 18th century from that of the first, as well as in some degree from that of all previous centuries. Among the authors of this generation whose writings belonged to other departments of thought than pure literature may be mentioned, in passing, the great historian, Edward Gibbon, whose *Decline and Fall of the Roman Empire* was published from 1776-1788, and Edmund Burke, whose political speeches and pamphlets possess a true literary quality.

The romantic poets had addressed the imagination rather than the heart. It was reserved for two men—a contrast to one another in almost every respect—to bring once more into British song a strong individual feeling, and with it a new warmth and directness of speech. These were William Cowper (1731–1800) and Robert Burns (1759–1796). Cowper spoke out of his own life-experience, his agony, his love, his worship and despair; and straightway the varnish that had glittered over all our poetry since the time of Dryden melted away. Cowper had scribbled verses when he was a young law student at the Middle Temple in London, and he had contributed to the *Olney Hymns*, published in 1779 by his friend and pastor, the Rev. John Newton; but he only began to write poetry in earnest when he was nearly fifty years old. In 1782, the date of his first volume, he said, in a letter to a friend, that he had read but one English poet during the past twenty years. Perhaps, therefore, of all English poets of equal culture, Cowper owed the least impulse to books and the most to the need of uttering his inmost thoughts and feelings. Cowper had a most unhappy life. As a child he was shy, sensitive, and sickly, and suffered much from bullying and fagging at a school whither he was sent after his mother's death. This happened when he was six years old;

and in his affecting lines written *On Receipt of My Mother's Picture*, he speaks of himself as a

Wretch even then, life's journey just begun.

In 1763 he became insane and was sent to an asylum, where he spent a year. Judicious treatment restored him to sanity, but he came out a broken man and remained for the rest of his life an invalid, unfitted for any active occupation. His disease took the form of religious melancholy. He had two recurrences of madness, and both times made attempts upon his life. At Huntingdon, and afterward at Olney, in Buckinghamshire, he found a home with the Unwin family, whose kindness did all which the most soothing and delicate care could do to heal his wounded spirit. His two poems *To Mary Unwin*, together with the lines on his mother's picture, were almost the first examples of deep and tender sentiment in the lyrical poetry of the last century. Cowper found relief from the black thoughts that beset him only in an ordered round of quiet household occupations. He corresponded indefatigably, took long walks through the neighborhood, read, sang, and conversed with Mrs. Unwin and his friend, Lady Austin, and amused himself with carpentry, gardening, and raising pets, especially hares, of which gentle animals he grew very fond. All these simple tastes, in which he found for a time a refuge and a sheltered happiness, are reflected in his best poem, *The Task*, 1785. Cowper is the poet of the family affections, of domestic life, and rural retirement; the laureate of the fireside, the tea-table, the evening lamp, the garden, the green-house, and the rabbit-coop. He draws with elegance and precision a chair, a clock, a harpsichord, a barometer, a piece of needle-work. But Cowper was an outdoor as well as an indoor man. The Olney landscape was tame, a fat, agricultural region, where the sluggish Ouse wound between plowed fields and the horizon was bounded by low hills. Nevertheless Cowper's natural descriptions are at once more distinct and more imaginative than Thomson's. *The Task* reflects, also, the new philanthropic spirit, the enthusiasm of humanity, the feeling of the brotherhood of men to which Rousseau had given expression in France, and which issued in the French Revolution. In England this was the time of Wilberforce, the antislavery agitator; of Whitefield, the eloquent revival preacher; of John and Charles Wesley, and of the Evangelical and Methodist movements which gave new life to the English Church. John Newton, the curate of Olney and the keeper of Cowper's conscience, was one of the leaders of the Evangelicals; and Cowper's first volume of *Table Talk* and other poems, 1782, written under Newton's inspiration, was a series of sermons in verse, somewhat intolerant of all worldly enjoyments, such as hunting, dancing, and theaters. "God made the country and man made the town," he wrote. He was a moralizing poet, and his morality was sometimes that of the invalid and the recluse. Byron called him a "coddled poet." And, indeed, there is a suspicion of gruel and dressing-gowns about him. He lived much among women, and his sufferings had refined him to a feminine delicacy. But there is no sickliness in his poetry, and he retained a charming playful humor—displayed in his excellent comic ballad *John Gilpin ;* and Mrs. Browning has sung of him,

How, when one by one sweet sounds and wandering lights departed,
He bore no less a loving face, because so broken-hearted.

At the close of the year 1786 a young Scotchman, named Samuel Rose, called upon Cowper at Olney, and left with him a small volume, which had appeared at Edinburgh during the past summer, entitled *Poems chiefly in the Scottish Dialect by Robert Burns.* Cowper read the book through twice, and, though somewhat bothered by the dialect, pronounced it a "very extraordinary production." This momentary flash, as of an electric spark, marks the contact not only of the two chief British poets of their generation, but of two literatures. Scotch poets, like Thomson and

Beattie, had written in southern English, and, as Carlyle said, *in vacuo*, that is, with nothing specially national in their work. Burns's sweet though rugged Doric first secured the vernacular poetry of his country a hearing beyond the border. He had, to be sure, a whole literature of popular songs and ballads behind him, and his immediate models were Allan Ramsay and Robert Ferguson ; but these remained provincial, while Burns became universal.

He was born in Ayrshire, on the banks of "bonny Doon," in a clay biggin not far from "Alloway's auld haunted kirk," the scene of the witch dance in *Tam O'Shanter*. His father was a hard-headed, God-fearing tenant farmer, whose life and that of his sons was a harsh struggle with poverty. The crops failed ; the landlord pressed for his rent ; for weeks at a time the family tasted no meat ; yet this life of toil was lightened by love and homely pleasures. In the *Cotter's Saturday Night* Burns has drawn a beautiful picture of his parents' household, the rest that came at the week's end, and the family worship about the "wee bit ingle, blinkin' bonnily." Robert was handsome, wild, and witty. He was universally susceptible, and his first songs, like his last, were of "the lasses." His head had been stuffed, in boyhood, with "tales and songs concerning devils, ghosts, fairies, brownies, witches, warlocks, spunkies, kelpies, elf-candles, dead-lights," etc., told him by one Jenny Wilson, an old woman who lived in the family. His ear was full of ancient Scottish tunes, and as soon as he fell in love he began to make poetry as naturally as a bird sings. He composed his verses while following the plow or working in the stack-yard ; or, at evening, balancing on two legs of his chair and watching the light of a peat fire play over the reeky walls of the cottage. Burns's love songs are in many keys, ranging from strains of the most pure and exalted passion, like *Ae Fond Kiss* and *To Mary in Heaven*, to such loose ditties as *When Januar Winds*, and *Green Grow the Rashes O*.

Burns liked a glass almost as well as a lass, and at Mauch-line, where he carried on a farm with his brother Gilbert, after their father's death, he began to seek a questionable re-lief from the pressure of daily toil and unkind fates, in the convivialities of the tavern. There, among the wits of the Mauchline Club, farmers' sons, shepherds from the uplands, and the smugglers who swarmed over the west coast, he would discuss politics and farming, recite his verses, and join in the singing and ranting, while

> Bousin o'er the nappy
> And gettin' fou and unco happy.

To these experiences we owe not only those excellent drinking songs, *John Barleycorn* and *Willie Brewed a Peck o' Maut*, but the headlong fun of *Tam O'Shanter*, the visions, grotesquely terrible, of *Death and Dr. Hornbook*, and the dramatic humor of the *Jolly Beggars*. Cowper had cele-brated "the cup which cheers but not inebriates." Burns sang the praises of *Scotch Drink*. Cowper was a stranger to Burns's high animal spirits, and his robust enjoyment of life. He had affections, but no passions. At Mauchline, Burns, whose irregularities did not escape the censure of the kirk, became involved, through his friendship with Gavin Hamil-ton, in the controversy between the Old Light and New Light clergy. His *Holy Fair, Holy Tulzie, Twa Herds, Holy Willie's Prayer*, and *Address to the Unco Gude*, are satires against bigotry and hypocrisy. But in spite of the rollicking profanity of his language, and the violence of his rebound against the austere religion of Scotland, Burns was at bottom deeply impressible by religious ideas, as may be seen from his *Prayer under the Pressure of Violent Anguish*, and *Prayer in Prospect of Death*.

His farm turned out a failure, and he was on the eve of sailing for Jamaica, when the favor with which his volume of poems was received stayed his departure, and turned his steps to Edinburgh. There the peasant poet was lionized

for a winter season by the learned and polite society of the
Scotch capital, with results in the end not altogether favor-
able to Burns's best interests. For when society finally
turned the cold shoulder on him he had to go back to farming
again, carrying with him a bitter sense of injustice and neg-
lect. He leased a farm at Ellisland, in 1788, and some friends
procured his appointment as exciseman for his district. But
poverty, disappointment, irregular habits, and broken health
clouded his last years, and brought him to an untimely death
at the age of thirty-seven. He continued, however, to pour
forth songs of unequaled sweetness and force. "The man
sank," said Coleridge, "but the poet was bright to the last."

Burns is the best of British song-writers. His songs are
singable; they are not merely lyrical poems. They were
meant to be sung, and they are sung. They were mostly set
to old Scottish airs, and sometimes they were built up from
ancient fragments of anonymous popular poetry, a chorus,
or stanza, or even a single line. Such are, for example, *Auld
Lang Syne*, *My Heart's in the Highlands*, and *Landlady,
Count the Lawin*. Burns had a great, warm heart. His sins
were sins of passion, and sprang from the same generous
soil that nourished his impulsive virtues. His elementary
qualities as a poet were sincerity, a healthy openness to all
impressions of the beautiful, and a sympathy which em-
braced men, animals, and the dumb objects of nature. His
tenderness toward flowers and the brute creation may be read
in his lines *To a Mountain Daisy*, *To a Mouse*, and *The
Auld Farmer's New Year's Morning Salutation to his Auld
Mare Maggie*. Next after love and good fellowship, patriotism is the most frequent motive of his song. Of his
national anthem, *Scots wha hae wi' Wallace bled*, Carlyle
said: "So long as there is warm blood in the heart of
Scotchman, or man, it will move in fierce thrills under this
war ode."

Burns's politics were a singular mixture of sentimental

Toryism with practical democracy. A romantic glamour was thrown over the fortunes of the exiled Stuarts, and to have been "out" in '45 with the Young Pretender was a popular thing in parts of Scotland. To this purely poetic loyalty may be attributed such Jacobite ballads of Burns as *Over the Water to Charlie*. But his sober convictions were on the side of liberty and human brotherhood, and are expressed in *The Twa Dogs*, the *First Epistle to Davie*, and *A Man's a Man for a' that*. His sympathy with the Revolution led him to send four pieces of ordnance, taken from a captured smuggler, as a present to the French Convention, a piece of bravado which got him into difficulties with his superiors in the excise. The poetry which Burns wrote, not in dialect, but in the classical English, is in the stilted manner of his century, and his prose correspondence betrays his lack of culture by its constant lapse into rhetorical affectation and fine writing.

---

1. James Thomson. The Castle of Indolence.
2. The Poems of Thomas Gray.
3. William Collins. Odes.
4. The Six Chief Lives from Johnson's Lives of the Poets. Edited by Matthew Arnold. Macmillan, 1878.
5. Boswell's Life of Johnson [abridged]. Henry Holt & Co., 1878.
6. Samuel Richardson. Clarissa Harlowe.
7. Henry Fielding. Tom Jones.
8. Tobias Smollett. Humphrey Clinker.
9. Lawrence Sterne. Tristram Shandy.
10. Oliver Goldsmith. Vicar of Wakefield and Deserted Village.
11. William Cowper. The Task and John Gilpin. (Globe Edition.) London: Macmillan & Co., 1879.
12. The Poems and Songs of Robert Burns. (Globe Edition.) London: Macmillan & Co., 1884.

CHAPTER VII.

FROM THE FRENCH REVOLUTION TO THE DEATH OF SCOTT.

1789–1832.

The burst of creative activity at the opening of the 19th century has but one parallel in English literary history, namely, the somewhat similar flowering out of the national genius in the time of Elizabeth and the first two Stuart kings. The later age gave birth to no supreme poets, like Shakspere and Milton. It produced no *Hamlet* and no *Paradise Lost ;* but it offers a greater number of important writers, a higher average of excellence, and a wider range and variety of literary work than any preceding era. Wordsworth, Coleridge, Scott, Byron, Shelley, and Keats are all great names ; while Southey, Landor, Moore, Lamb, and De Quincey would be noteworthy figures at any period, and deserve a fuller mention than can be here accorded them. But in so crowded a generation, selection becomes increasingly needful, and in the present chapter, accordingly, the emphasis will be laid upon the first-named group as not only the most important, but the most representative of the various tendencies of their time.

The conditions of literary work in this century have been almost unduly stimulating. The rapid advance in population, wealth, education, and the means of communication has vastly increased the number of readers. Every one who has any thing to say can say it in print, and is sure of some sort of a hearing. A special feature of the time is the multiplication of periodicals. The great London dailies, like the *Times* and the *Morning Post,* which were started during the

WORDSWORTH.

BYRON.

SHELLEY.

KEATS.

last quarter of the 18th century, were something quite new in journalism. The first of the modern reviews, the *Edinburgh*, was established in 1802, as the organ of the Whig party in Scotland. This was followed by the London *Quarterly*, in 1808, and by *Blackwood's Magazine*, in 1817, both in the Tory interest. The first editor of the *Edinburgh* was Francis Jeffrey, who assembled about him a distinguished corps of contributors, including the versatile Henry Brougham, afterward a great parliamentary orator and lord chancellor of England, and the Rev. Sydney Smith, whose witty sayings are still current. The first editor of the *Quarterly* was William Gifford, a satirist, who wrote the *Baviad* and *Mæviad* in ridicule of literary affectations. He was succeeded in 1824 by John Gibson Lockhart, the son-in-law of Walter Scott, and the author of an excellent *Life of Scott. Blackwood's* was edited by John Wilson, Professor of Moral Philosophy in the University of Edinburgh, who, under the pen-name of "Christopher North," contributed to his magazine a series of brilliant imaginary dialogues between famous characters of the day, entitled *Noctes Ambrosianæ*, because they were supposed to take place at Ambrose's tavern in Edinburgh. These papers were full of a profuse, headlong eloquence, of humor, literary criticism, and personalities interspersed with songs expressive of a roystering and convivial Toryism and an uproarious contempt for Whigs and cockneys. These reviews and magazines, and others which sprang up beside them, became the *nuclei* about which the wit and scholarship of both parties gathered. Political controversy under the Regency and the reign of George IV. was thus carried on more regularly by permanent organs, and no longer so largely by privateering, in the shape of pamphlets, like Swift's *Public Spirit of the Allies*, Johnson's *Taxation No Tyranny*, and Burke's *Reflections on the Revolution in France.* Nor did politics by any means usurp the columns of the reviews. Literature, art, science, the whole circle of human effort and achievement passed under review. *Blackwood's, Fraser's,* and the other monthlies published stories, poetry, criticism, and correspondence—every thing, in short, which enters into the make-up of our magazines to-day, except illustrations.

Two main influences, of foreign origin, have left their trace in the English writers of the first thirty years of the 19th century, the one communicated by contact with the new German literature of the latter half of the 18th century, and in particular with the writings of Goethe, Schiller, and Kant; the other springing from the events of the French Revolution. The influence of German upon English literature in the 19th century was more intellectual and less formal than that of the Italian in the 16th and of the French in the 18th. In other words, the German writers furnished the English with ideas and ways of feeling rather than with models of style. Goethe and Schiller did not become subjects for literary imitation as Molière, Racine, and Boileau had become in Pope's time. It was reserved for a later generation and for Thomas Carlyle to domesticate the diction of German prose. But the nature and extent of this influence can, perhaps, best be noted when we come to take up the authors of the time one by one.

The excitement caused by the French Revolution was something more obvious and immediate. When the Bastile fell, in 1789, the enthusiasm among the friends of liberty and human progress in England was hardly less intense than in France. It was the dawn of a new day; the shackles were stricken from the slave ; all men were free and all men were brothers, and radical young England sent up a shout that echoed the roar of the Paris mob. Wordsworth's lines on the *Fall of the Bastile,* Coleridge's *Fall of Robespierre* and *Ode to France,* and Southey's revolutionary drama, *Wat Tyler,* gave expression to the hopes and aspirations of the English democracy. In after life, Wordsworth, looking back regretfully to those years of promise, wrote his poem on the *French Revolution as it Appeared to Enthusiasts at its Commencement.*

> Bliss was it in that dawn to be alive;
> But to be young was very heaven. O times
> In which the meager, stale, forbidding ways
> Of custom, law, and statute took at once
> The attraction of a country in romance.

Those were the days in which Wordsworth, then an undergraduate at Cambridge, spent a college vacation in tramping through France, landing at Calais on the eve of the very day (July 14, 1790) on which Louis XVI. signalized the anniversary of the fall of the Bastile by taking the oath of fidelity to the new constitution. In the following year Wordsworth revisited France, where he spent thirteen months, forming an intimacy with the republican general, Beaupuis, at Orleans, and reaching Paris not long after the September massacres of 1792. Those were the days, too, in which young Southey and young Coleridge, having married sisters at Bristol, were planning a "Pantisocracy," or ideal community, on the banks of the Susquehannah, and denouncing the British government for going to war with the French Republic. This group of poets, who had met one another first in the south of England, came afterward to be called the Lake Poets, from their residence in the mountainous lake country of Westmoreland and Cumberland, with which their names, and that of Wordsworth, especially, are forever associated. The so-called "Lakers" did not, properly speaking, constitute a school of poetry. They differed greatly from one another in mind and art. But they were connected by social ties and by religious and political sympathies. The excesses of the French Revolution, and the usurpation of Napoleon disappointed them, as it did many other English liberals, and drove them into the ranks of the reactionaries. Advancing years brought conservatism, and they became in time loyal Tories and orthodox churchmen.

William Wordsworth (1770–1850), the chief of the three, and, perhaps, on the whole, the greatest English poet since Milton, published his *Lyrical Ballads* in 1798. The volume contained a few pieces by his friend Coleridge—among them the *Ancient Mariner*—and its appearance may fairly be said to mark an epoch in the history of English poetry. Wordsworth regarded himself as a reformer of poetry; and in the preface to the second edition of the *Lyrical Ballads*, he defended the theory on which they were composed. His innovations were twofold: in subject-matter and in diction. "The principal object which I proposed to myself in these poems," he said, "was to choose incidents and situations from common life. Low and rustic life was generally chosen, because, in that condition, the essential passions of the heart find a better soil in which they can attain their maturity . . . and are incorporated with the beautiful and permanent forms of nature." Wordsworth discarded, in theory, the poetic diction of his predecessors, and professed to use "a selection of the real language of men in a state of vivid sensation." He adopted, he said, the language of men in rustic life, "because such men hourly communicate with the best objects from which the best part of language is originally derived."

In the matter of poetic diction Wordsworth did not, in his practice, adhere to the doctrine of this preface. Many of his most admired poems, such as the *Lines written near Tintern Abbey*, the great *Ode on the Intimations of Immortality*, the *Sonnets*, and many parts of his longest poems, *The Excursion* and *The Prelude*, deal with philosophic thought and highly intellectualized emotions. In all of these and in many others the language is rich, stately, involved, and as remote from the "real language" of Westmoreland shepherds as is the epic blank verse of Milton. On the other hand, in those of his poems which were consciously written in illustration of his theory, the affectation of simplicity, coupled with a defective sense of humor, sometimes led him to the selection of vulgar and trivial themes, and the use of language which is bald, childish, or even ludicrous. His simplicity is too often the simplicity of Mother Goose rather than of Chaucer. Instances of this occur in such poems as *Peter Bell*, the *Idiot Boy, Goody Blake and Harry Gill, Simon Lee*, and the *Wagoner*. But there are multitudes of Wordsworth's ballads and lyrics which are simple without being silly, and which, in their homeliness and clear profundity, in their production of the strongest effects by the fewest strokes, are among the choicest modern examples of *pure*, as distinguished from decorated, art. Such are (out of many) *Ruth, Lucy, She was a Phantom of Delight, To a Highland Girl, The Reverie of Poor Susan, To the Cuckoo, The Solitary Reaper, We Are Seven, The Pet Lamb, The Fountain, The Two April Mornings, Resolution and Independence, The Thorn*, and *Yarrow Unvisited*.

Wordsworth was something of a Quaker in poetry, and loved the sober drabs and grays of life. Quietism was his literary religion, and the sensational was to him not merely vulgar, but almost wicked. "The human mind," he wrote, "is capable of being excited without the application of gross and violent stimulants." He disliked the far-fetched themes and high-colored style of Scott and Byron. He once told Landor that all of Scott's poetry together was not worth sixpence. From action and passion he turned away to sing the inward life of the soul and the outward life of nature. He said :

> To me the meanest flower that blows can give
> Thoughts that do often lie too deep for tears.

And again :

> Long have I loved what I behold.
> The night that charms, the day that cheers;
> The common growth of mother earth
> Suffices me—her tears, her mirth,
> Her humblest mirth and tears.

Wordsworth's life was outwardly uneventful. The companionship of the mountains and of his own thoughts, the sympathy of his household, the lives of the dalesmen and cottagers about him furnished him with all the stimulus that he required.

> Love had he found in huts where poor men lie;
> His only teachers had been woods and rills,
> The silence that is in the starry sky,
> The sleep that is among the lonely hills.

He read little, but reflected much, and made poetry daily, composing, by preference, out of doors, and dictating his verses to some member of his family. His favorite amanuensis was his sister Dorothy, a woman of fine gifts, to whom Wordsworth was indebted for some of his happiest inspirations. Her charming *Memorials of a Tour in the Scottish Highlands* records the origin of many of her brother's best poems. Throughout life Wordsworth was remarkably self-centered. The ridicule of the reviewers, against which he gradually made his way to public recognition, never disturbed his serene belief in himself, or in the divine message which he felt himself commissioned to deliver. He was a slow and serious person, a preacher as well as a poet, with a certain rigidity, not to say narrowness, of character. That plastic temperament which we associate with poetic genius Wordsworth either did not possess, or it hardened early. Whole sides of life were beyond the range of his sympathies. He touched life at fewer points than Byron and Scott, but touched it more profoundly. It is to him that we owe the phrase "plain living and high thinking," as also a most noble illustration of it in his own practice. His was the wisest and deepest spirit among the English poets of his generation, though hardly the most poetic. He wrote too much, and, attempting to make every petty incident or reflection the occasion of a poem, he finally reached the point of composing verses *On Seeing a Harp in the shape of a Needle Case*, and on other themes more worthy of Mrs. Sigourney. In parts of his long blank-verse poems, *The Excursion*, 1814, and *The Prelude*—which was printed after his death in 1850, though finished as early as 1806—the poetry wears very thin and its place is taken by prosaic, tedious didacticism. These two poems were designed as portions of a still more extended work, *The Recluse*, which was never completed. *The Excursion* consists mainly of philosophical discussions on nature and human life between a school-master, a solitary, and an itinerant peddler. *The Prelude* describes the development of Wordsworth's own genius. In parts of *The Excursion* the diction is fairly Shaksperian:

> The good die first,
> And they whose hearts are dry as summer dust
> Burn to the socket;

a passage not only beautiful in itself but dramatically true, in the mouth of the bereaved mother who utters it, to that human instinct which generalizes a private sorrow into a universal law. Much of *The Prelude* can hardly be called poetry at all, yet some of Wordsworth's loftiest poetry is buried among its dreary wastes, and now and then, in the midst of commonplaces, comes a flash of Miltonic splendor —like

> Golden cities ten months' journey deep
> Among Tartarian wilds.

Wordsworth is, above all things, the poet of nature. In this province he was not without forerunners. To say nothing of Burns and Cowper, there was George Crabbe, who had published his *Village* in 1783—fifteen years before the *Lyrical Ballads*—and whose last poem, *Tales of the Hall*, came out in 1819, five years after *The Excursion*. Byron called Crabbe "Nature's sternest painter, and her best." He was a minutely accurate delineator of the harsher aspects of rural life. He photographs a Gypsy camp; a common, with its geese and donkey; a salt marsh, a shabby village street, or tumble-down manse. But neither Crabbe nor Cowper has the imaginative lift of Wordsworth,

> The light that never was, on sea or land,
> The consecration, and the poet's dream.

In a note on a couplet in one of his earliest poems, descriptive of an oak-tree standing dark against the sunset, Wordsworth says: "I recollect distinctly the very spot where this struck me. The moment was important in my poetical history, for I date from it my consciousness of the infinite variety of natural appearances which had been unnoticed by the poets of any age or country, and I made a resolution to supply, in some degree, the deficiency." In later life he is said to have been impatient of any thing spoken or written by another about mountains, conceiving himself to have a monopoly of "the power of hills." But Wordsworth did not stop with natural description. Matthew Arnold has said that the office of modern poetry is the "moral interpretation of Nature." Such, at any rate, was Wordsworth's office. To him Nature was alive and divine. He felt, under the veil of phenomena,

> A presence that disturbs me with the joy
> Of elevated thought: a sense sublime
> Of something far more deeply interfused.

He approached, if he did not actually reach, the view of pantheism which identifies God with Nature; and the mysticism of the Idealists, who identify Nature with the soul of man. This tendency was not inspired in Wordsworth by German philosophy. He was no metaphysician. In his rambles with Coleridge about Nether Stowey and Alfoxden, when both were young, they had, indeed, discussed Spinoza. And in the autumn of 1798, after the publication of the *Lyrical Ballads*, the two friends went together to Germany, where Wordsworth spent half a year. But the literature and philosophy of Germany made little direct impression upon

Wordsworth. He disliked Goethe, and he quoted with approval the saying of the poet Klopstock, whom he met at Hamburg, that he placed the romanticist Bürger above both Goethe and Schiller.

It was through Samuel Taylor Coleridge (1772–1834), who was pre-eminently the *thinker* among the literary men of his generation, that the new German thought found its way into England. During the fourteen months which he spent in Germany—chiefly at Ratzburg and Göttingen—he had familiarized himself with the transcendental philosophy of Immanuel Kant and of his continuators, Fichte and Schelling, as well as with the general literature of Germany. On his return to England, he published, in 1800, a free translation of Schiller's *Wallenstein,* and through his writings, and more especially through his conversations, he became the conductor by which German philosophic ideas reached the English literary class.

Coleridge described himself as being from boyhood a bookworm and a day-dreamer. He remained through life an omnivorous, though unsystematic, reader. He was helpless in practical affairs, and his native indolence and procrastination were increased by his indulgence in the opium habit. On his return to England, in 1800, he went to reside at Keswick, in the Lake Country, with his brother-in-law, Southey, whose industry supported both families. During his last nineteen years Coleridge found an asylum under the roof of Mr. James Gilman, of Highgate, near London, whither many of the best young men in England were accustomed to resort to listen to Coleridge's wonderful talk. Talk, indeed, was the medium through which he mainly influenced his generation. It cost him an effort to put his thoughts on paper. His *Table Talk*—crowded with pregnant paragraphs—was taken down from his lips by his nephew, Henry Coleridge. His criticisms of Shakspere are nothing but notes, made here and there, from a course of lectures delivered before the Royal

Institute, and never fully written out. Though only hints and suggestions, they are, perhaps, the most penetrative and helpful Shaksperian criticisms in English. He was always forming projects and abandoning them. He projected a great work on Christian philosophy, which was to have been his *magnum opus*, but he never wrote it. He projected an epic poem on the fall of Jerusalem. " I schemed it at twenty-five," he said, "but, alas ! *venturum expectat*." What bade fair to be his best poem, *Christabel*, is a fragment. Another strangely beautiful poem, *Kubla Khan*—which came to him, he said, in sleep—is even more fragmentary. And the most important of his prose remains, his *Biographia Literaria*, 1817, a history of his own opinions, breaks off abruptly.

It was in his suggestiveness that Coleridge's great service to posterity resided. He was what J. S. Mill called a "seminal mind," and his thought had that power of stimulating thought in others which is the mark and the privilege of original genius. Many a man has owed to some sentence of Coleridge's, if not the awakening in himself of a new intellectual life, at least the starting of fruitful trains of reflection which have modified his whole view of certain great subjects. On every thing that he left is set the stamp of high mental authority. He was not, perhaps, primarily, he certainly was not exclusively, a poet. In theology, in philosophy, in political thought and literary criticism he set currents flowing which are flowing yet. The terminology of criticism, for example, is in his debt for many of those convenient distinctions—such as that between genius and talent, between wit and humor, between fancy and imagination—which are familiar enough now, but which he first introduced or enforced. His definitions and apothegms we meet everywhere. Such are, for example, the sayings: " Every man is born an Aristotelian or a Platonist." " Prose is words in their best order; poetry, the best words in the best order." And among the bits of subtle interpretation that abound in his writings may be mentioned his estimate of Wordsworth, in the *Biographia Literaria*, and his sketch of Hamlet's character—one with which he was personally in strong sympathy—in the *Lectures on Shakspere.*

The Broad Church party, in the English Church, among whose most eminent exponents have been W. Frederic Robertson, Arnold of Rugby, F. D. Maurice, Charles Kingsley, and the late Dean Stanley, traces its intellectual origin to Coleridge's *Aids to Reflection*, to his writings and conversations in general, and particularly to his ideal of a national clerisy, as set forth in his essay on *Church and State.*   In politics, as in religion, Coleridge's conservatism represents the reaction against the destructive spirit of the 18th century and the French Revolution.   To this root-and-branch democracy he opposed the view that every old belief, or institution, such as the throne or the Church, had served some need, and had a rational idea at the bottom of it, to which it might be again recalled, and made once more a benefit to society, instead of a curse and an anachronism.

As a poet, Coleridge has a sure, though slender, hold upon immortal fame.   No English poet has "sung so wildly well" as the singer of *Christabel* and the *Ancient Mariner.*   The former of these is, in form, a romance in a variety of meters, and in substance, a tale of supernatural possession, by which a lovely and innocent maiden is brought under the control of a witch.   Though unfinished and obscure in intention, it haunts the imagination with a mystic power.   Byron had seen *Christabel* in manuscript, and urged Coleridge to publish it.   He hated all the "Lakers," but when, on parting from Lady Byron, he wrote his song,

> Fare thee well, and if forever,
> Still forever fare thee well,

he prefixed to it the noble lines from Coleridge's poem, beginning

> Alas! they had been friends in youth.

In that weird ballad, the *Ancient Mariner*, the supernatural is handled with even greater subtlety than in *Christabel*. The reader is led to feel that amid the loneliness of the tropic sea the line between the earthly and the unearthly vanishes, and the poet leaves him to discover for himself whether the spectral shapes that the mariner saw were merely the visions of the calenture, or a glimpse of the world of spirits. Coleridge is one of our most perfect metrists. The poet Swinburne—than whom there can be no higher authority on this point (though he is rather given to exaggeration)—pronounces *Kubla Khan*, "for absolute melody and splendor, the first poem in the language."

Robert Southey, the third member of this group, was a diligent worker, and one of the most voluminous of English writers. As a poet, he was lacking in inspiration, and his big oriental epics, *Thalaba*, 1801, and the *Curse of Kehama*, 1810, are little better than wax-work. Of his numerous works in prose, the *Life of Nelson* is, perhaps, the best, and is an excellent biography.

Several other authors were more or less closely associated with the Lake Poets by residence or social affiliation. John Wilson, the editor of *Blackwood's*, lived for some time, when a young man, at Elleray, on the banks of Windermere. He was an athletic man of outdoor habits, an enthusiastic sportsman, and a lover of natural scenery. His admiration of Wordsworth was thought to have led him to imitation of the latter, in his *Isle of Palms*, 1812, and his other poetry.

One of Wilson's companions, in his mountain walks, was Thomas De Quincey, who had been led by his reverence for Wordsworth and Coleridge to take up his residence, in 1808, at Grasmere, where he occupied for many years the cottage from which Wordsworth had removed to Allan Bank. De Quincey was a shy, bookish man, of erratic, nocturnal habits, who impresses one, personally, as a child of genius, with a child's helplessness and a child's sharp observation. He was, above all things, a magazinist. All his writings, with one exception, appeared first in the shape of contributions to periodicals; and his essays, literary criticisms, and miscellaneous papers are exceedingly rich and varied. The most famous of them was his *Confessions of an English Opium Eater*, published as a serial in the *London Magazine*, in 1821. He had begun to take opium, as a cure for the toothache, when a student at Oxford, where he resided from 1803 to 1808. By 1816 he had risen to eight thousand drops of laudanum a day. For several years after this he experienced the acutest misery, and his will suffered an entire paralysis. In 1821 he succeeded in reducing his dose to a comparatively small allowance, and in shaking off his torpor so as to become capable of literary work. The most impressive effect of the opium habit was seen in his dreams, in the unnatural expansion of space and time, and the infinite repetition of the same objects. His sleep was filled with dim, vast images ; measureless cavalcades deploying to the sound of orchestral music; an endless succession of vaulted halls, with staircases climbing to heaven, up which toiled eternally the same solitary figure. "Then came sudden alarms, hurrying to and fro; trepidations of innumerable fugitives; darkness and light; tempest and human faces." Many of De Quincey's papers were autobiographical, but there is always something baffling in these reminiscences. In the interminable wanderings of his pen—for which, perhaps, opium was responsible—he appears to lose all trace of facts or of any continuous story. Every actual experience of his life seems to have been taken up into a realm of dream, and there distorted till the reader sees not the real figures, but the enormous, grotesque shadows of them, executing wild dances on a screen. An instance of this process is described by himself in his *Vision of Sudden Death*. But his unworldliness and faculty of vision-seeing were not inconsistent with the keenness of judgment and the justness and delicacy of perception displayed in his

Biographical Sketches of Wordsworth, Coleridge, and other contemporaries: in his critical papers on *Pope, Milton, Lessing, Homer and the Homeridæ*: his essay on *Style;* and his *Brief Appraisal of the Greek Literature.* His curious scholarship is seen in his articles on the *Toilet of a Hebrew Lady,* and the *Casuistry of Roman Meals;* his ironical and somewhat elaborate humor in his essay on *Murder Considered as One of the Fine Arts.* Of his narrative pieces the most remarkable is his *Revolt of the Tartars,* describing the flight of a Kalmuck tribe of six hundred thousand souls from Russia to the Chinese frontier: a great hegira or anabasis, which extended for four thousand miles over desert steppes infested with foes, occupied six months' time, and left nearly half of the tribe dead upon the way. The subject was suited to De Quincey's imagination. It was like one of his own opium visions, and he handled it with a dignity and force which make the history not altogether unworthy of comparison with Thucydides's great chapter on the Sicilian Expedition.

An intimate friend of Southey was Walter Savage Landor, a man of kingly nature, of a leonine presence, with a most stormy and unreasonable temper, and yet with the courtliest graces of manner, and with—said Emerson—"a wonderful brain, despotic, violent, and inexhaustible." He inherited wealth, and lived a great part of his life at Florence, where he died in 1864, in his ninetieth year. Dickens, who knew him at Bath, in the latter part of his life, made a kindly caricature of him as Lawrence Boythorn, in *Bleak House,* whose "combination of superficial ferocity and inherent tenderness," testifies Henry Crabb Robinson, in his *Diary,* was true to the life. Landor is the most purely classical of English writers. Not merely his themes, but his whole way of thinking was pagan and antique. He composed indifferently in English or Latin, preferring the latter, if any thing, in obedience to his instinct for compression and exclusiveness. Thus, portions of his narrative poem, *Gebir*, 1798, were written originally in Latin and he added a Latin version, *Gebirius*, to the English edition. In like manner his *Hellenics*, 1847, were mainly translations from his Latin *Idyllia Heroica*, written years before. The Hellenic clearness and repose which were absent from his life, Landor sought in his art. His poems, in their restraint, their objectivity, their aloofness from modern feeling, have something chill and artificial. The verse of poets like Byron and Wordsworth is alive ; the blood runs in it. But Landor's polished, clean-cut *intaglios* have been well described as "written in marble." He was a master of fine and solid prose. His *Pericles and Aspasia* consists of a series of letters passing between the great Athenian demagogue ; the hetaira, Aspasia ; her friend, Cleone of Miletus ; Anaxagoras, the philosopher, and Pericles's nephew, Alcibiades. In this masterpiece, the intellectual life of Athens, at its period of highest refinement, is brought before the reader with singular vividness, and he is made to breathe an atmosphere of high-bred grace, delicate wit, and thoughtful sentiment, expressed in English "of Attic choice." The *Imaginary Conversations*, 1824–1846, were Platonic dialogues between a great variety of historical characters ; between, for example, Dante and Beatrice, Washington and Franklin, Queen Elizabeth and Cecil, Xenophon and Cyrus the Younger, Bonaparte and the president of the Senate. Landor's writings have never been popular ; they address an aristocracy of scholars ; and Byron—whom Landor disliked and considered vulgar—sneered at him as a writer who "cultivated much private renown in the shape of Latin verses." He said of himself that he "never contended with a contemporary, but walked alone on the far Eastern uplands, meditating and remembering."

A school-mate of Coleridge at Christ's Hospital, and his friend and correspondent through life, was Charles Lamb, one of the most charming of English essayists. He was a bachelor, who lived alone with his sister Mary, a lovable and intellectual woman, but subject to recurring attacks of madness. Lamb was " a notched and cropped scrivener, a votary of the desk;" a clerk, that is, in the employ of the East India Company. He was of antiquarian tastes, an ardent playgoer, a lover of whist and of the London streets ; and these tastes are reflected in his *Essays of Elia*, contributed to the *London Magazine* and reprinted in book form in 1823. From his mousing among the Elizabethan dramatists and such old humorists as Burton and Fuller, his own style imbibed a peculiar quaintness and pungency. His *Specimens of English Dramatic Poets*, 1808, is admirable for its critical insight. In 1802 he paid a visit to Coleridge at Keswick, in the Lake Country ; but he felt or affected a whimsical horror of the mountains, and said, " Fleet Street and the Strand are better to live in." Among the best of his essays are *Dream Children, Poor Relations, The Artificial Comedy of the Last Century, Old China, Roast Pig, A Defense of Chimney-sweeps, A Complaint of the Decay of Beggars in the Metropolis*, and *The Old Benchers of the Inner Temple*.

The romantic movement, preluded by Gray, Collins, Chatterton, Macpherson, and others, culminated in Walter Scott (1721–1832). His passion for the mediæval was excited by reading Percy's *Reliques* when he was a boy ; and in one of his school themes he maintained that Ariosto was a greater poet than Homer. He began early to collect manuscript ballads, suits of armor, pieces of old plate, border-horns, and similar relics. He learned Italian in order to read the romancers—Ariosto, Tasso, Pulci, and Boiardo—preferring them to Dante. He studied Gothic architecture, heraldry, and the art of fortification, and made drawings of famous ruins and battle-fields. In particular he read eagerly every thing that he could lay hands on relating to the history, legends, and antiquities of the Scottish border—the vale of Tweed, Teviotdale, Ettrick Forest, and the Yarrow, of all which land he became the laureate, as Burns had been of

Ayrshire and the "West Country." Scott, like Wordsworth, was an outdoor poet. He spent much time in the saddle, and was fond of horses, dogs, hunting, and salmon-fishing. He had a keen eye for the beauties of natural scenery, though "more especially," he admits, "when combined with ancient ruins or remains of our forefathers' piety or splendor." He had the historic imagination, and, in creating the historical novel, he was the first to throw a poetic glamour over European annals. In 1803 Wordsworth visited Scott at Lasswade, near Edinburgh ; and Scott afterward returned the visit at Grasmere. Wordsworth noted that his guest was "full of anecdote, and averse from disquisition." The Englishman was a moralist and much given to "disquisition," while the Scotchman was, above all things, a *raconteur*, and, perhaps, on the whole, the foremost of British story-tellers. Scott's Toryism, too, was of a different stripe from Wordsworth's, being rather the result of sentiment and imagination than of philosophy and reflection. His mind struck deep root in the past; his local attachments and family pride were intense. Abbotsford was his darling, and the expenses of this domain and of the baronial hospitality which he there extended to all comers were among the causes of his bankruptcy. The enormous toil which he exacted of himself, to pay off the debt of £117,000, contracted by the failure of his publishers, cost him his life. It is said that he was more gratified when the Prince Regent created him a baronet, in 1820, than by the public recognition that he acquired as the author of the Waverley Novels.

Scott was attracted by the romantic side of German literature. His first published poem was a translation made in 1796 from Bürger's wild ballad, *Leonora*. He followed this up with versions of the same poet's *Wilde Jäger*, of Goethe's violent drama of feudal life, *Götz Von Berlichingen*, and with other translations from the German, of a similar class. On his horseback trips through the border, where he studied

the primitive manners of the Liddesdale people, and took
down old ballads from the recitation of ancient dames and
cottagers, he amassed the materials for his *Minstrelsy of the
Scottish Border*, 1802.   But the first of his original poems
was the *Lay of the Last Minstrel*, published in 1805, and
followed, in quick sucession by *Marmion*, the *Lady of the
Lake, Rokeby*, the *Lord of the Isles*, and a volume of ballads
and lyrical pieces, all issued during the years 1806–1814.
The popularity won by this series of metrical romances was
immediate and wide-spread.   Nothing so fresh or so brilliant
had appeared in English poetry for nearly two centuries.
The reader was hurried along through scenes of rapid action,
whose effect was heightened by wild landscapes and picturesque manners.   The pleasure was a passive one.   There was
no deep thinking to perplex, no subtler beauties to pause
upon ; the feelings were stirred pleasantly, but not deeply;
the effect was on the surface.   The spell employed was novelty—or, at most, wonder—and the chief emotion aroused was
breathless interest in the progress of the story.   Carlyle
said that Scott's genius was *in extenso*, rather than *in intenso*,
and that its great praise was its healthiness. This is true of
his verse, but not altogether so of his prose, which exhibits
deeper qualities.   Some of Scott's most perfect poems, too,
are his shorter ballads, like *Jock o' Hazeldean*, and *Proud
Maisie is in the Wood*, which have a greater intensity and
compression than his metrical tales.

From 1814 to 1831 Scott wrote and published the *Waverley* novels, some thirty in number; if we consider the amount
of work done, the speed with which it was done, and the
general average of excellence maintained, perhaps the most
marvelous literary feat on record.   The series was issued
anonymously, and takes its name from the first number:
Waverley, or 'Tis Sixty Years Since.   This was founded
upon the rising of the clans, in 1745, in support of the Young
Pretender, Charles Edward Stuart, and it revealed to the

English public that almost foreign country which lay just across their threshold, the Scottish Highlands. The *Waverley* novels remain, as a whole, unequaled as historical fiction, although here and there a single novel, like George Eliot's *Romola*, or Thackeray's *Henry Esmond*, or Kingsley's *Hypatia*, may have attained a place beside the best of them. They were a novelty when they appeared. English prose fiction had somewhat declined since the time of Fielding and Goldsmith. There were truthful, though rather tame, delineations of provincial life, like Jane Austen's *Sense and Sensibility*, 1811, and *Pride and Prejudice*, 1813; or Maria Edgeworth's *Popular Tales*, 1804. On the other hand, there were Gothic romances, like the *Monk* of Matthew Gregory Lewis, to whose *Tales of Wonder* some of Scott's translations from the German had been contributed; or like Anne Radcliffe's *Mysteries of Udolpho*. The great original of this school of fiction was Horace Walpole's *Castle of Otranto*, 1765; an absurd tale of secret trap-doors, subterranean vaults, apparitions of monstrous mailed figures and colossal helmets, pictures that descend from their frames, and hollow voices that proclaim the ruin of ancient families.

Scott used the machinery of romance, but he was not merely a romancer, or an historical novelist even, and it is not, as Carlyle implies, the buff-belts and jerkins which principally interest us in his heroes. *Ivanhoe* and *Kenilworth* and the *Talisman* are, indeed, romances pure and simple, and very good romances at that. But, in novels such as *Rob Roy*, the *Antiquary*, the *Heart of Midlothian*, and the *Bride of Lammermoor*, Scott drew from contemporary life, and from his intimate knowledge of Scotch character. The story is there, with its entanglement of plot and its exciting adventures, but there are also, as truly as in Shakspere, though not in the same degree, the observation of life, the knowledge of men, the power of dramatic creation. No writer awakens in his readers a warmer personal affection than Walter Scott, the brave, honest, kindly gentleman; the noblest figure among the literary men of his generation.

Another Scotch poet was Thomas Campbell, whose *Pleasures of Hope*, 1799, was written in Pope's couplet, and in the stilted diction of the 18th century. *Gertrude of Wyoming*, 1809, a long narrative poem in Spenserian stanza, is untrue to the scenery and life of Pennsylvania, where its scene is laid. But Campbell turned his rhetorical manner and his clanking, martial verse to fine advantage in such pieces as *Hohenlinden*, *Ye Mariners of England*, and the *Battle of the Baltic*. These have the true lyric fire, and rank among the best English war-songs.

When Scott was asked why he had left off writing poetry, he answered, "Byron *bet* me." George Gordon Byron (1788–1824) was a young man of twenty-four when, on his return from a two years' sauntering through Portugal, Spain, Albania, Greece, and the Levant, he published, in the first two cantos of *Childe Harold*, 1812, a sort of poetic itinerary of his experiences and impressions. The poem took, rather to its author's surprise, who said that he woke one morning and found himself famous. *Childe Harold* opened a new field to poetry: the romance of travel, the picturesque aspects of foreign scenery, manners, and costumes. It is instructive of the difference between the two ages, in poetic sensibility to such things, to compare Byron's glowing imagery with Addison's tame *Letter from Italy*, written a century before. *Childe Harold* was followed by a series of metrical tales, the *Giaour*, the *Bride of Abydos*, the *Corsair*, *Lara*, the *Siege of Corinth*, *Parisina*, and the *Prisoner of Chillon*, all written in the years 1813–1816. These poems at once took the place of Scott's in popular interest, dazzling a public that had begun to weary of chivalry romances with pictures of Eastern life, with incidents as exciting as Scott's, descriptions as highly colored, and a much greater intensity of passion. So far as they depended for this interest upon the novelty of their accessories, the effect was a temporary one. Seraglios, divans, bulbuls, Gulistans, Zuleikas, and other oriental properties deluged English poetry for a time, and then subsided; even as the tide of moss-troopers, sorcerers, hermits, and feudal castles had already had its rise and fall.

But there was a deeper reason for the impression made by Byron's poetry upon his contemporaries. He laid his finger right on the sore spot in modern life. He had the disease with which the time was sick, the world-weariness, the desperation which proceeded from " passion incapable of being converted into action." We find this tone in much of the literature which followed the failure of the French Revolution and the Napoleonic wars. From the irritations of that period, the disappointment of high hopes for the future of the race, the growing religious disbelief, and the revolt of democracy and free thought against conservative reaction, sprang what Southey called the " Satanic school," which spoke its loudest word in Byron. Titanic is the better word, for the rebellion was not against God, but Jupiter; that is, against the State, Church, and society of Byron's day; against George III., the Tory cabinet of Lord Castlereagh, the Duke of Wellington, the bench of bishops, London gossip, the British constitution, and British cant. In these poems of Byron, and in his dramatic experiments, *Manfred* and *Cain*, there is a single figure—the figure of Byron under various masks—and one pervading mood, a restless and sardonic gloom, a weariness of life, a love of solitude, and a melancholy exaltation in the presence of the wilderness and the sea. Byron's hero is always represented as a man originally noble, whom some great wrong, by others, or some mysterious crime of his own, has blasted and embittered, and who carries about the world a seared heart and a somber brow. Harold—who may stand as a type of all his heroes—has run "through sin's labyrinth," and feeling the "fullness of satiety," is drawn abroad to roam, " the wandering exile of

his own dark mind." The loss of a capacity for pure, un-
jaded emotion is the constant burden of Byron's lament;

> No more, no more, O never more on me
> The freshness of the heart shall fall like dew :

and again,

> O could I feel as I have felt—or be what I have been,
> Or weep as I could once have wept, o'er many a vanished scene ;
> As springs in deserts found seem sweet, all brackish tho' they be,
> So, midst the withered waste of life, those tears would flow to me.

This mood was sincere in Byron; but by cultivating it, and
posing too long in one attitude, he became self-conscious and
theatrical, and much of his serious poetry has a false ring.
His example infected the minor poetry of the time, and it
was quite natural that Thackeray—who represented a generation that had a very different ideal of the heroic—should
be provoked into describing Byron as "a big sulky dandy."

Byron was well fitted by birth and temperament to be the
spokesman of this fierce discontent. He inherited from his
mother a haughty and violent temper, and profligate tendencies from his father. He was through life a spoiled
child, whose main characteristic was willfulness. He liked
to shock people by exaggerating his wickedness, or by perversely maintaining the wrong side of a dispute. But he
had traits of bravery and generosity. Women loved him,
and he made strong friends. There was a careless charm
about him which fascinated natures as unlike each other as
Shelley and Scott. By the death of the fifth Lord Byron
without issue, Byron came into a title and estates at the age
of ten. Though a liberal in politics he had aristocratic feelings, and was vain of his rank as he was of his beauty. He
was educated at Harrow and at Trinity College, Cambridge,
where he was idle and dissipated, but did a great deal of
miscellaneous reading. He took some of his Cambridge set
—Hobhouse, Matthews, and others—to Newstead Abbey, his
ancestral seat, where they filled the ancient cloisters with

eccentric orgies. Byron was strikingly handsome. His face had a spiritual paleness and a classic regularity, and his dark hair curled closely to his head. A deformity in one of his feet was a mortification to him, and impaired his activity in many ways, although he prided himself upon his powers as a swimmer.

In 1815, when at the height of his literary and social *éclat* in London, he married. . In February of the following year he was separated from Lady Byron, and left England forever, pursued by the execrations of outraged respectability. In this chorus of abuse there was mingled a share of cant; but Byron got, on the whole, what he deserved. From Switzerland, where he spent a summer by Lake Leman, with the Shelleys; from Venice, Ravenna, Pisa, and Rome, scandalous reports of his intrigues and his wild debaucheries were wafted back to England, and with these came poem after poem, full of burning genius, pride, scorn, and anguish, and all hurling defiance at English public opinion. The third and fourth cantos of *Childe Harold*, 1816–1818, were a great advance upon the first two, and contain the best of Byron's serious poetry. He has written his name all over the continent of Europe, and on a hundred memorable spots has made the scenery his own. On the field of Waterloo, on "the castled crag of Drachenfels," "by the blue rushing of the arrowy Rhone," in Venice on the Bridge of Sighs, in the Coliseum at Rome, and among the "Isles of Greece," the tourist is compelled to see with Byron's eyes and under the associations of his pilgrimage. In his later poems, such as *Beppo*, 1818, and *Don Juan*, 1819–1823, he passed into his second manner, a mocking cynicism gaining ground upon the somewhat stagey gloom of his early poetry—Mephistophiles gradually elbowing out Satan. *Don Juan*, though morally the worst, is intellectually the most vital and representative of Byron's poems. It takes up into itself most fully the life of the time; exhibits most thoroughly the characteristic alternations of Byron's moods and the prodigal resources of wit, passion, and understanding, which—rather than imagination—were his prominent qualities as a poet. The hero, a graceless, amorous stripling, goes wandering from Spain to the Greek islands and Constantinople, thence to St. Petersburg, and finally to England. Every-where his seductions are successful, and Byron uses him as a means of exposing the weakness of the human heart and the rottenness of society in all countries. In 1823, breaking away from his life of selfish indulgence in Italy, Byron threw himself into the cause of Grecian liberty, which he had sung so gloriously in the *Isles of Greece.* He died at Missolonghi, in the following year, of a fever contracted by exposure and overwork.

Byron was a great poet but not a great literary artist. He wrote negligently and with the ease of assured strength; his mind gathering heat as it moved, and pouring itself forth in reckless profusion. His work is diffuse and imperfect; much of it is melodrama or speech-making, rather than true poetry. But, on the other hand, much, very much of it is unexcelled as the direct, strong, sincere utterance of personal feeling. Such is the quality of his best lyrics, like *When We Two Parted,* the *Elegy on Thyrza, Stanzas to Augusta, She Walks in Beauty,* and of innumerable passages, lyrical and descriptive, in his longer poems. He had not the wisdom of Wordsworth, nor the rich and subtle imagination of Coleridge, Shelley, and Keats when they were at their best. But he had greater body and motive force than any of them. He is the strongest personality among English poets since Milton, though his strength was wasted by want of restraint and self-culture. In Milton the passion was there, but it was held in check by the will and the artistic conscience, made subordinate to good ends, ripened by long reflection, and finally uttered in forms of perfect and harmonious beauty. Byron's love of Nature was quite different in kind from Wordsworth's. Of all English

poets he has sung most lyrically of that national theme, the
sea; as witness, among many other passages, the famous
apostrophe to the ocean which closes *Childe Harold*, and the
opening of the third canto in the same poem,

> Once more upon the waters, etc.

He had a passion for night and storm, because they made
him forget himself.

> Most glorious night!
> Thou wert not sent for slumber!   Let me be
> A sharer in thy fierce and far delight,
> A portion of the tempest and of thee!

Byron's literary executor and biographer was the Irish
poet, Thomas Moore, a born song-writer, whose *Irish Melodies*, set to old native airs, are, like Burns's, genuine, spontaneous singing, and run naturally to music.   Songs such as
the *Meeting of the Waters*, *The Harp of Tara*, *Those Evening Bells*, the *Light of Other Days*, *Araby's Daughter*, and
the *Last Rose of Summer* were, and still are, popular favorites.   Moore's Oriental romance, *Lalla Rookh*, 1817, is overladen with ornament and with a sugary sentiment that clogs
the palate.   He had the quick Irish wit, sensibility rather
than passion, and fancy rather than imagination.

Byron's friend, Percy Bysshe Shelley (1792–1822), was
also in fiery revolt against all conventions and institutions,
though his revolt proceeded not, as in Byron's case, from the
turbulence of passions which brooked no restraint, but rather
from an intellectual impatience of any kind of control.   He
was not, like Byron, a sensual man, but temperate and chaste.
He was, indeed, in his life and in his poetry, as nearly a dis-
embodied spirit as a human creature can be.   The German
poet, Heine, said that liberty was the religion of this century,
and of this religion Shelley was a worshiper.   His rebellion
against authority began early.   He refused to fag at Eton,
and was expelled from Oxford for publishing a tract on the
Necessity of Atheism.   At nineteen, he ran away with Har-

riet Westbrook, and was married to her in Scotland. Three years later he deserted her for Mary Godwin, with whom he eloped to Switzerland. Two years after this his first wife drowned herself in the Serpentine, and Shelley was then formally wedded to Mary Godwin. All this is rather startling, in the bare statement of it, yet it is not inconsistent with the many testimonies that exist to Shelley's singular purity and beauty of character, testimonies borne out by the evidence of his own writings. Impulse with him took the place of conscience. Moral law, accompanied by the sanction of power, and imposed by outside authority, he rejected as a form of tyranny. His nature lacked robustness and ballast. Byron, who was at the bottom intensely practical, said that Shelley's philosophy was too spiritual and romantic.. Hazlitt, himself a Radical, wrote of Shelley: "He has a fire in his eye, a fever in his blood, a maggot in his brain, a hectic flutter in his speech, which mark out the philosophic fanatic. He is sanguine-complexioned and shrill-voiced." It was, perhaps, with some recollection of this last-mentioned trait of Shelley the man, that Carlyle wrote of Shelley the poet, that " the sound of him was shrieky," and that he had " filled the earth with an inarticulate wailing."

His career as a poet began, characteristically enough, with the publication, while at Oxford, of a volume of political rimes, entitled *Margaret Nicholson's Remains*, Margaret Nicholson being the crazy woman who tried to stab George III. His boyish poem, *Queen Mab*, was published in 1813; *Alastor* in 1816, and the *Revolt of Islam*—his longest—in 1818, all before he was twenty-one. These were filled with splendid, though unsubstantial, imagery, but they were abstract in subject, and had the faults of incoherence and formlessness which make Shelley's longer poems wearisome and confusing. They sought to embody his social creed of perfectionism, as well as a certain vague pantheistic system of belief in a spirit of love in nature and man, whose presence is a constant source of obscurity in Shelley's verse. In 1818 he went to Italy, where the last four years of his life were passed, and where, under the influences of Italian art and poetry, his writing became deeper and stronger. He was fond of yachting, and spent much of his time upon the Mediterranean. In the summer of 1822 his boat was swamped in a squall, off the Gulf of Spezzia, and Shelley's drowned body was washed ashore, and burned in the presence of Byron and Leigh Hunt. The ashes were entombed in the Protestant cemetery at Rome, with the epitaph, *Cor cordium.*

Shelley's best and maturest work, nearly all of which was done in Italy, includes his tragedy, *The Cenci*, 1819, and his lyrical drama, *Prometheus Unbound*, 1821. The first of these has a unity and a definiteness of contour unusual with Shelley, and is, with the exception of some of Robert Browning's, the best English tragedy since Otway. Prometheus represented to Shelley's mind the human spirit fighting against divine oppression, and in his portrayal of this figure he kept in mind not only the *Prometheus* of Æschylus, but the Satan of *Paradise Lost.* Indeed, in this poem, Shelley came nearer to the sublime than any English poet since Milton. Yet it is in lyrical, rather than in dramatic, quality that *Prometheus Unbound* is great. If Shelley be not, as his latest editor, Mr. Forman, claims him to be, the foremost of English lyrical poets, he is at least the most lyrical of them. He had, in a supreme degree, the "lyric cry." His vibrant nature trembled to every breath of emotion, and his nerves craved ever newer shocks; to pant, to quiver, to thrill, to grow faint in the spasm of intense sensation. The feminine cast observable in Shelley's portrait is borne out by this tremulous sensibility in his verse. It is curious how often he uses the metaphor of wings: of the winged spirit, soaring, like his skylark, till lost in music, rapture, light, and then falling back to earth. Three successive moods—longing, ecstasy, and the revulsion of despair—are expressed in many of his lyrics; as in the *Hymn to the Spirit of Nature* in *Prometheus*, in the ode *To a Skylark*, and in the *Lines to an Indian Air*—Edgar Poe's favorite. His passionate desire to lose himself in Nature, to become one with that spirit of love and beauty in the universe which was to him in place of God, is expressed in the *Ode to the West Wind*, his most perfect poem :

> Make me thy lyre, even as the forest is;
>   What if my leaves are falling like its own!
> The tumult of thy mighty harmonies
>   Will take from both a deep autumnal tone
> Sweet, though in sadness. Be thou, Spirit fierce,
>   My spirit! be thou me, impetuous one!

In the lyrical pieces already mentioned, together with *Adonais*, the lines *Written in the Euganean Hills*, *Epipsychidion*, *Stanzas Written in Dejection near Naples*, *A Dream of the Unknown*, and many others, Shelley's lyrical genius reaches a rarer loveliness and a more faultless art than Byron's ever attained, though it lacks the directness and momentum of Byron.

In Shelley's longer poems, intoxicated with the music of his own singing, he abandons himself wholly to the guidance of his imagination, and the verse seems to go on of itself, like the enchanted boat in *Alastor*, with no one at the helm. Vision succeeds vision in glorious but bewildering profusion; ideal landscapes and cities of cloud " pinnacled dim in the intense inane." These poems are like the water-falls in the Yosemite, which, tumbling from a height of several thousand feet, are shattered into foam by the air, and waved about over the valley. Very beautiful is this descending spray, and the rainbow dwells in its bosom; but there is no longer any stream, nothing but an iridescent mist. The word *ethereal* best expresses the quality of Shelley's genius. His poetry is full of atmospheric effects; of the tricks which light plays with the fluid elements of water and air; of stars, clouds, rain, dew, mist, frost, wind, the foam of seas, the phases of the moon, the green shadows of waves, the shapes of flames, the "golden lightning of the setting sun." Nature, in Shelley, wants homeliness and relief. While poets like Wordsworth and Burns let in an ideal light upon the rough fields of earth, Shelley escapes into a "moonlight-colored" realm of shadows and dreams, among whose abstractions the heart turns cold. One bit of Wordsworth's mountain turf is worth them all.

By the death of John Keats (1796–1821), whose elegy Shelley sang in *Adonais*, English poetry suffered an irreparable loss. His *Endymion*, 1818, though disfigured by mawkishness and by some affectations of manner, was rich in promise. Its faults were those of youth, the faults of exuberance and of a sensibility, which time corrects. *Hyperion*, 1820, promised to be his masterpiece, but he left it unfinished—"a Titanic torso"—because, as he said, "there were too many Miltonic inversions in it." The subject was the displacement by Phœbus Apollo of the ancient sun-god, Hyperion, the last of the Titans who retained his dominion. It was a theme of great capabilities, and the poem was begun by Keats with a strength of conception which leads to the belief that here was once more a really epic genius, had fate suffered it to mature. The fragment, as it stands—"that inlet to severe magnificence"—proves how rapidly Keats's diction was clarifying. He had learned to string up his loose chords. There is nothing maudlin in *Hyperion ;* all there is in whole tones and in the grand manner, "as sublime as Æschylus," said Byron, with the grave, antique simplicity, and something of modern sweetness interfused.

Keats's father was a groom in a London livery-stable. The poet was apprenticed at fifteen to a surgeon. At school he had studied Latin but not Greek. He, who of all the English poets had the most purely Hellenic spirit, made acquaintance with Greek literature and art only through the medium of classical dictionaries, translations, and popular mythologies ; and later through the marbles and casts in the British Museum. His friend, the artist Haydon, lent him a copy of Chapman's Homer, and the impression that it made upon him he recorded in his sonnet, *On First Looking into Chapman's Homer*. Other poems of the same inspiration are his three sonnets, *To Homer*, *On Seeing the Elgin Marbles*, *On a Picture of Leander*, *Lamia*, and the beautiful *Ode on a Grecian Urn*. But Keats's art was retrospective and eclectic, the blossom of a double root ; and " golden-tongued Romance with serene lute " had her part in him, as well as the classics. In his seventeenth year he had read the *Faerie Queene*, and from Spenser he went on to a study of Chaucer, Shakspere and Milton. Then he took up Italian and read Ariosto. The influence of these studies is seen in his poem, *Isabella, or the Pot of Basil*, taken from a story of Boccaccio ; in his wild ballad, *La Belle Dame sans Merci;* and in his love tale, the *Eve of St. Agnes*, with its wealth of mediæval adornment. In the *Ode to Autumn*, and *Ode to a Nightingale*, the Hellenic choiceness is found touched with the warmer hues of romance.

There is something deeply tragic in the short story of Keats's life. The seeds of consumption were in him ; he felt the stirrings of a potent genius, but he knew that he could not wait for it to unfold, but must die

> Before high-piled books in charactry
> Hold like rich garners the full-ripened grain.

His disease was aggravated, possibly, by the stupid brutality with which the reviewers had treated *Endymion;* and certainly by the hopeless love which devoured him. " The very thing which I want to live most for," he wrote, " will be a great occasion of my death. If I had any chance of recovery, this passion would kill me." In the autumn of 1820, his disease gaining apace, he went on a sailing vessel to Italy, accompanied by a single friend, a young artist named Severn. The change was of no avail, and he died at Rome a few weeks after, in his twenty-sixth year.

Keats was, above all things, the *artist*, with that love of the beautiful and that instinct for its reproduction which are the artist's divinest gifts. He cared little about the politics and philosophy of his day, and he did not make his poetry the vehicle of ideas. It was sensuous poetry, the poetry of youth and gladness. But if he had lived, and if, with wider knowledge of men and deeper experience of life, he had attained to Wordsworth's spiritual insight and to Byron's power of passion and understanding, he would have become a greater poet than either. For he had a style—a "natural magic"—which only needed the chastening touch of a finer culture to make it superior to any thing in modern English poetry, and to force us back to Milton or Shakspere for a comparison. His tombstone, not far from Shelley's, bears the inscription of his own choosing : "Here lies one whose name was writ in water." But it would be within the limits of truth to say that it is written in large characters on most of our contemporary poetry. " Wordsworth," says Lowell, "has influenced most the ideas of succeeding poets ; Keats their forms." And he has influenced these out of all proportion to the amount which he left, or to his intellectual range, by virtue of the exquisite quality of his *technique.*

---

1. Mrs. Oliphant's Literary History of England, 18th–19th Centuries. London: Macmillan & Co., 1883.

2. Wordsworth's Poems. Chosen and edited by Matthew Arnold. London, 1879.

3. Poetry of Byron. Chosen and arranged by Matthew Arnold. London, 1881.

4. Shelley. Julian and Maddalo, Prometheus Unbound, The Cenci, Lyrical Pieces.

5. Landor. Pericles and Aspasia.

6. Coleridge. Table-Talk, Notes on Shakspere, The Ancient Mariner, Christabel, Love, Ode to France, Ode to the Departing Year, Kubla Khan, Hymn before Sunrise in the Vale of Chamouni, Youth and Age, Frost at Midnight.

7. De Quincey. Confessions of an English Opium Eater, Flight of a Tartar Tribe, Biographical Sketches.

8. Scott. Waverley, Heart of Midlothian, Bride of Lammermoor, Rob Roy, Antiquary, Marmion, Lady of the Lake.

9. Keats. Hyperion, Eve of St. Agnes, Lyrical Pieces. Boston: J. R. Osgood, 1871.

SOUTHEY. SCOTT.

COLERIDGE. MACAULAY

CHAPTER VIII.

FROM THE DEATH OF SCOTT TO THE PRESENT TIME.

1832–1893.

THE literature of the past fifty years is too close to our eyes to enable the critic to pronounce a final judgment, or the literary historian to get a true perspective. Many of the principal writers of the time are still living, and many others have been dead but a few years. This concluding chapter, therefore, will be devoted to the consideration of the few who stand forth, incontestably, as the leaders of literary thought, and who seem likely, under all future changes of fashion and taste, to remain representatives of their generation. As regards *form*, the most striking fact in the history of the period under review is the immense preponderance in its imaginative literature of prose fiction, of the novel of real life. The novel has become to the solitary reader of to-day what the stage play was to the audiences of Elizabeth's reign, or the periodical essay, like the *Tatler* and *Spectator*, to the clubs and breakfast-tables of Queen Anne's. And if its criticism of life is less concentrated and brilliant than the drama gives, it is far more searching and minute. No period has ever left in its literary records so complete a picture of its whole society as the period which is just closing. At any other time than the present, the names of authors like Charlotte Brontë, Charles Kingsley, and Charles Reade—names which are here merely mentioned in passing —besides many others which want of space forbids us even to mention—would be of capital importance. As it is, we must limit our review to the three acknowledged masters of modern English fiction, Charles Dickens (1812–1870),

William Makepeace Thackeray (1811–1863), and "George Eliot" (Mary Ann Evans, 1819–1880).

It is sometimes helpful to reduce a great writer to his lowest term, in order to see what the prevailing bent of his genius is. This lowest term may often be found in his early work, before experience of the world has overlaid his original impulse with foreign accretions. Dickens was much more than a humorist, Thackeray than a satirist, and George Eliot than a moralist; but they had their starting-points respectively in humor, in burlesque, and in strong ethical and religious feeling. Dickens began with a broadly comic series of papers, contributed to the *Old Magazine* and the *Evening Chronicle*, and reprinted in book form, in 1836, as *Sketches by Boz*. The success of these suggested to a firm of publishers the preparation of a number of similar sketches of the misadventures of cockney sportsmen, to accompany plates by the comic draughtsman, Mr. R. Seymour. This suggestion resulted in the *Pickwick Papers*, published in monthly installments in 1836–1837. The series grew, under Dickens's hand, into a continuous though rather loosely strung narrative of the doings of a set of characters, conceived with such exuberant and novel humor that it took the public by storm and raised its author at once to fame. *Pickwick* is by no means Dickens's best, but it is his most characteristic and most popular book. At the time that he wrote these early sketches he was a reporter for the *Morning Chronicle*. His naturally acute powers of observation had been trained in this pursuit to the utmost efficiency, and there always continued to be about his descriptive writing a reportorial and newspaper air. He had the eye for effect, the sharp fidelity to detail, the instinct for rapidly seizing upon and exaggerating the salient point, which are developed by the requirements of modern journalism. Dickens knew London as no one else has ever known it, and, in particular, he knew its hideous and grotesque recesses, with the strange developments of human nature that abide there; slums like Tom-all-Alone's, in *Bleak House;* the river-side haunts of Rogue Riderhood, in *Our Mutual Friend;* as well as the old inns, like the "White Hart," and the "dusky purlieus of the law." As a man, his favorite occupation was walking the streets, where, as a child, he had picked up the most valuable part of his education. His tramps about London—often after nightfall—sometimes extended to fifteen miles in a day. He knew, too, the shifts of poverty. His father—some traits of whom are preserved in Mr. Micawber—was imprisoned for debt in the Marshalsea prison, where his wife took lodging with him, while Charles, then a boy of ten, was employed at six shillings a week to cover blacking-pots in Warner's blacking warehouse. The hardships and loneliness of this part of his life are told under a thin disguise in Dickens's masterpiece, *David Copperfield*, the most autobiographical of his novels. From these young experiences he gained that insight into the lives of the lower classes and that sympathy with children and with the poor which shine out in his pathetic sketches of Little Nell, in *The Old Curiosity Shop;* of Paul Dombey; of poor Jo, in *Bleak House;* of "the Marchioness," and a hundred other figures.

In *Oliver Twist*, contributed, during 1837–1838, to *Bentley's Miscellany*, a monthly magazine of which Dickens was editor, he produced his first regular novel. In this story of the criminal classes the author showed a tragic power which he had not hitherto exhibited. Thenceforward his career was a series of dazzling successes. It is impossible here to particularize his numerous novels, sketches, short tales, and "Christmas Stories"—the latter a fashion which he inaugurated, and which has produced a whole literature in itself. In *Nicholas Nickleby*, 1839; *Master Humphrey's Clock*, 1840; *Martin Chuzzlewit*, 1844; *Dombey and Son*, 1848; *David Copperfield*, 1850, and *Bleak House*, 1853, there is no falling off in strength. The last named was, in some respects, and especially in the skillful construction of the plot, his best novel. In some of his latest books, as *Great Expectations*, 1861, and *Our Mutual Friend*, 1865, there are signs of a decline. This showed itself in an unnatural exaggeration of characters and motives, and a painful straining after humorous effects; faults, indeed, from which Dickens was never wholly free. There was a histrionic side to him, which came out in his fondness for private theatricals, in which he exhibited remarkable talent, and in the dramatic action which he introduced into the delightful public readings from his works that he gave before vast audiences all over the United Kingdom, and in his two visits to America. It is not surprising, either, to learn that upon the stage his preference was for melodrama and farce. His own serious writing was always dangerously close to the melodramatic, and his humor to the farcical. There is much false art, bad taste, and even vulgarity in Dickens. He was never quite a gentleman, and never succeeded well in drawing gentlemen or ladies. In the region of low comedy he is easily the most original, the most inexhaustible, the most wonderful, of modern humorists. Creations such as Mrs. Nickleby, Mr. Micawber, Sam Weller, Sairy Gamp, take rank with Falstaff and Dogberry; while many others, like Dick Swiveller, Stiggins, Chadband, Mrs. Jellyby, and Julia Mills, are almost equally good. In the innumerable swarm of minor characters with which he has enriched our comic literature there is no indistinctness. Indeed, the objection that has been made to him is that his characters are too distinct—that he puts labels on them; that they are often mere personifications of a single trick of speech or manner, which becomes tedious and unnatural by repetition. Thus, Grandfather Smallweed is always settling down into his cushion, and having to be shaken up; Mr. Jellyby is always sitting with his head against the wall; Peggotty is always bursting her buttons off, etc. As Dickens's humorous characters tend perpetually to run into caricatures and grotesques, so his sentiment, from the same excess, slops over too frequently into "gush," and into a too deliberate and protracted attack upon the pity. A favorite humorous device in his style is a stately and roundabout way of telling a trivial incident, as where, for example, Mr. Roker "muttered certain unpleasant invocations concerning his own eyes, limbs, and circulating fluids;" or where the drunken man who is singing comic songs in the Fleet received from Mr. Smangle "a gentle intimation, through the medium of the water-jug, that his audience were not musically disposed." This manner was original with Dickens, though he may have taken a hint of it from the mock heroic language of *Jonathan Wild;* but as practiced by a thousand imitators, ever since, it has gradually become a burden.

It would not be the whole truth to say that the difference between the humor of Thackeray and Dickens is the same as between that of Shakspere and Ben Jonson. Yet it is true that the "humors" of Ben Jonson have an analogy with the extremer instances of Dickens's character sketches in this respect, namely, that they are both studies of the eccentric, the abnormal, the whimsical, rather than of the typical and universal; studies of manners, rather than of whole characters. And it is easily conceivable that, at no distant day, the oddities of Captain Cuttle, Deportment Turveydrop, Mark Tapley, and Newman Noggs will seem as far-fetched and impossible as those of Captain Otter, Fastidious Brisk and Sir Amorous La-Foole.

When Dickens was looking about for some one to take Seymour's place as illustrator of *Pickwick,* Thackeray applied for the job, but without success. He was then a young man of twenty-five, and still hesitating between art and literature. He had begun to draw caricatures with his pencil when a school-boy at the Charter House, and to scribble them with his pen when a student at Cambridge,

editing *The Snob,* a weekly under-graduate paper, and
parodying the prize poem *Timbuctoo* of his contemporary at
the university, Alfred Tennyson. Then he went abroad
to study art, passing a season at Weimar, where he met
Goethe and filled the albums of the young Saxon ladies with
caricatures; afterward living a bohemian existence in the
Latin quarter at Paris, studying art in a desultory way,
and seeing men and cities ; accumulating portfolios full
of sketches, but laying up stores of material to be used
afterward to greater advantage when he should settle upon
his true medium of expression. By 1837, having lost his
fortune of five hundred pounds a year in speculation and
gambling, he began to contribute to *Fraser's,* and thereafter
to the *New Monthly,* Cruikshank's *Comic Almanac, Punch,*
and other periodicals, clever burlesques, art criticisms by
"Michael Angelo Titmarsh," *Yellowplush Papers,* and all
manner of skits, satirical character sketches, and humorous
tales, like the *Great Hoggarty Diamond* and the *Luck of
Barry Lyndon.* Some of these were collected in the *Paris
Sketch-Book,* 1840, and the *Irish Sketch-Book,* 1843 ; but
Thackeray was slow in winning recognition, and it was not
until the publication of his first great novel, *Vanity Fair,*
in monthly parts, during 1846–1848, that he achieved any
thing like the general reputation that Dickens had reached
at a bound. *Vanity Fair* described itself, on its title-page,
as "a novel without a hero." It was also a novel without a
plot—in the sense in which *Bleak House* or *Nicholas Nickleby* had a plot—and in that respect it set the fashion for the
latest school of realistic fiction, being a transcript of life,
without necessary beginning or end. Indeed, one of the
pleasantest things to a reader of Thackeray is the way which
his characters have of re-appearing, as old acquaintances, in
his different books; just as, in real life, people drop out of
mind and then turn up again in other years and places.
Vanity Fair is Thackeray's masterpiece, but it is not the

best introduction to his writings. There are no illusions in
it, and, to a young reader fresh from Scott's romances or
Dickens's sympathetic extravagances, it will seem hard and
repellent. But men who, like Thackeray, have seen life and
tasted its bitterness and felt its hollowness know how to
prize it. Thackeray does not merely expose the cant, the
emptiness, the self-seeking, the false pretenses, flunkeyism,
and snobbery—the " mean admiration of mean things "—in
the great world of London society ; his keen, unsparing
vision detects the base alloy in the purest natures. There
are no " heroes " in his books, no perfect characters. Even
his good women, such as Helen and Laura Pendennis, are
capable of cruel injustice toward less fortunate sisters, like
little Fanny ; and Amelia Sedley is led, by blind feminine instinct, to snub and tyrannize over poor Dobbin. The shabby
miseries of life, the numbing and belittling influences of failure and poverty on the most generous natures, are the tragic
themes which Thackeray handles by preference. He has
been called a cynic, but the boyish playfulness of his humor
and his kindly spirit are incompatible with cynicism. Charlotte Bronté said that Fielding was the vulture and Thackeray the eagle. The comparison would have been truer if
made between Swift and Thackeray. Swift was a cynic ; his
pen was driven by hate, but Thackeray's by love, and it was
not in bitterness but in sadness that the latter laid bare
the wickedness of the world. He was himself a thorough
man of the world, and he had that dislike for a display of
feeling which characterizes the modern Englishman. But
behind his satiric mask he concealed the manliest tenderness,
and a reverence for every thing in human nature that is good
and true. Thackeray's other great novels are *Pendennis*, 1849 ;
Henry Esmond, 1852, and *The Newcomes*, 1855—the last
of which contains his most lovable character, the pathetic
and immortal figure of Colonel Newcome, a creation worthy
to stand, in its dignity and its sublime weakness, by the side

of Don Quixote. It was alleged against Thackeray that he made all his good characters, like Major Dobbin and Amelia Sedley and Colonel Newcome, intellectually feeble, and his brilliant characters, like Becky Sharp and Lord Steyne and Blanche Amory, morally bad. This is not entirely true, but the other complaint—that his women are inferior to his men—is true in a general way. Somewhat inferior to his other novels were *The Virginians,* 1858, and *The Adventures of Philip,* 1862. All of these were stories of contemporary life, except *Henry Esmond* and its sequel, *The Virginians,* which, though not precisely historical fictions, introduced historical figures, such as Washington and the Earl of Peterborough. Their period of action was the 18th century, and the dialogue was a cunning imitation of the language of that time. Thackeray was strongly attracted by the 18th century. His literary teachers were Addison, Swift, Steele, Gay, Johnson, Richardson, Goldsmith, Fielding, Smollett, and Sterne, and his special master and model was Fielding. He projected a history of the century, and his studies in this kind took shape in his two charming series of lectures on *The English Humorists* and *The Four Georges.* These he delivered in England and in America, to which country he, like Dickens, made two several visits.

Thackeray's genius was, perhaps, less astonishing than Dickens's; less fertile, spontaneous, and inventive; but his art is sounder, and his delineation of character more truthful. After one has formed a taste for his books, Dickens's sentiment will seem overdone, and much of his humor will have the air of buffoonery. Thackeray had the advantage in another particular : he described the life of the upper classes, and Dickens of the lower. It may be true that the latter offers richer material to the novelist, in the play of elementary passions and in strong native developments of character. It is true, also, that Thackeray approached "society" rather

to satirize it than to set forth its agreeableness. Yet, after all, it is "the great world" which he describes, that world upon which the broadening and refining processes of a high civilization have done their utmost, and which, consequently, must possess an intellectual interest superior to any thing in the life of London thieves, traveling showmen, and coachees. Thackeray is the equal of Swift as a satirist, of Dickens as a humorist, and of Scott as a novelist. The one element lacking in him—and which Scott had in a high degree—is the poetic imagination. "I have no brains above my eyes" he said ; "I describe what I see." Hence there is wanting in his creations that final charm which Shakspere's have. For what the eyes see is not all.

The great woman who wrote under the pen-name of George Eliot was a humorist, too. She had a rich, deep humor of her own, and a wit that crystallized into sayings which are not epigrams only because their wisdom strikes more than their smartness. But humor was not, as with Thackeray and Dickens, her point of view. A country girl, the daughter of a land agent and surveyor at Nuneaton, in Warwickshire, her early letters and journals exhibit a Calvinistic gravity and moral severity. Later, when her truth to her convictions led her to renounce the Christian belief, she carried into positivism the same religious earnestness, and wrote the one English hymn of the religion of humanity:

O, let me join the choir invisible, etc.

Her first published work was a translation of Strauss's *Leben Jesu*, 1846. In 1851 she went to London and became one of the editors of the Radical organ, the *Westminster Review*. Here she formed a connection—a marriage in all but the name—with George Henry Lewes, who was, like herself, a freethinker, and who published, among other things, a *Biographical History of Philosophy*. Lewes had also written fiction, and it was at his suggestion that his wife undertook story writing. Her *Scenes of Clerical Life* were contributed to *Blackwood's Magazine* for 1857, and published in book form in the following year. *Adam Bede* followed in 1859, the *Mill on the Floss* in 1860, *Silas Marner* in 1861, *Romola* in 1863, *Felix Holt* in 1866, and *Middlemarch* in 1872. All of these, except *Romola*, are tales of provincial and largely of domestic life in the midland counties. *Romola* is an historical novel, the scene of which is Florence in the 15th century; the Florence of Macchiavelli and of Savonarola.

George Eliot's method was very different from that of Thackeray or Dickens. She did not crowd her canvas with the swarming life of cities. Her figures are comparatively few, and they are selected from the middle-class families of rural parishes or small towns, amid that atmosphere of "fine old leisure;" whose disappearance she lamented. Her drama is a still-life drama, intensely and profoundly inward. Character is the stuff that she works in, and she deals with it more subtly than Thackeray. With him the tragedy is produced by the pressure of society and its false standards upon the individual; with her, by the malign influence of individuals upon one another. She watches "the stealthy convergence of human fates," the intersection at various angles of the planes of character, the power that the lower nature has to thwart, stupefy, or corrupt the higher, which has become entangled with it in the mesh of destiny. At the bottom of every one of her stories there is a problem of the conscience or the intellect. In this respect she resembles Hawthorne, though she is not, like him, a romancer, but a realist.

There is a melancholy philosophy in her books, most of which are tales of failure or frustration. The *Mill on the Floss* contains a large element of autobiography, and its heroine, Maggie Tulliver, is, perhaps, her idealized self. Her aspirations after a fuller and nobler existence are condemned to struggle against the resistance of a narrow, provincial environment, and the pressure of untoward fates. She is tempted to seek an escape even through a desperate throwing off of moral obligations, and is driven back to her duty only to die by a sudden stroke of destiny. "Life is a bad business," wrote George Eliot, in a letter to a friend, "and we must make the most of it." *Adam Bede* is, in construction, the most perfect of her novels, and *Silas Marner* of her shorter stories. Her analytic habit gained more and more upon her as she wrote. *Middlemarch*, in some respects her greatest book, lacks the unity of her earlier novels, and the story tends to become subordinate to the working out of character studies and social problems. The philosophic speculations which she shared with her husband were seemingly unfavorable to her artistic growth, a circumstance which becomes apparent in her last novel, *Daniel Deronda*, 1877. Finally in the *Impressions of Theophrastus Such*, 1879, she abandoned narrative altogether, and recurred to that type of "character" books which we have met as a flourishing department of literature in the 17th century, represented by such works as Earle's *Microcosmographie* and Fuller's *Holy and Profane State*. The moral of George Eliot's writings is not obtruded. She never made the artistic mistake of writing a novel of purpose, or what the Germans call a *tendenz-roman;* as Dickens did, for example, when he attacked imprisonment for debt, in *Pickwick;* the poor laws, in *Oliver Twist;* the Court of Chancery, in *Bleak House;* and the Circumlocution office, in *Little Dorrit.*

Next to the novel, the essay has been the most overflowing literary form used by the writers of this generation—a form characteristic, it may be, of an age which "lectures, not creates." It is not the essay of Bacon, nor yet of Addison, nor of Lamb, but attempts a complete treatment. Indeed, many longish books, like Carlyle's *Heroes and Hero Worship* and Ruskin's *Modern Painters*, are, in spirit, rather literary essays than formal treatises. The most popular essayist and historian of his time was Thomas Babington Macaulay

(1800–1859), an active and versatile man, who won splendid success in many fields of labor. He was prominent in public life as one of the leading orators and writers of the Whig party. He sat many times in the House of Commons, as member for Calne, for Leeds, and for Edinburgh, and took a distinguished part in the debates on the Reform bill of 1832. He held office in several Whig governments, and during his four years' service in British India, as member of the Supreme Council of Calcutta, he did valuable work in promoting education in that province, and in codifying the Indian penal law. After his return to England, and especially after the publication of his *History of England from The Accession of James II.*, honors and appointments of all kinds were showered upon him. In 1857 he was raised to the peerage as Baron Macaulay of Rothley.

Macaulay's equipment, as a writer on historical and biographical subjects, was, in some points, unique. His reading was prodigious, and his memory so tenacious that it was said, with but little exaggeration, that he never forgot any thing that he had read. He could repeat the whole of *Paradise Lost* by heart, and thought it probable that he could rewrite *Sir Charles Grandison* from memory. In his books, in his speeches in the House of Commons, and in private conversation—for he was an eager and fluent talker, running on often for hours at a stretch—he was never at a loss to fortify and illustrate his positions by citation after citation of dates, names, facts of all kinds, and passages quoted *verbatim* from his multifarious reading. The first of Macaulay's writings to attract general notice was his article on *Milton*, printed in the August number of the *Edinburgh Review* for 1825. The editor, Lord Jeffrey, in acknowledging the receipt of the manuscript, wrote to his new contributor, " The more I think, the less I can conceive where you picked up that style." That celebrated style—about which so much has since been written—was an index to the mental character of its owner.

Macaulay was of a confident, sanguine, impetuous nature. He had great common sense, and he saw what he saw quickly and clearly, but he did not see very far below the surface. He wrote with the conviction of an advocate, and the easy omniscience of a man whose learning is really nothing more than "general information" raised to a very high power, rather than with the subtle penetration of an original or truly philosophic intellect, like Coleridge's or De Quincey's. He always had at hand explanations of events or of characters which were admirably easy and simple—too simple, indeed, for the complicated phenomena which they professed to explain. His style was clear, animated, showy, and even its faults were of an exciting kind. It was his habit to give piquancy to his writing by putting things concretely. Thus, instead of saying, in general terms—as Hume or Gibbon might have done—that the Normans and Saxons began to mingle about 1200, he says: "The great-grandsons of those who had fought under William and the great grandsons of those who had fought under Harold began to draw near to each other." Macaulay was a great scene painter, who neglected delicate truths of detail for exaggerated distemper effects. He used the rhetorical machinery of climax and hyperbole for all that it was worth, and he "made points"— as in his essay on *Bacon*—by creating antithesis. In his *History of England* he inaugurated the picturesque method of historical writing. The book was as fascinating as any novel. Macaulay, like Scott, had the historic imagination, though his method of turning history into romance was very different from Scott's. Among his essays the best are those which, like the ones on *Lord Clive*, *Warren Hastings*, and *Frederick the Great*, deal with historical subjects; or those which deal with literary subjects under their public historic relations, such as the essays on *Addison*, *Bunyan*, and *The Comic Dramatists of the Restoration*. "I have never written a page of criticism on poetry, or the fine arts," wrote

Macaulay, " which I would not burn if I had the power."
Nevertheless his own *Lays of Ancient Rome*, 1842, are good,
stirring verse of the emphatic and declamatory kind, though
their quality may be rather rhetorical than poetic.

Our critical time has not forborne to criticize itself, and
perhaps the writer who impressed himself most strongly upon
his generation was the one who railed most desperately
against the " spirit of the age." Thomas Carlyle (1795–
1881) was occupied between 1822 and 1830 chiefly in imparting to the British public a knowledge of German literature. He published, among other things, a *Life of Schiller*,
a translation of Goethe's *Wilhelm Meister*, and two volumes
of translations from the German romancers—Tieck, Hoffmann,
Richter, and Fouqué—and contributed to the *Edinburgh*
and *Foreign Review* articles on Goethe, Werner, Novalis,
Richter, German playwrights, the *Nibelungen Lied*, etc.
His own diction became more and more tinctured with Ger-
manisms.   There was something Gothic in his taste, which
was attracted by the lawless, the grotesque, and the whimsical in the writings of Jean Paul Richter. His favorite
among English humorists was Sterne, who has a share of these
same qualities. He spoke disparagingly of " the sensuous
literature of the Greeks," and preferred the Norse to the
Hellenic mythology. Even in his admirable critical essays
on Burns, on Richter, on Scott, Diderot, and Voltaire, which
are free from his later mannerism—written in English, and
not in Carlylese—his sense of spirit is always more lively
than his sense of form. He finally became so impatient of
art as to maintain—half-seriously—the paradox that Shakspere would have done better to write in prose. In three of
these early essays—on the *Signs of the Times*, 1829 ; on
History, 1830, and on *Characteristics*, 1831—are to be found
the germs of all his later writings. The first of these was
an arraignment of the mechanical spirit of the age. In
every province of thought he discovered too great a reliance

upon systems, institutions, machinery, instead of upon men. Thus, in religion, we have Bible societies, "machines for converting the heathen." "In defect of Raphaels and Angelos and Mozarts, we have royal academies of painting, sculpture, music." In like manner, he complains, government is a machine. "Its duties and faults are not those of a father, but of an active parish-constable." Against the "police theory," as distinguished from the "paternal" theory, of government, Carlyle protested with ever shriller iteration. In *Chartism*, 1839, *Past and Present*, 1843, and *Latterday Pamphlets*, 1850, he denounced this *laissez faire* idea. The business of government, he repeated, is to govern; but this view makes it its business to refrain from governing. He fought most fiercely against the conclusions of political economy, "the dismal science" which, he said, affirmed that men were guided exclusively by their stomachs. He protested, too, against the Utilitarians, followers of Bentham and Mill, with their "greatest happiness principle," which reduced virtue to a profit-and-loss account. Carlyle took issue with modern liberalism; he ridiculed the self-gratulation of the time, all the talk about progress of the species, unexampled prosperity, etc. But he was reactionary without being conservative. He had studied the French Revolution, and he saw the fateful, irresistible approach of democracy. He had no faith in government "by counting noses," and he hated talking Parliaments; but neither did he put trust in an aristocracy that spent its time in "preserving the game." What he wanted was a great individual ruler; a real king or hero; and this doctrine he set forth afterward most fully in *Hero Worship*, 1841, and illustrated in his lives of representative heroes, such as his *Cromwell's Letters and Speeches*, 1845, and his great *History of Frederick the Great*, 1858–1865. Cromwell and Frederick were well enough; but as Carlyle grew older his admiration for mere force grew, and his latest hero was none other than that infamous Dr. Francia, the South American dictator, whose career of bloody and crafty crime horrified the civilized world.

The essay on *History* was a protest against the scientific view of history which attempts to explain away and account for the wonderful. "Wonder," he wrote in *Sartor Resartus*, "is the basis of all worship." He defined history as "the essence of innumerable biographies." "Mr. Carlyle," said the Italian patriot, Mazzini, "comprehends only the individual. The nationality of Italy is, in his eyes, the glory of having produced Dante and Christopher Columbus." This trait comes out in his greatest book, *The French Revolution*, 1837, which is a mighty tragedy enacted by a few leading characters—Mirabeau, Danton, Napoleon. He loved to emphasize the superiority of history over fiction as dramatic material. The third of the three essays mentioned was a Jeremiad on the morbid self-consciousness of the age, which shows itself, in religion and philosophy, as skepticism and introspective metaphysics ; and in literature, as sentimentalism, and "view-hunting."

But Carlyle's epoch-making book was *Sartor Resartus* (The Tailor Retailored), published in *Fraser's Magazine* for 1833–1834, and first reprinted in book form in America. This was a satire upon shams, conventions, the.disguises which overlie the most spiritual realities of the soul. It purported to be the life and "clothes-philosophy" of a certain Diogenes Teufelsdröckh, Professor *der Allerlei Wissenschaft*—of things in general—in the University of Weissnichtwo. "Society," said Carlyle, "is founded upon cloth," following the suggestions of Lear's speech to the naked bedlam beggar: "Thou art the thing itself : unaccommodated man is no more but such a poor, bare, forked animal as thou art ;" and borrowing also, perhaps, an ironical hint from a paragraph in Swift's *Tale of a Tub:* "A sect was established who held the universe to be a large suit of

GEO. ELIOT.

FROUDE.

BROWNING.

TENNYSON.

clothes. . . . . If certain ermines or furs be placed in a certain
position, we style them a judge ; and so an apt conjunction
of lawn and black satin we entitle a bishop." In *Sartor
Resartus* Carlyle let himself go. It was willful, uncouth,
amorphous, titanic. There was something monstrous in the
combination—the hot heart of the Scot married to the transcendental dream of Germany. It was not English, said the
reviewers ; it was not sense ; it was disfigured by obscurity
and "mysticism." Nevertheless even the thin-witted and
the dry-witted had to acknowledge the powerful beauty of
many chapters and passages, rich with humor, eloquence,
poetry, deep-hearted tenderness, or passionate scorn.

Carlyle was a voracious reader, and the plunder of whole
literatures is strewn over his pages. He flung about the resources of the language with a giant's strength, and made
new words at every turn. The concreteness and the swarming fertility of his mind are evidenced by his enormous vocabulary, computed greatly to exceed Shakspere's, or any
other single writer's in the English tongue. His style lacks
the crowning grace of simplicity and repose. It astonishes,
but it also fatigues.

Carlyle's influence has consisted more in his attitude than
in any special truth which he has preached. It has been the
influence of a moralist, of a practical rather than a speculative philosopher. "The end of man," he wrote, "is an
action, not a thought." He has not been able to persuade the
time that it is going wrong, but his criticisms have been whole-
somely corrective of its self-conceit. In a democratic age he
has insisted upon the undemocratic virtues of obedience, silence, and reverence. *Ehrfurcht*, reverence—the text of his
address to the students of Edinburgh University in 1866—
is the last word of his philosophy.

In 1830 Alfred Tennyson (1809–1892), a young graduate of
Cambridge, published a thin duodecimo of 154 pages entitled
Poems, Chiefly Lyrical. The pieces in this little volume,

such as the *Sleeping Beauty, Ode to Memory,* and *Recollections of the Arabian Nights,* were full of color, fragrance, melody; but they had a dream-like character, and were without definite theme, resembling an artist's studies, or exercises in music—a few touches of the brush, a few sweet chords, but no *aria*. A number of them—*Claribel, Lilian, Adeline, Isabel, Mariana, Madeline*—were sketches of women; not character portraits, like Browning's *Men and Women,* but impressions of temperament, of delicately differentiated types of feminine beauty. In *Mariana,* expanded from a hint of the forsaken maid in Shakspere's *Measure for Measure,* "Mariana at the moated grange," the poet showed an art then peculiar, but since grown familiar, of heightening the central feeling by landscape accessories. The level waste, the stagnant sluices, the neglected garden, the wind in the single poplar, re-enforce, by their monotonous sympathy, the loneliness, the hopeless waiting and weariness of life in the one human figure of the poem. In *Mariana,* the *Ode to Memory,* and the *Dying Swan,* it was the fens of Cambridge and of his native Lincolnshire that furnished Tennyson's scenery.

> Stretched wide and wild, the waste enormous marsh,
> Where from the frequent bridge,
> Like emblems of infinity,
> The trenched waters run from sky to sky.

A second collection, published in 1833, exhibited a greater scope and variety, but was still in his earlier manner. The studies of feminine types were continued in *Margaret, Fatima, Eleanore, Mariana in the South,* and *A Dream of Fair Women,* suggested by Chaucer's *Legend of Good Women.* In the *Lady of Shalott* the poet first touched the Arthurian legends. The subject is the same as that of *Elaine,* in the *Idylls of the King,* but the treatment is shadowy, and even allegorical. In *Œnone* and the *Lotus Eaters* he handled Homeric subjects, but in a romantic fashion which contrasts markedly with the style of his later pieces, *Ulysses* and *Ti-thonus*. These last have the true classic severity, and are among the noblest specimens of weighty and sonorous blank verse in modern poetry. In general, Tennyson's art is un-classical. It is rich, ornate, composite; not statuesque so much as picturesque. He is a great painter, and the critics complain that in passages calling for movement and action —a battle, a tournament, or the like—his figures stand still as in a tableau; and they contrast such passages unfavorably with scenes of the same kind in Scott, and with Browning's spirited ballad, *How we brought the Good News from Ghent to Aix*. In the *Palace of Art* these elaborate pictorial effects were combined with allegory; in the *Lotus Eaters*, with that expressive treatment of landscape noted in *Mariana ;* the lotus land, "in which it seemed always afternoon," re-flecting and promoting the enchanted indolence of the he-roes. Two of the pieces in this 1833 volume, the *May Queen* and the *Miller's Daughter*, were Tennyson's first poems of the affections, and as ballads of simple rustic life they anticipated his more perfect idyls in blank verse, such as *Dora*, the *Brook*, *Edwin Morris*, and the *Gardener's Daughter*. The songs in the *Miller's Daughter* had a more spontaneous lyrical movement than any thing he had yet published, and foretokened the lovely songs which interlude the divisions of the *Princess*, the famous *Bugle Song*, the no-less famous *Cradle Song*, and the rest. In 1833 Tennyson's friend, Arthur Hallam, died, and the effect of this great sor-row upon the poet was to deepen and strengthen the character of his genius. It turned his mind in upon itself, and set it brooding over questions which his poetry had so far left un-touched ; the meaning of life and death, the uses of adver-sity, the future of the race, the immortality of the soul, and the dealings of God with mankind.

> Thou madest Death: and, lo, thy foot
> Is on the skull which thou hast made.

His elegy on Hallam, *In Memoriam*, was not published till 1850. He kept it by him all those years, adding section after section, gathering up into it whatever reflections crystallized about its central theme. It is his most intellectual and most individual work; a great song of sorrow and consolation. In 1842 he published a third collection of poems, among which were *Locksley Hall*, displaying a new strength of passion ; *Ulysses*, suggested by a passage in Dante: pieces of a speculative cast, like the *Two Voices* and the *Vision of Sin;* the song *Break, Break, Break*, which preluded *In Memoriam;* and, lastly, some additional gropings toward the subject of the Arthurian romance, such as *Sir Galahad, Sir Launcelot and Queen Guinevere*, and *Morte d'Arthur*. The last was in blank verse, and, as afterward incorporated in the *Passing of Arthur*, forms one of the best passages in the *Idylls of the King*. The *Princess, a Medley*, published in 1849, represents the eclectic character of Tennyson's art; a mediæval tale with an admixture of modern sentiment, and with the very modern problem of woman's sphere for its theme. The first four *Idylls of the King*, 1859, with those since added, constitute, when taken together, an epic poem on the old story of King Arthur. Tennyson went to Malory's *Morte Darthur* for his material, but the outline of the first idyl, *Enid*, was taken from Lady Charlotte Guest's translation of the Welsh *Mabinogion*. In the idyl of *Guinevere* Tennyson's genius reached its high-water mark. The interview between Arthur and his fallen queen is marked by a moral sublimity and a tragic intensity which move the soul as nobly as any scene in modern literature. Here, at least, the art is pure and not "decorated;" the effect is produced by the simplest means, and all is just, natural, and grand. *Maud*—a love novel in verse—published in 1855, and considerably enlarged in 1856, had great sweetness and beauty, particularly in its lyrical portions, but it was uneven in execution, imperfect in design, and marred by lapses into mawkishness and excess in language. Since 1860 Tennyson has added little of permanent value to his work. His dramatic experiments, like *Queen Mary*, are not, on the whole, successful, though it would be unjust to deny dramatic power to the poet who has written, upon one hand, *Guinevere* and the *Passing of Arthur*, and upon the other the homely dialectic monologue of the *Northern Farmer*.

When we tire of Tennyson's smooth perfection, of an art that is over exquisite, and a beauty that is well-nigh too beautiful, and crave a rougher touch, and a meaning that will not yield itself too readily, we turn to the thorny pages of his great contemporary, Robert Browning (1812–1889). Dr. Holmes says that Tennyson is white meat and Browning is dark meat. A masculine taste, it is inferred, is shown in a preference for the gamier flavor. Browning makes us think; his poems are puzzles, and furnish business for "Browning Societies." There are no Tennyson societies, because Tennyson is his own interpreter. Intellect in a poet may display itself quite as properly in the construction of his poem as in its content; we value a building for its architecture, and not entirely for the amount of timber in it. Browning's thought never wears so thin as Tennyson's sometimes does in his latest verse, where the trick of his style goes on of itself with nothing behind it. Tennyson, at his worst, is weak. Browning, when not at his best, is hoarse. Hoarseness, in itself, is no sign of strength. In Browning, however, the failure is in art, not in thought.

He chooses his subjects from abnormal character types, such as are presented, for example, in *Caliban upon Setebos*, the *Grammarian's Funeral, My Last Duchess* and *Mr. Sludge, the Medium*. These are all psychological studies, in which the poet gets into the inner consciousness of a monster, a pedant, a criminal, and a quack, and gives their point of view. They are dramatic soliloquies; but the poet's self-identification with each of his creations, in turn, remains incomplete. His curious, analytic observation, his way of looking at the soul from outside, gives a doubleness to the monologues in his *Dramatic Lyrics*, 1845, *Men and Women*, 1855, *Dramatis Personæ*, 1864, and other collections of the kind. The words are the words of Caliban or Mr. Sludge; but the voice is the voice of Robert Browning. His first complete poem, *Paracelsus*, 1835, aimed to give the true inwardness of the career of the famous 16th century doctor, whose name became a synonym with charlatan. His second, *Sordello*, 1840, traced the struggles of an Italian poet who lived before Dante, and could not reconcile his life with his art. *Paracelsus* was hard, but *Sordello* was incomprehensible. Browning has denied that he was ever perversely crabbed or obscure. Every great artist must be allowed to say things in his own way, and obscurity has its artistic uses, as the Gothic builders knew. But there are two kinds of obscurity in literature. One is inseparable from the subtlety and difficulty of the thought or the compression and pregnant indirectness of the phrase. · Instances of this occur in the clear deeps of Dante, Shakspere, and Goethe. The other comes from a vice of style, a willfully enigmatic and unnatural way of expressing thought. Both kinds of obscurity exist in Browning. He was a deep and subtle thinker, but he was also a very eccentric writer; abrupt, harsh, disjointed. It has been well said that the reader of Browning learns a new dialect. But one need not grudge the labor that is rewarded with an intellectual pleasure so peculiar and so stimulating. The odd, grotesque impression made by his poetry arises, in part, from his desire to use the artistic values of ugliness, as well as of obscurity; to avoid the shallow prettiness that comes from blinking the disagreeable truth: not to leave the saltness out of the sea. Whenever he emerges into clearness, as he does in hundreds of places, he is a poet of great qualities. There are a fire and a swing in his *Cavalier Tunes*, and in pieces like the *Glove* and the *Lost*

Leader; and humor in such ballads as the *Pied Piper of Hamelin* and the *Soliloquy of the Spanish Cloister*, which appeal to the most conservative reader. He seldom deals directly in the pathetic, but now and then, as in *Evelyn Hope*, the *Last Ride Together*, or the *Incident of the French Camp*, a tenderness comes over the strong verse

> as sheathes
> A film the mother eagle's eye
> When her bruised eaglet breathes.

Perhaps the most astonishing example of Browning's mental vigor is the huge composition, entitled *The Ring and the Book*, 1868; a narrative poem in twenty-one thousand lines in which the same story is repeated eleven times in eleven different ways. It is the story of a criminal trial which occurred at Rome about 1700, the trial of one Count Guido for the murder of his young wife. First the poet tells the tale himself; then he tells what one half the world said and what the other; then he gives the deposition of the dying girl, the testimony of witnesses, the speech made by the count in his own defense, the arguments of counsel, etc., and, finally, the judgment of the pope. So wonderful are Browning's resources in casuistry, and so cunningly does he ravel the intricate motives at play in this tragedy and lay bare the secrets of the heart, that the interest increases at each repetition of the tale. He studied the Middle Age carefully, not for its picturesque externals, its feudalisms, chivalries, and the like; but because he found it a rich quarry of spiritual monstrosities, strange outcroppings of fanaticism, superstition, and moral and mental distortion of all shapes. It furnished him especially with a great variety of ecclesiastical types, such as are painted in *Fra Lippo Lippi*, *The Heretic's Tragedy*, and *The Bishop Orders his Tomb in St. Praxed's Church.*

Browning's dramatic instinct always attracted him to the stage. His tragedy, *Strafford* (1837), was written for

Macready, and put on at Covent Garden Theater, but without pronounced success. He wrote many fine dramatic poems, like *Pippa Passes, Colombe's Birthday*, and *In a Balcony;* and at least two good acting plays, *Luria* and *A Blot in the Scutcheon.* The last named has recently been given to the American public, with Lawrence Barrett's careful and intelligent presentation of the leading role. The motive of the tragedy is somewhat strained and fantastic, but it is, notwithstanding, very effective on the stage. It gives one an unwonted thrill to listen to a play, by a contemporary English writer, which is really literature. One gets a faint idea of what it must have been to assist at the first night of *Hamlet.*

————

1. English Literature in the Reign of Victoria. Henry Morley. (Tauchnitz Series.)

2. Victorian Poets. E. C. Stedman. Boston: Houghton, Mifflin & Co., 1886.

3. Dickens. Pickwick Papers, Nicholas Nickleby, David Copperfield, Bleak House, Tale of Two Cities.

4. Thackeray. Vanity Fair, Pendennis, Henry Esmond, The Newcomes.

5. George Eliot. Scenes of Clerical Life, Mill on the Floss, Silas Marner, Romola, Adam Bede, Middlemarch.

6. Macaulay. Essays, Lays of Ancient Rome.

7. Carlyle. Sartor Resartus, French Revolution, Essays on History, Signs of the Times, Characteristics, Burns, Scott, Voltaire, and Goethe.

8. The Works of Alfred Tennyson. London: Stranham & Co., 1872. 6 vols.

9. Selections from the Poetical Works of Robert Browning. London: Smith, Elder & Co., 1880. 2 vols.

APPENDIX.

APPENDIX.

APPENDIX.

GEOFFREY CHAUCER.

The Prioress.

[From the general prologue to the Canterbury Tales.]

There was also a nonne, a prioresse,
That of hire smiling was ful simple and coy;
Hire gretest othe n'as but by Seint Eloy;
And she was cleped [1] madame Eglentine.
Ful wel she sange the servicē devine,
Entunēd in hire nose ful swetēly;
And Frenche she spake ful fayre and fetisly [2]
After the scole of Stratford-attē-Bowe, [3]
For Frenche of Paris was to hire unknowe.
At metē was she wel ytaught withalle;
She lette no morsel from hire lippēs falle,
Ne wette hire fingres in hire saucē depe.
Wel coude she carie a morsel, and wel kepe,
Thatte no drope ne fell upon hire brest.
In curtesie was sette ful moche hire lest. [4]
Hire over lippē wipēd she so clene
That in hire cuppē was no ferthing [5] seue
Of gresē, whan she dronken hadde hire draught.
Ful semēly after hire mete she raught. [6]
And sikerly [7] she was of grete disport
And ful plesánt and amiable of port,
And peinēd hire to contrefeten chere
Of court, [8] and ben estatelich of manére
And to ben holden digne [9] of reverence.
But for to speken of hire conscience,

---

[1] Called. [2] Neatly. [3] Stratford on the Bow (river): a small village where such French as was spoken would be provincial. [4] Delight. [5] Farthing, bit. [6] Reached. [7] Surely. [8] Took pains to imitate court manners. [9] Worthy.

She was so charitable and so pitoús,
She woldë wepe if that she saw a mous
Caughte in a trappe, if it were ded or bledde.
Of smalë houndës hadde she, that she fedde
With rosted flesh and milk and wastel brede.[1]
But sore wept she if on of hem were dede,
Or if men smote it with a yerdë[2] smert:[3]
And all was conscience and tendre herte.

PALAMON'S FAREWELL TO EMELIE.

[From the Knightes Tale.]

Naught may the woful spirit in myn herte
Declare o[4] point of all my sorwes smerte
To you, my lady, that I lovë most.
But I bequethe the service of my gost
To you aboven every crëatúre,
Sin[5] that my lif no may no lenger dure.
Alas the wo! alas the peinës stronge
That I for you have suffered, and so longe!
Alas the deth! alas min Emelie!
Alas departing of our compagnie!
Alas min hertës quene! alas my wif!
Min hertës ladie, ender of my lif!
What is this world? what axen[6] men to have?
Now with his love, now in his coldë grave
Alone withouten any compagnie.
Farewel my swete, farewel min Emelie,
And softë take me in your armës twey,[7]
For love of God, and herkeneth[8] what I sey.

EMELIE IN THE GARDEN.

[From the Knightes Tale.]

Thus passeth yere by yere, and day by day,
Till it felle onës in a morwe[9] of May
That Emelie, that fayrer was to sene[10]
Than is the lilie upon his stalkë grene,
And fresher than the May with flourës newe,
(For with the rosë colour strof hire hewe;

---

[1] Fine bread.   [2] Stick.   [3] Smartly.   [4] One.   [5] Since.   [6] Ask.   [7] Two.
[8] Hearken.   [9] Morning.   [10] See.

I n'ot [1] which was the finer of hem two)
Er it was day, as she was wont to do,
She was arisen and all redy dight,[2]
For May wol have no slogardie a-night.
The seson priketh every gentil herte,
And maketh him out of his slepe to sterte,
And sayth, "Arise, and do thin observánce."
This maketh Emelie han remembránce
To dou honoúr to May, and for to rise.
Yclothĕd was she fresh for to devise.[3]
Hire yelwe here was broided in a tresse
Behind hire back, a yerdĕ long I gesse.
And in the gardin at the sonne uprist [4]
She walketh up and doun wher as hire list.[5]
She gathereth floures, partie white and red,
To make a sotel [6] gerlond for hire hed,
And as an angel hevenlich she song.

ALISON.

[From the Millere's Tale.]

Fayre was this yongĕ wif, and therwithal
As any wesel hire body gent and smal [7]
A seint [8] she werĕd, barrĕd al of silk,
A barm-cloth [9] eke as white as morne milk [10]
Upon hire lendĕs [11] ful of many a gore,
White was hire smok, and brouded [12] al before
And eke behind on hire colére [13] aboute
Of cole-black silk within and eke withoute.
The tapĕs of hire whitĕ volupere [14]
Were of the samĕ suit of hire colére;
Hire fillet brode of silk and set ful hye;
And sikerly [15] she had a likerous [16] eye,
Ful smal ypulled [17] were hire browĕs two,
And they were bent and black as any slo,
She was wel morĕ blisful on to see
Than is the newĕ perjenetĕ [18] tree,

---

[1] Know not.   [2] Dressed.   [3] Describe.   [4] Sunrise.   [5] Wherever it pleases her.
[6] Subtle, cunningly enwoven.   [7] Trim and slim.   [8] Girdle.   [9] Apron.   [10] Morning's milk.   [11] Loins.   [12] Embroidered.   [13] Collar.   [14] Cap.   [15] Surely.   [16] Wanton.
[17] Trimmed fine.   [18] Young pear.

And softer than the wolle is of a wether.
And by hire girdle heng a purse of lether,
Tasseled with silk and perlĕd with latoun,[1]
In all this world to seken up and doun
Ther n'is no man so wise that coude thenche[2]
So gay a popelot[3] or swiche[4] a wenche.
Ful brighter was the shining of hire hewe
Than in the tour, the noble yforged newe.
But of hire song, it was as loud and yerne[5]
As any swalow sitting on a berne.
Thereto she coudĕ skip and make a game
As any kid or calf folowing his dame.
Hire mouth was swete as braket[6] or the meth,[7]
Or horde of apples laid in hay or heth.
Winsing[8] she was, as is a jolly colt,
Long as a mast, and upright as a bolt.
A broche she bare upon hire low colére,
As brode as is the bosse of a bokelére.[9]
Hire shoon were lacĕd on hire leggĕs hie;
She was a primerole,[10] a piggesnie,[11]
For any lord, to liggen[12] in his bedde,
Or yet for any good yemán[13] to wedde.

ANONYMOUS BALLADS OF THE SIXTEENTH AND SEVENTEENTH CENTURIES.

WALY, WALY BUT LOVE BE BONNY.

O waly,[14] waly up the bank,
  And waly, waly down the brae,[15]
And waly, waly yon burn[16] side,
  Where I and my love wont to gae.

I lean'd my back unto an aik,[17]
  I thought it was a trusty tree;
But first it bow'd and syne[18] it brak,
  Sae my true love did lightly me.

---

[1] Ornamented with pearl-shaped beads of a metal resembling brass.   [2] Think.
[3] Puppet.   [4] Such.   [5] Brisk.   [6] A sweet drink of ale, honey, and spice.   [7] Mead.
[8] Skittish.   [9] Buckler.   [10] Primrose.   [11] Pansy.   [12] Lie.   [13] Yeoman.   [14] An exclamation of sorrow, woe! alas!   [15] Hillside.   [16] Brook.   [17] Oak.   [18] Then.

O waly, waly but love be bonny,
   A little time while it is new;
But when 'tis auld it waxeth cauld,
   And fades away like the morning dew.

O wherefore should I busk [1] my head?
   Or wherefore should I kame [2] my hair?
For my true love has me forsook,
   And says he'll never love me mair.

Now Arthur-Seat shall be my bed,
   The sheets shall ne'er be fyl'd by me;
Saint Anton's well [3] shall be my drink,
   Sinn my true love has forsaken me.

Martinmas' wind, when wilt thou blaw
   And shake the green leaves off the tree?
O gentle death, when wilt thou come?
   For of my life I'm aweary.

'Tis not the frost that freezes fell,
   Nor blawing snow's inclemency;
'Tis not sic cauld that makes me cry,
   But my love's heart grown cauld to me.

When we came in by Glasgow town
   We were a comely sight to see;
My love was clad in the black velvet,
   And I myself in cramasie. [4]

But had I wist, before I kissed,
   That love had been sae ill to win,
I'd lock'd my heart in a case of gold,
   And pin'd it with a silver pin.

Oh, oh, if my young babe were born,
   And set upon the nurse's knee,
And I myself were dead and gane,
   And the green grass growing over me!

[1] Adorn.   [2] Comb.   [3] At the foot of Arthur's-Seat, a cliff near Edinburgh.
[4] Crimson.

THE TWO CORBIES.[1]

As I was walking all alane
I heard twa corbies making a mane;
The tane unto the t'other say,
" Where sall we gang and dine to-day ?"

"In behint yon auld fail[2] dyke,
I wot there lies a new-slain knight;
And naebody kens that he lies there
But his hawk, his hound, and lady fair.

"His hound is to the hunting gane,
His hawk to fetch the wild fowl hame,
His lady's ta'en another mate,
So we may mak our dinner sweet.

"Ye'll sit on his white hause-bane,[3]
And I'll pick out his bonny blue een;
Wi' ae[4] lock o' his gowden hair,
We'll theck[5] our nest when it grows bare.

"Mony a one for him makes mane,
But nane sall ken where he is gane;
O'er his white banes, when they are bare,
The wind sall blow for evermair."

BONNIE GEORGE CAMPBELL.

Hie upon Highlands and low upon Tay,
Bonnie George Campbell rade out on a day.
Saddled and bridled and gallant rade he;
Hame cam' his horse, but never cam' he.

Out came his auld mother, greeting[6] fu' sair;
And out cam' his bonnie bride, riving her hair.
Saddled and bridled and booted rade he;
Toom[7] hame cam' the saddle, but never cam' he.

" My meadow lies green and my corn is unshorn;
My barn is to bigg[8] and my babie's unborn."
Saddled and bridled and booted rade he;
Toom cam' the saddle, but never cam' he.

---

[1] The two ravens.   [2] Turf.   [3] Neck-bone.   [4] One.   [5] Thach.   [6] Weeping.
[7] Empty.   [8] Build.

EDMUND SPENSER.

THE SUITOR'S LIFE.

Full little knowest thou that hast not tride,
What hell it is in suing long to bide;
To lose good days that might be better spent;
To wast long nights in pensive discontent:
To speed to-day, to be put back to-morrow;
To feed on hope, to pine with feare and sorrow;
To have thy prince's grace, yet want her peere's[1]:
To have thy asking, yet waite manie yeers,
To fret thy soule with crosses and with cares;
To eate thy heart through comfortlesse dispaires:
To fawne, to crowche, to waite, to ride, to ronne,
To spend, to give, to want, to be undone!

THE MUSIC OF THE BOWER OF BLISS.

[From the *Faerie Queene*. Book II. Canto XII.]

Eftsoones they heard a most melodious sound,
Of all that mote[2] delight a daintie eare,
Such as attonce[3] might not on living ground,
Save in this paradise, be heard elsewhere:
Right hard it was for wight which did it heare,
To read what manner of music that mote[2] bee;
For all that pleasing is to living eare
Was there consorted in one harmonee;
Birdes, voices, instruments, windes, waters, all agree.

The joyous birdes, shrouded in chearefull shade,
Their notes unto the voyce attempred sweet;
Th' angelicall soft trembling voyces made
To th' instruments divine respondence meet;
The silver sounding instruments did meet
With the base[4] murmure of the waters fall;
The waters fall with difference discreet,
Now soft, now loud, unto the wind did call;
The gentle warbling wind low answerèd to all. . . .

[1] A reference to Lord Burleigh's hostility to the poet   [2] Might.   [3] At once.   [4] Bass.

The whiles some one did chaunt this lovely lay;
Ah! see, whoso fayre thing doest faine [1] to see,
In springing flowre the image of thy day!
Ah! see the virgin rose, how sweetly shee
Doth first peepe foorth with bashfull modestee,
That fairer seemes the lesse ye see her may!
.Lo! see, soone after how more bold and free
Her barëd bosome she doth broad display;
Lo! see, soone after how she fades and falls away.

So passeth, in the passing of a day,
Of mortall life the leafe, the bud, the flowre;
Ne more doth florish after first decay,
That earst [2] was sought to deck both bed and bowre
Of many a lady, and many a paramowre!
Gather therefore the rose whilst yet is prime, [3]
For soone comes age that will her pride deflowre:
Gather the rose of love whilst yet is time,
Whilst loving thou mayst lovëd be with equall crime.

The House of Sleep.

[From the *Faerie Queene*. Book I. Canto I.

He, making speedy way through spersëd ayre,
And through the world of waters wide and deepe,
To Morpheus' house doth hastily repaire:
Amid the bowels of the earth full steepe
And low, where dawning day doth never peepe,
His dwelling is; there Tethys his wet bed
Doth ever wash, and Cynthia still doth steepe
In silver deaw his ever-drouping hed,
Whiles sad Night over him her mantle black doth spred. . . .

And more to lulle him in his slumber soft,
A trickling streame from high rock tumbling downe,
And ever-drizling raine upon the loft,
Mixt with a murmuring winde, much like the sowne
Of swarming bees, did cast him in a swowne.
No other noyse, nor people's troublous cryes,
As still are wont t'annoy the wallëd towne,
Might there be heard; but careless quiet lyes
Wrapt in eternall silence farre from enimyes.

[1] Rejoice.   [2] First, formerly.   [3] Spring.

WILLIAM SHAKSPERE.

SONNET XC.

Then hate me when thou wilt: if ever, now:
  Now, while the world is bent my deeds to cross,
Join with the spite of fortune, make me bow,
  And do not drop in for an after loss.
Ah! do not when my heart hath scaped this sorrow,
  Come in the rearward of a conquered woe;
Give not a windy night a rainy morrow,
  To linger out a purposed overthrow.
If thou wilt leave me, do not leave me last,
  When other petty griefs have done their spite;
But in the onset come: So shall I taste
  At first the very worst of fortune's might;
And other strains of woe, which now seem woe,
  Compared with loss of thee, will not seem so.

SONG.

[From *As You Like It*.]

Blow, blow, thou winter wind,
Thou art not so unkind
    As man's ingratitude;
Thy tooth is not so keen,
Because thou art not seen
    Although thy breath be rude.
Heigh ho! Sing heigh ho! unto the green holly:
Most friendship is feigning, most loving mere folly.
Then heigh ho! the holly!
This life is most jolly.

Freeze, freeze thou bitter sky,
Thou dost not bite so nigh
    As benefits forgot;
Though thou the waters warp,
Thy sting is not so sharp
    As friend remembered not.
Heigh ho! sing heigh ho! etc.

THE SLEEP OF KINGS.

[From *Henry IV.*—Part II.]

How many thousand of my poorest subjects
Are at this hour asleep! O sleep, O gentle sleep,
Nature's soft nurse, how have I frighted thee,
That thou no more wilt weigh my eyelids down,
And steep my senses in forgetfulness?
Why rather, sleep, liest thou in smoky cribs,
Upon uneasy pallets stretching thee,
And hushed with buzzing night-flies to thy slumber,
Than in the perfumed chambers of the great,
Under the canopy of costly state,
And lull'd with sounds of sweetest melody?
O thou dull god, why liest thou with the vile,
In loathsome beds; and leav'st the kingly couch,
A watch-case, or a common 'larum bell?
Wilt thou upon the high and giddy mast
Seal up the ship-boy's eyes, and rock his brains
In cradle of the rude imperious surge;
And in the visitation of the winds,
Who take the ruffian billows by the top,
Curling their monstrous heads, and hanging them
With deaf'ning clamors in the slippery clouds,
That, with the hurly, death itself awakes?
Can'st thou, O partial sleep! give thy repose
To the wet sea-boy in an hour so rude;
And, in the calmest and most stillest night,
With all appliances and means to boot,
Deny it to a king? Then, happy low-lie-down!
Uneasy lies the head that wears a crown.

FALSTAFF AND BARDOLPH.

[From *Henry IV.*—Part I.]

Falstaff. Bardolph, am I not fallen away vilely since this last action? do I
not bate? do I not dwindle?

Why, my skin hangs about me like an old lady's loose gown; I am
wither'd like an an old apple-John.

Well, I'll repent, and that suddenly, while I am in some liking; I shall be out of heart shortly, and then I shall have no strength to repent. An I have not forgotten what the inside of a church is made of, I am a pepper-corn, a brewer's horse: the inside of a church! Company, villainous company hath been the spoil of me:

Bardolph. Sir John, you are so fretful, you cannot live long.

Fal. Why, there it is. Come, sing me a bawdy song; make me merry. I was as virtuously given, as a gentleman need to be; virtuous enough; swore little; diced, not above seven times a week; paid money that I borrowed, three or four times; lived well, and in good compass: and now I live out of all order, out of all compass.

Bard. Why you are so fat, Sir John, that you must needs be out of all compass; out of all reasonable compass, Sir John.

Fal. Do thou amend thy face, and I'll amend my life: Thou art our admiral, thou bearest the lantern in the poop—but 'tis in the nose of thee; thou art the knight of the burning lamp.

Bard. Why, Sir John, my face does you no harm.

Fal. No, I'll be sworn; I make as good use of it as many a man doth of a death's head or a *memento mori:* I never see thy face but I think upon hell-fire, and Dives that lived in purple; for there he is in his robes, burning, burning. If thou wert anyway given to virtue, I would swear by thy face; my oath should be: By this fire: but thou art altogether given over; and wert indeed, but for the light of thy face, the son of utter darkness. When thou runn'st up Gad's Hill in the night to catch my horse, if I did not think thou hadst been an *ignis fatuus*, or a ball of wildfire, there's no purchase in money. O, thou art a perpetual triumph, an everlasting bonfire-light! Thou hast saved me a thousand marks in links and torches, walking with thee in the night betwixt tavern and tavern; but the sack that thou hast drunk me, would have bought me lights as good cheap, at the dearest chandler's in Europe. I have maintained that Salamander of yours with fire, any time this two and thirty years; Heaven reward me for it!

THE SEVEN AGES OF MAN.

[From *As You Like It.*]

Jacques.   All the world's a stage,
And all the men and women merely players:
They have their exits and their entrances;
And one man in his time plays many parts,
His acts being seven ages. At first, the infant,
Mewling and puking in the nurse's arms;

Then the whining school-boy, with his satchel,
And shining morning face, creeping like snail
Unwillingly to school: and then, the lover,
Sighing like furnace, with a woeful ballad
Made to his mistress' eyebrow: Then a soldier,
Full of strange oaths and bearded like a pard,
Jealous in honor, sudden and quick in quarrel,
Seeking the bubble reputation
Even in the cannon's mouth: And then the justice,
In fair round belly, with good capon lined,
With eyes severe and beard of formal cut,
Full of wise saws and modern instances;
And so he plays his part.   The sixth age shifts
Into the lean and slippered pantaloon,
With spectacles on nose and pouch on side;
His youthful hose, well-saved, a world too wide
For his shrunk shank; and his big manly voice,
Turning again toward childish treble, pipes
And whistles in his sound.   Last scene of all,
That ends this strange eventful history,
Is second childishness and mere oblivion,
Sans [1] teeth, sans eyes, sans taste, sans every thing.

HAMLET'S SOLILOQUY.

To be, or not to be, that is the question:
Whether 'tis nobler in the mind, to suffer
The slings and arrows of outrageous fortune;
Or to take arms against a sea of troubles,
And, by opposing, end them?   To die—to sleep—
No more; and, by a sleep, to say we end
The heart-ache, and the thousand natural shocks
That flesh is heir to—'tis a consummation
Devoutly to be wished: to die, to sleep;
To sleep! perchance to dream; ay, there's the rub;
For in that sleep of death what dreams may come,
When we have shuffled off this mortal coil,
Must give us pause: there's the respect,
That makes calamity of so long life:
For who would bear the whips and scorns of time,
The oppressor's wrong, the proud man's contumely,

[1] Without.

The pangs of disprized love, the law's delay,
The insolence of office and the spurns
That patient merit of the unworthy takes,
When he himself might his quietus take
With a bare bodkin?[1] Who would fardels[2] bear,
To grunt and sweat under a weary life;
But that the dread of something after death,
The undiscovered country, from whose bourn
No traveller returns, puzzles the will;
And makes us rather bear those ills we have,
Than fly to others that we know not of?
Thus conscience does make cowards of us all;
And thus the native hue of resolution
Is sicklied o'er with the pale cast of thought,
And enterprises of great pith and moment,
With this regard, their currents turn away
And lose the name of action.

DETACHED PASSAGES FROM THE PLAYS.

To-morrow, and to-morrow, and to-morrow,
Creeps in this petty pace from day to day,
To the last syllable of recorded time;
And all our yesterdays have lighted fools
The way to dusty death. Out, out, brief candle!
Life's but a walking shadow; a poor player,
That struts and frets his hour upon the stage,
And then is heard no more: it is a tale
Told by an idiot, full of sound and fury,
Signifying nothing.

Our revels now are ended: these our actors,
As I foretold you, were all spirits, and
Are melted into air, into thin air:
And like the baseless fabric of this vision,
The cloud-capped towers, the gorgeous palaces,
The solemn temples, the great globe itself—
Yea, all which it inherit, shall dissolve,
And, like this insubstantial pageant faded,
Leave not a rack[3] behind. We are such stuff
As dreams are made on, and our little life
Is rounded[4] with a sleep.

[1] Small sword.   [2] Burdens.   [3] Cloud.   [4] Encompassed.

Ay, but to die, and go we know not where;
To lie in cold obstruction and to rot;
This sensible warm motion to become
A kneaded clod; and the delighted spirit
To bathe in fiery floods, or to reside
In thrilling regions of thick-ribbed ice;
To be imprisoned in the viewless winds,
And blown with restless violence round about
The pendent world; or to be worse than worst
Of those that lawless and uncertain thoughts
Imagine howling! 'tis too horrible!

O who can hold a fire in his hand,
By thinking on the frosty Caucasus?
Or cloy the hungry edge of appetite
By bare imagination of a feast?
Or wallow naked in December snow,
By thinking on fantastic summer's heat?
O no! the apprehension of the good
Gives but the greater feeling to the worse.

     She never told her love,
But let concealment, like a worm i' the bud,
Feed on her damask cheek; she pined in thought,
And with a green and yellow melancholy,
She sat, like patience on a monument,
Smiling at grief.

Ah me! for aught that ever I could read,
Could ever·hear by tale or history,
The course of true love never did run smooth:
But either it was different in blood;
Or, if there were a sympathy in choice,
War, death, or sickness did lay siege to it;
Making it momentary as a sound,
Swift as a shadow, short as any dream,
Brief as the lightning in the collied [1] night,
That, in a spleen, [2] unfolds both heaven and earth,
And ere a man hath power to say, Behold!
The jaws of darkness do devour it up:
So quick bright things come to confusion.

  [1] Black.   [2] Caprice, whim.

FRANCIS BACON.

OF DEATH.

[From the Essays.]

MEN fear death as children fear to go in the dark; and as that natural fear in children is increased with tales, so is the other. Certainly, the contemplation of death, as the wages of sin, and passage to another world, is holy and religious; but the fear of it, as a tribute due unto nature, is weak. Yet in religious meditations there is sometimes mixture of vanity and of superstition. You shall read in some of the friars' books of mortification, that a man should think with himself what the pain is, if he have but his finger's end pressed or tortured; and thereby imagine what the pains of death are, when the whole body is corrupted and dissolved; when many times death passeth with less pain than the torture of a limb; for the most vital parts are not the quickest of sense. And by him that spake only as a philosopher and natural man, it was well said, *Pompa mortis magis terret quam mors ipsa.*[1] Groans and convulsions, and a discolored face, and friends weeping, and blacks and obsequies, and the like, show death terrible. It is worthy the observing, that there is no passion in the mind of man so weak but it mates and masters the fear of death, and therefore death is no such terrible enemy, when a man hath so many attendants about him that can win the combat of him. Revenge triumphs over death; love slights it; honor aspireth to it; grief flieth to it; fear preoccupateth[2] it. It is as natural to die as to be born; and to a little infant perhaps the one is as painful as the other. He that dies in an earnest pursuit is like one that is wounded in hot blood: who, for the time, scarce feels the hurt; and therefore a mind fixed and bent upon somewhat that is good doth avert the dolours of death; but, above all, believe it, the sweetest canticle is *Nunc dimittis,*[3] when a man hath obtained worthy ends and expectations. Death hath this also, that it openeth the gate to good fame, and extinguisheth envy: *Extinctus amabitur idem.*[4]

OF STUDIES.

Studies serve for delight, for ornament, and for ability. Their chief use for delight is in privateness and retiring: for ornament, is in discourse; and for ability, is in the judgment and disposition of business; for expert men can execute, and perhaps judge of particulars, one by one; but the general counsels, and the plots and marshaling of affairs come best from

---

[1] The shows of death terrify more than death itself.   [2] Anticipates.
[3] Now thou dismissest us.   [4] The same man will be loved when dead.

those that are learned. To spend too much time in studies, is sloth; to use them too much for ornament, is affectation; to make judgment wholly by their rules, is the humor of a scholar: they perfect nature, and are perfected by experience: for natural abilities are like natural plants, that need pruning by study; and studies themselves do give forth directions too much at large, except they be bounded in by experience. Crafty men contemn studies, simple men admire them, and wise men use them; for they teach not their own use; but that is a wisdom without them and above them, won by observation. Read not to contradict and confute, nor to believe and take for granted, nor to find talk and discourse, but to weigh and consider. Some books are to be tasted, others to be swallowed, and some few to be chewed and digested; that is, some books are to be read only in parts ; others to be read, but not curiously; [1] and some few to be read wholly, and with diligence and attention. Some books also may be read by deputy, and extracts made of them by others; but that would be only in the less important arguments,[2] and the meaner sorts of books; else distilled books are, like common distilled waters, flashy things. Reading maketh a full man, conference a ready man, and writing an exact man; and therefore, if a man write little, he had need have a great memory; if he confer little, he had need have a present wit; and if he read little, he had need have much cunning, to seem to know that he doth not. Histories make men wise; poets, witty; the mathematics, subtile; natural philosophy, deep; moral, grave; logic and rhetoric, able to contend: *Abeunt studia in mores;*[3] nay, there is no stand or impediment in the wit, but may be wrought out by fit studies: like as diseases of the body may have appropriate exercises—bowling is good for the stone and reins, shooting for the lungs and breast, gentle walking for the stomach, riding for the head and the like; so, if a man's wit be wandering, let him study the mathematics; for in demonstrations, if his wit be called away never so little, he must begin again; if his wit be not apt to distinguish or find differences, let him study the school-men, for they are *Cymini sectores*;[4] if he be not apt to beat over matters, and to call up one thing to prove and illustrate another, let him study the lawyers' cases: so every defect of the mind may have a special receipt.

Of Adversity.

It was a high speech of Seneca (after the manner of the Stoics), that " the good things which belong to prosperity are to be wished, but the good things that belong to adversity are to be admired "—*Bona rerum secundarum optabilia, adversarum mirabilia.* Certainly, if miracles be the command

[1] Attentively.   [2] Subjects.   [3] Studies pass into the character.   [4] Hair-splitters.

over Nature, they appear most in adversity. It is yet a higher speech of his than the other (much too high for a heathen), "It is true greatness to have in one the frailty of a man and the security of a god"—*Vere magnum habere fragilitatem hominis, securitatem dei.* This would have done better in poesy, where transcendencies are more allowed; and the poets indeed have been busy with it; for it is in effect the thing which is figured in that strange fiction of the ancient poets, which seemeth not to be without mystery;[1] nay, and to have some approach to the state of a Christian; "that Hercules, when he went to unbind *Prometheus* (by whom human nature is represented), sailed the length of the great ocean in an earthen pot or pitcher," lively describing Christian resolution, that saileth in the frail bark of the flesh through the waves of the world. But, to speak in a *mean,*[2] the virtue of prosperity is temperance, the virtue of adversity is fortitude, which in morals is the more heroical virtue. Prosperity is the blessing of the Old Testament, adversity is the blessing of the New, which carrieth the greater benediction, and the clearer revelation of God's favor. Yet, even in the Old Testament, if you listen to David's harp, you shall hear as many hearse-like airs as carols; and the pencil of the Holy Ghost hath labored more in describing the afflictions of Job than the felicities of Solomon. Prosperity is not without many fears and distastes; and adversity is not without comforts and hopes. We see in needle-works and embroideries it is more pleasing to have a lively work upon a sad and solemn ground, than to have a dark and melancholy work upon a lightsome ground: judge, therefore, of the pleasure of the heart by the pleasure of the eye. Certainly virtue is like precious odors, most fragrant when they are incensed[3] or crushed: for prosperity doth best discover vice, but adversity doth best discover virtue.

BEN JONSON.

SONG TO CELIA.

Drink to me only with thine eyes,
    And I will pledge with mine;
Or leave a kiss but in the cup,
    And I'll not look for wine.
The thirst that from the soul doth rise
    Doth ask a drink divine;
But might I of Jove's nectar sup
    I would not change for thine.

[1] An allegorical meaning.   [2] Moderately, that is, without poetic figures.   [3] Burnt.

I sent thee late a rosy wreath,
  Not so much honoring thee,
As giving it a hope, that there
  It could not withered be.
But thou thereon did'st only breathe
  And sent'st it back to me:
Since when it grows and smells, I swear,
  Not of itself, but thee.

Long Life.

It is not growing like a tree
  In bulk, doth make men better be;
Or standing long an oak, three hundred year,
To fall a log at last, dry, bald, and sere:
      A lily of a day
      Is fairer far in May,
Although it fall and die that night;
It was the plant and flower of light.
In small proportions we just beauty see;
And in short measures life may perfect be.

Epitaph on the Countess of Pembroke.

Underneath this sable hearse
Lies the subject of all verse,
Sidney's sister, Pembroke's mother;
Death, ere thou hast slain another,
Learn'd and fair and good as she,
Time shall throw a dart at thee.

The Thankless Muse.

[From *The Poetaster.*]

O this would make a learned and liberal soul
To rive his stainéd quill up to the back,
And damn his long-watched labours to the fire—
Things that were born when none, but the still night
And his dumb candle, saw his pinching throes;
Were not his own free merit a more crown,
Unto his travails than their reeling claps.[1]

[1] Applauses.

This 'tis that strikes me silent, seals my lips,
And apts me rather to sleep out my time,
Than I would waste it in contemnéd strifes
With these vile Ibidés,[1] these unclean birds
That make their mouths their clysters, and still purge
From their hot entrails. But I leave the monsters
To their own fate. And, since the Comic Muse
Hath proved so ominous to me, I will try
If tragedy have a more kind aspect:
Her favors in my next I will pursue,
Where, if I prove the pleasure but of one,
So he judicious be, he shall be alone
A theater unto me. Once I'll 'say[2]
To strike the ear of time in those fresh strains,
  As shall, beside the cunning of their ground,
Give cause to some of wonder, some despite,
  And more despair to imitate their sound.
I, that spend half my nights and all my days
  Here in a cell, to get a dark pale face,
To come forth worth the ivy or the bays,
  And in this age can hope no other grace—
Leave me! There's something come into my thought
That must and shall be sung high and aloof,
Safe from the wolf's black jaw and the dull ass's hoof.[3]

JOHN FLETCHER AND FRANCIS BEAUMONT.

A SONG OF TRUE LOVE DEAD.

[From *The Maid's Tragedy.*]

Lay a garland on my hearse
  Of the dismal yew;
Maidens willow branches bear;
  Say I died true:
My love was false, but I was firm
  From my hour of birth:
Upon my buried body lie
  Lightly, gentle earth.

Plural of ibis.   [2] That is, I will try once for all.   [3] That is, envy and stupidity.

A SONG OF CRUEL LOVE.[1]

[From *Rollo, Duke of Normandy.*]

Take, oh take those lips away,
  That so sweetly were forsworn,
And those eyes, the break of day,
  Lights that do mislead the morn;
But my kisses bring again,
Seals of love, though sealed in vain.

Hide, oh hide those hills of snow,
  Which thy frozen bosom bears,
On whose tops the pinks that grow
  Are of those that April wears;
But first set my poor heart free,
Bound in those icy chains by thee.

SWEET MELANCHOLY.[2]

[From *The Nice Valor.*]

Hence, all your vain delights,
As short as are the nights
    Wherein you spend your folly!
There's naught in this life sweet,
If man were wise to see't,
    But only melancholy:
    O sweetest melancholy!

Welcome, folded arms and fixéd eyes,
A sigh that piercing mortifies,
A look that's fastened on the ground,
A tongue chained up without a sound!
Fountain-heads and pathless groves,
Places which pale passion loves,
Moonlight walks when all the fowls
Are warmly housed, save bats and owls,
A midnight bell, a parting groan,
These are the sounds we feed upon;
Then stretch our bones in a still gloomy valley:
Nothing's so dainty sweet as lovely melancholy.

[1] The first stanza of this song was probably Shakspere's.   [2] This should be compared with Milton's *Il Penseroso*.

CÆSAR'S LAMENT OVER POMPEY.

[From *The False One.*]

O thou conqueror,
Thou glory of the world once, now the pity:
Thou awe of nations, wherefore didst thou fall thus?
What poor fate followed thee and plucked thee on
To trust thy sacred life to an Egyptian?
The life and light of Rome to a blind stranger
That honorable war ne'er taught a nobleness,
Nor worthy circumstance showed what a man was?
That never heard thy name sung but in banquets
And loose lascivious pleasures?   To a boy
That had no faith to comprehend thy greatness,
No study of thy life to know thy goodness?   .   .   .
Egyptians, dare you think your high pyrámidēs,
Built to out-dure the sun, as you suppose,
Where your unworthy kings lie raked in ashes,
Are monuments fit for him?   No, brood of Nilus,
Nothing can cover his high fame but heaven;
No pyramid set off his memories,
But the eternal substance of his greatness,
To which I leave him.

JOHN MILTON.

FAME.

[From *Lycidas.*]

Alas! what boots it with incessant care
To tend the homely, slighted, shepherd's trade,
And strictly meditate the thankless Muse?
Were it not better done, as others use,
To sport with Amaryllis in the shade,
Or with the tangles of Neæra's hair?
Fame is the spur that the clear spirit doth raise
(That last infirmity of noble mind)
To scorn delights and live laborious days;
But the fair guerdon when we hope to find,

And think to burst out into sudden blaze,
Comes the blind Fury with the abhorred shears,[1]
And slits the thin-spun life.   "But not the praise,"
Phœbus replied, and touched my trembling ears:
"Fame is no plant that grows on mortal soil,
Nor in the glistering foil
Set off to the world, nor in broad rumour lies,
But lives and spreads aloft by those pure eyes
And perfect witness of all-judging Jove;
As he pronounces lastly on each deed,
Of so much fame in heaven expect thy meed."

The Pleasures of Melancholy.

[From *Il Penseroso*.]

Sweet bird that shun'st the noise of folly,
Most musical, most melancholy!
Thee, chauntress, oft the woods among
I woo, to hear thy even-song;
And, missing thee, I walk unseen
On the dry smooth-shaven green,
To behold the wandering moon,
Riding near her highest noon,
Like one that had been led astray
Through the heaven's wide pathless way,
And oft, as if her head she bowed,
Stooping through a fleecy cloud.
Oft, on a plat of rising ground,
I hear the far-off curfew sound,
Over some wide-watered shore,
Swinging slow with sullen roar;
Or, if the air will not permit,
Some still removèd place will fit,
Where glowing embers through the room
Teach light to counterfeit a gloom,
Far from all resort of mirth,
Save the cricket on the hearth,
Or the bellman's drowsy charm[2]
To bless the doors from nightly harm. . . .
    But let my due feet never fail
To walk the studious cloister's pale,

---

[1] Atropos, the fate who cuts the thread of life.   [2] The watchman's call.

And love the high embowèd roof,
With antique pillars massy-proof,
And storied windows richly dight,
Casting a dim religious light.
There let the pealing organ blow,
To the full-voiced quire below,
In service high and anthem clear,
As may with sweetness, through mine ear,
Dissolve me into ecstsies,
And bring all Heaven before mine eyes.
      And may at last my weary age
Find out the peaceful hermitage,
The hairy gown and mossy cell,
Where I may sit and rightly spell
Of every star that heaven doth shew,
And every herb that sips the dew,
Till old experience do attain
To something like prophetic strain.
      These pleasures, Melancholy, give ;
And I with thee will choose to live.

THE PROTECTION OF CONSCIENCE.

[From *Comus*.]

Scene: A wild wood; night.

Lady: My brothers, when they saw me wearied out
      With this long way, resolving here to lodge
      Under the spreading favor of these pines,
      Stepped, as they said, to the next thicket-side
      To bring me berries, or such cooling fruit
      As the kind hospitable woods provide.
      They left me then when the grey-hooded Even,
      Like a sad votarist in palmer's weed,
      Rose from the hindmost wheels of Phœbus' wain.
      But where they are, and why they came not back,
      Is now the labor of my thoughts.   'Tis likeliest
      They had engaged their wandering steps too far ;
      And envious darkness, ere they could return,
      Had stolen them from me.   Else, O thievish Night,
      Why shouldst thou, but for some felonious end,

In thy dark lantern thus close up the stars
That Nature hung in heaven, and filled their lamps
With everlasting oil, to give due light
To the misled and lonely traveller?
This is the place, as well as I may guess,
Whence even now the tumult of loud mirth
Was rife, and perfect in my listening ear;
Yet nought but single darkness do I find.
What might this be?   A thousand fantasies
Begin to throng into my memory,
Of calling shapes and beckoning shadows dire,
And airy tongues that syllable men's names
On sands and shores and desert wildernesses.
These thoughts may startle well, but not astound
The virtuous mind, that ever walks attended
By a strong siding champion, Conscience.
O, welcome, pure-eyed Faith, white-handed Hope,
Thou hovering angel girt with golden wings,
And thou unblemished form of Chastity!
I see ye visibly, and now believe
That He, the Supreme Good, to whom all things ill
Are but as slavish officers of vengeance,
Would send a glistening guardian, if need were,
To keep my life and honor unassailed. . . .
Was I deceived, or did a sable cloud
Turn forth her silver lining on the night?
I did not err: there does a sable cloud
Turn forth her silver lining on the night,
And casts a gleam over this tufted grove.

INVOCATION TO LIGHT.

[From *Paradise Lost*.]

        Thee I revisit safe,
And feel thy sovereign vital lamp; but thou
Revisitest not these eyes, that roll in vain
To find thy piercing ray, and find no dawn;
So thick a drop serene[1] hath quenched their orbs,
Or dim suffusion veiled.   Yet not the more
Cease I to wander where the Muses haunt
Clear spring, or shady grove, or sunny hill,

---

[1] The *gutta serena*, or cataract.

Smit with the love of sacred song; but chief
Thee, Sion, and the flowery brooks beneath,
That wash thy hallowed feet, and warbling flow,
Nightly I visit: nor sometimes forget
Those other two equalled with me in fate,
So were I equalled with them in renown,
Blind Thamyris and blind Mæonides,[1]
And Tiresias and Phineus, prophets old:
Then feed on thoughts that voluntary move
Harmonious numbers; as the wakeful bird
Sings darkling, and in shadiest covert hid
Tunes her nocturnal note.   Thus with the year
Seasons return, but not to me returns
Day, or the sweet approach of even or morn,
Or sight of vernal bloom, or summer's rose,
Or flocks, or herds, or human face divine;
But cloud instead, and ever-during dark,
Surrounds me, from the cheerful ways of men
Cut off, and for the book of knowledge fair
Presented with a univresal blank
Of nature's works, to me expunged and rased,
And wisdom at one entrance quite shut out.
So much the rather thou, celestial Light,
Shine inward, and the mind through all her powers
Irraiate; there plant eyes, all mist from thence
Purge and disperse, that I may see and tell
Of things invisible to mortal sight.

SATAN.

[From *Paradise Lost.*]

He scarce had ceased when the superior Fiend
Was moving toward the shore: his ponderous shield,
Etherial temper, massy, large and round,
Behind him cast; the broad circumference
Hung on his shoulders like the moon, whose orb
Through optic glass the Tuscan artist[2] views
At evening from the top of Fesole,[3]
Or in Valdamo, to descry new lands,
Rivers or mountains on her spotty globe.
His spear (to equal which the tallest pine

---

[1] Homer.   [2] Galileo.   [3] A hill near Florence.

Hewn on Norwegian hills, to be the mast
Of some great ammiral, were but a wand)
He walked with, to support uneasy steps
Over the burning marle, not like those steps
On heaven's azure; and the torrid clime
Smote on him sore beside, vaulted with fire.
Nathless he so endured, till on the beach
Of that inflamèd sea he stood, and called
His legions, angel-forms, who lay entranced
Thick as autumnal leaves that strew the brooks
In Vallombrosa, where the Etrurian shades
High over-arched embower, or scattered sedge
Afloat, when with fierce winds Orion armed
Hath vexed the Red Sea coast, whose waves o'erthrew
Busiris and his Memphian chivalry,
While with perfidious hatred they pursued
The sojourners of Goshen, who beheld
From the safe shore their floating carcasses
And broken chariot-wheels: so thick bestrewn,
Abject and lost lay these, covering the flood,
Under amazement of their hideous change.

ON THE LATE MASSACRE IN PIEDMONT.[1]

Avenge, O Lord, thy slaughtered saints, whose bones
　　Lie scattered on the Alpine mountains cold;
　　Even them who kept thy truth so pure of old,
　　When all our fathers worshipped stocks and stones,
Forget not: in thy book record their groans
　　Who were thy sheep, and in their ancient fold
　　Slain by the bloody Piedmontese, that rolled
　　Mother with infant down the rocks. Their moans
The vales redoubled to the hills, and they
　　To heaven. Their martyred blood and ashes sow
O'er all the Italian fields, where still doth sway
The triple Tyrant,[2] that from these may grow
　　A hundred-fold, who, having learnt thy way,
　　Early may fly the Babylonian woe.[3]

[1] This sonnet refers to the persecution instituted in 1655 by the Duke of Savoy against the Vaudois Protestants.　[2] The Pope, who wore the triple crown or tiara.
[3] The Papacy, with which the Protestant reformers identified Babylon the Great, the "Scarlet Woman" of Revelation.

SIR THOMAS BROWNE.

THE VANITY OF MONUMENTS.

[From *Urn Burial*]

There is no antidote against the opium of time, which temporally considereth all things. Our fathers find their graves in our short memories, and sadly tell us how we may be buried in our survivors. Grave-stones tell truth scarce forty years. Generations pass while some trees stand, and old families last not three oaks. . . . The iniquity[1] of oblivion blindly scattereth her poppy, and deals with the memory of men without distinction to merit of perpetuity. Who can but pity the founder of the pyramids? Herostratus lives, that burnt the temple of Diana, he is almost lost that built it. Time hath spared the epitaph of Adrian's horse, confounded that of himself. In vain we compute our felicities by the advantage of our good names, since bad have equal durations and Thersites[2] is like to live as long as Agamemnon. Who knows whether the best of men be known, or whether there be not more remarkable persons forgot than any that stand remembered in the known account of time? Without the favor of the everlasting register, the first man had been as unknown as the last, and Methusaleh's long life had been his only chronicle.

Oblivion is not to be hired.[3] The greater part must be content to be as though they had not been, to be found in the register of God, not in the record of man. Twenty-seven names make up the first story, and the reported names ever since contain not one living century. The number of the dead long exceedeth all that shall live. The night of time far surpasseth the day, and who knows when was the equinox? Every hour adds unto that current arithmetic which scarce stands one moment. And since death must be the Lucina[4] of life, and even pagans could doubt whether thus to live were to die; since our longest sun sets at right descensions and makes but winter arches, and, therefore, it cannot be long before we lie down in darkness and have our light in ashes. Since the brother[5] of death daily haunts us with dying mementoes, and time that grows old in itself bids us hope no long duration; diuturnity is a dream and folly of expectation. . . .

There is nothing strictly immortal but immortality. Whatever hath no beginning may be confident of no end. All others have a dependent being and within the reach of destruction, which is the peculiar of that necessary essence that cannot destroy itself, and the highest strain of omnipo-

[1] Injustice.   [2] See Shakspere's *Troilus and Cressida*.   [3] That is, bribed, bought off.   [4] The goddess of childbirth. We must die to be born again.   [5] Sleep.

tency, to be so powerfully constituted as not to suffer even from the power of itself.   But the sufficiency of Christian immortality frustrates all earthly glory, and the quality of either state after death makes a folly of posthumous memory.   God, who can only[1] destroy our souls, and hath assured our resurrection, either of our bodies or names hath directly promised no duration. Wherein there is so much of chance that the boldest expectants have found unhappy frustrations, and to hold long subsistence seems but a scape[2] in oblivion.   But man is a noble animàl, splendid in ashes and pompous in the grave, solemnizing nativities and deaths with equal lustre, nor omitting ceremonies of bravery [3] in the infamy of his nature.

JOHN DRYDEN.

THE CHARACTER OF ZIMRI.[4]

[From *Absalom and Achitophel.*]

In the first rank of these did Zimri stand,
A man so various that he seemed to be
Not one, but all mankind's epitome:
Stiff in opinions, always in the wrong,
Was every thing by turns, and nothing long;
But in the course of one revolving moon
Was chymist, fiddler, statesman, and buffoon;
Then all for women, painting, rhyming, drinking,
Besides ten thousand freaks that died in thinking,
Blest madman, who could every hour employ
With something new to wish or to enjoy!
Railing and praising were his usual themes,
And both, to show his judgment, in extremes:
So over-violent or over-civil
That every man with him was God or Devil.
In squandering wealth was his peculiar art;
Nothing went unrewarded but desert.
Beggared by fools whom still he found[5] too late,
He had his jest, and they had his estate.
He laughed himself from court; then sought relief
By forming parties, but could ne'er be chief:

[1] That is, the only one who can.   [2] Freak   [3] Ostentation.   [4] This is a satirical sketch of George Villiers, Duke of Buckingham.   [5] Found out, detected.

For spite of him, the weight of business fell
To Absalom and wise Achitophel.[1]
Thus, wicked but in will, of means bereft,
He left not faction, but of that was left.

THE CHEATS OF HOPE.

[From *Aurengzebe*.]

When I consider life, 'tis all a cheat;
Yet, fooled with hope, men favor the deceit,
Trust on, and think to-morrow will repay;
To-morrow's falser than the former day,
Lies worse, and while it says we shall be blest
With some new joys, cuts off what we possessed.
Strange cozenage! none would live past years again,
Yet all hope pleasure in what yet remain,
And from the dregs of life think to receive
What the first sprightly running could not give.
I'm tired of waiting for this chymic[2] gold
Which fools us young and beggars us when old.

JONATHAN SWIFT.

THE EMPEROR OF LILLIPUT.

[From *Gulliver's Travels*.]

He is taller by almost the breadth of my nail than any of his court; which alone is enough to strike an awe into the beholders. His features are strong and masculine, with an Austrian lip and arched nose, his complexion olive, his countenance erect, his body and limbs well proportioned, all his motions graceful, and his deportment majestic. He was then past his prime, being twenty-eight years and three quarters old, of which he had reigned about seven in great felicity, and generally victorious. For the better convenience of beholding him, I lay on my side, so that my face was parallel to his, and he stood but three yards off; however, I have had him since many times in my hand, and therefore cannot be deceived in the descrip-

---

[1] The Duke of Monmouth and the Earl of Shaftesbury.   [2] The gold which the alchemists tried to make from base metals.

tion. His dress was very plain and simple, and the fashion of it between the Asiatic and the European; but he had on his head a light helmet of gold, adorned with jewels and a plume on the crest. He held his sword drawn in his hand to defend himself, if I should happen to break loose; it was almost three inches long: the hilt and scabbard were gold enriched with diamonds. His voice was shrill, but very clear and articulate, and I could distinctly hear it, when I stood up.

.

THE STRULDBRUGS.

[From *Gulliver's Travels.*]

One day in much good company, I was asked by a person of quality whether I had seen any of their *Struldbrugs*, or immortals? I said I had not, and desired he would explain to me what he meant by such an appellation, applied to a mortal creature. He told me that sometimes, though very rarely, a child happened to be born in a family with a red circular spot in the forehead, directly over the left eyebrow, which was an infallible mark that it should never die. . . . He said these births were so rare that he did not believe there could be above eleven hundred *Struldbrugs* of both sexes in the whole kingdom; of which he computed about fifty in the metropolis, and among the rest, a young girl born about three years ago ;·that these productions were not peculiar to any family, but a mere effect of chance; and the children of the *Struldbrugs* themselves were equally mortal with the rest of the people. . . . After this preface, he gave me a particular account of the *Struldbrugs* among them. He said they commonly acted like mortals till about thirty years old; after which, by degrees, they grew melancholy and dejected, increasing in both till they came to fourscore. This he learned from their own confession; for otherwise, there not being above two or three of that species born in an age, they were too few to form a general observation by. When they came to fourscore years, which is reckoned the extremity of living in this country, they had not only all the follies and infirmities of other old men, but many more, which arose from the dreadful prospect of never dying. They were not only opinionative, peevish, covetous, morose, vain, talkative, but incapable of friendship and dead to all natural affection, which never descended below their grandchildren. Envy and impotent desires are their prevailing passions. But those objects against which their envy seems principally directed are the vices of the younger sort and the deaths of the old. By reflecting on the former, they find themselves cut off from all possibility of pleasure; and whenever they see a funeral they lament and repine that others are gone to a harbor of rest, to which they themselves never can hope to arrive. They have no remembrance of any thing but what they learned and observed in their youth and middle age, and even that is very imperfect. And for the truth or particulars of any fact, it is safer to depend on common tradition than upon their best recollections. The least miserable among them appear to be those who turn to dotage and entirely lose their memories; these meet with more pity and assistance, because they want many bad qualities which abound in others. . . . At ninety, they lose their teeth and hair; they have at that age no distinction of taste, but eat and drink whatever they can get, without relish or appetite. The diseases they were subject to still continue, without increasing or diminishing. In talking, they forget the common appellation of things, and the names of persons, even of those who are their nearest friends and relatives. For the same reason they never can amuse themselves with reading, because their memory will not serve to carry them from the beginning of a sentence to the end; and by this defect they are deprived of the only entertainment whereof they might otherwise be capable. . . . They are despised and hated by all sorts of people; when one of them is born, it is reckoned ominous, and their birth is recorded very particularly. . . . They were the most mortifying sight I ever beheld; and the women were homelier than the men Beside the usual deformities in extreme old age, they acquired an additional ghastliness, in proportion to their number of years, which is not to be described; and among half a dozen I soon distinguished which was the eldest, although there was not above a century or two between them.

ALEXANDER POPE.

A CHARACTER OF ADDISON.

[From the *Epistle to Dr. Arbuthnot*.]

Peace to all such! but were there one whose fires
True genius kindles and fair fame inspires;
Blest with each talent and each art to please,
And born to write, converse, and live with ease:
Should such a man, too fond to rule alone,
Bear, like the Turk, no brother near the throne;
View him with scornful, yet with jealous eyes,
And hate, for arts that caused himself to rise;
Damn with faint praise, assent with civil leer,
And, without sneering, teach the rest to sneer;
Willing to wound, and yet afraid to strike,
Just hint a fault and hesitate dislike;

Alike reserved to blame or to commend,
A timorous foe and a suspicious friend;
Dreading even fools, by flatterers besieged;
And so obliging that he ne'er obliged;
Like *Cato*,[1] give his little Senate laws,
And sit attentive to his own applause;
While wits and templars [2] every sentence raise,
And wonder with a foolish face of praise—
Who but must laugh if such a man there be?
Who would not weep if Atticus were he?

An Ornament to Her Sex.

[From the *Epistle of the Characters of Women.*]

See how the world its veterans rewards!
A youth of frolic, an old age of cards;
Fair to no purpose, artful to no end,
Young without lovers, old without a friend;
A fop their passion, but their prize a sot;
Alive, ridiculous, and dead, forgot.
Ah! Friend,[3] to dazzle let the vain design;
To raise the thought and touch the heart be thine!
That charm shall grow, while what fatigues the Ring [4]
Flaunts and goes down, an unregarded thing.
So when the sun's broad beam has tired the sight,
All mild ascends the moon's more sober light,
Serene in virgin majesty she shines,
And unobserved, the glaring orb declines.
Oh! blest with temper, whose unclouded ray
Can make to-morrow cheerful as to-day;
She who can love a sister's charms, or hear
Sighs for a daughter with unwounded ear;
She who ne'er answers till a husband cools,
Or, if she rules him, never shows she rules;
Charms by accepting, by submitting sways,
Yet has her humour most when she obeys;
Let fops or fortune fly which way they will,
Disdains all loss of tickets or Codille; [5]

---

[1] A reference to Addison's tragedy of *Cato*.   [2] Young lawyers resident in the temple. See Spenser's *Prothalamion*.   [3] Martha Blount, a dear friend of the poet's.
[4] The fashionable promenade in Hyde Park.   [5] The "pool" in the game of ombre.

Spleen, vapours, or small-pox, above them all,
And mistress of herself though china fall. . . .
Be this a woman's fame: with this unblest,
Toasts live a scorn, and queens may die a jest.
This Phœbus promised (I forget the year)
When those blue eyes first opened on the sphere;
Ascendant Phœbus watched that hour with care,
Averted half your parents' simple prayer;
And gave you beauty, but denied the pelf
That buys your sex a tyrant o'er itself.
The generous God who wit and gold refines,
And ripens spirits as he ripens mines,
Kept dross for duchesses, the world shall know it,
To you gave sense, good-humour, and a poet.

JOSEPH ADDISON.

SIGNOR NICOLINI AND THE LION.

[From the *Spectator*.]

There is nothing that of late years has afforded matter of greater amusement to the town than Signor Nicolini's combat with a lion in the Haymarket, which has been very often exhibited to the general satisfaction of
most of the nobility and gentry in the kingdom of Great Britain. . . . But
before I communicate my discoveries I must acquaint the reader that upon
my walking behind the scenes last winter, as I was thinking on something
else, I accidentally jostled against a monstrous animal that extremely
startled me, and, upon my nearer survey of it, appeared to be a lion ram-
pant. The lion, seeing me very much surprised, told me in a gentle voice
that I might come by him if I pleased; "for," says he, "I do not intend to
hurt any body." I thanked him very kindly and passed by him, and in a
little time after saw him leap upon the stage and act his part with very
great applause. It has been observed by several that the lion has changed
his manner of acting twice or thrice since his first appearance, which will
not seem strange when I acquaint the reader that the lion has been changed
upon the audience three several times.

The first lion was a candle-snuffer, who, being a fellow of a testy, choleric
temper, overdid his part, and would not suffer himself to be killed so easily
as he ought to have done; besides, it was observed of him that he grew

more surly every time he came out of the lion; and having dropt some words in ordinary conversation, as if he had not fought his best, and that he suffered himself to be thrown upon his back in the scuffle, and that he would wrestle with Mr. Nicolini for what he pleased, out of his lion's skin, it was thought proper to discard him; and it is verily believed to this day that had he been brought upon the stage another time he would certainly have done mischief. Besides, it was objected against the first lion that he reared himself so high upon his hinder paws, and walked in so erect a position, that he looked more like an old man than a lion.

The second lion was a tailor by trade, who belonged to the play-house, and had the character of a mild and peaceful man in his profession. If the former was too furious, this was too sheepish, for his part; inasmuch that, after a short, modest walk upon the stage, he would fall at the first touch of 'Hydaspes'[1] without grappling with him and giving him an opportunity of showing his variety of Italian trips; it is said, indeed, that he once gave him a rip in his flesh-colored doublet; but this was only to make work for himself in his private character of a tailor. I must not omit that it was this second lion who treated me with so much humanity behind the scenes.

The acting lion at present is, as I am informed, a country gentleman who does it for his diversion, but desires his name may be concealed. He says very handsomely, in his own excuse, that he does not act for gain, that he indulges an innocent pleasure in it, and that it is better to pass away an evening in this manner than in gaming and drinking; but at the same time says, with a very agreeable raillery upon himself, that if his name should be known the ill-natured world might call him *the ass in the lion's skin*. This gentleman's temper is made out of such a happy mixture of the mild and the choleric that he outdoes both his predecessors, and has drawn together greater audiences than have been known in the memory of man.

I must not conclude my narrative without taking notice of a groundless report that has been raised to a gentleman's disadvantage, of whom I must declare myself an admirer; namely, that Signor Nicolini and the lion have been seen sitting peaceably by one another and smoking a pipe together behind the scenes, by which their common enemies would insinuate that it is but a sham combat which they represent upon the stage; but upon inquiry I find that if any such correspondence has passed between them it was not till the combat was over, when the lion was to be looked upon as dead, according to the received rules of the drama. Besides, this is what is practiced every day in Westminster Hall, where nothing is more usual than to see a couple of lawyers, who have been tearing each other to pieces in the court, embracing one another as soon as they are out of it.

[1] In the opera of *Hydaspes*, presented at the Haymarket in 1710, the hero, whose part was taken by Signor Nicolini, kills a lion in the amphitheater.

SAMUEL JOHNSON.

DETACHED PASSAGES FROM BOSWELL'S LIFE.

We talked of the education of children, and I asked him what he thought was best to teach them first. *Johnson:* Sir, it is no matter what you teach them first, any more than what leg you shall put into your breeches first. Sir, while you are considering which of two things you should teach your child first, another boy has learnt them both.

Sir, a woman's preaching is like a dog's walking on his hind legs. It is not done well, but you are surprised to see it done at all.

A gentleman who had been very unhappy in marriage married immediately after his wife died. Johnson said it was a triumph of hope over experience.

He would not allow Scotland to derive any credit from Lord Mansfield, for he was educated in England. "Much," said he, "may be made of a Scotchman if he be *caught* young." *Johnson:* An old tutor of a college said to one of his pupils, "Read over your compositions, and wherever you meet with a passage which you think is particularly fine strike it out." A gentleman who introduced his brother to Dr. Johnson was earnest to recommend him to the doctor's notice, which he did by saying: "When we have sat together some time you'll find my brother grow very entertaining."

"Sir," said Johnson, "I can wait."

"Greek, sir," said he, "is like lace; every man gets as much of it as he can."

Lord Lucan tells a very good story, that when the sale of Thrale's brewery was going forward, Johnson appeared bustling about with an inkhorn and pen in his button-hole, like an exciseman, and on being asked what he really considered to be the value of the property which was to be disposed of, answered, "We are not here to sell a parcel of boilers and vats, but the potentiality of growing rich beyond the dreams of avarice."

Johnson: My dear friend, clear your *mind* of cant. You may *talk* as other people do; you may say to a man, "Sir, I am your most humble servant." You are *not* his most humble servant. You may say, "These are bad times; it is a melancholy thing to be reserved to such times." You don't mind the times. You tell a man, "I am sorry you had such bad weather the last day of your journey and were so much wet." You don't care sixpence whether he is wet or dry. You may *talk* in this manner; it is a mode of talking in society, but don't *think* foolishly.

A lively saying of Dr. Johnson to Miss Hannah More, who had expressed a wonder that the poet who had written *Paradise Lost* should write such poor sonnets: "Milton, madam, was a genius that could cut a colossus from a rock, but could not carve heads upon cherry-stones."

A gentleman having said that a *congé d'elire* has not, perhaps, the force of

a command, but may be considered only as a strong recommendation:
"Sir," replied Johnson, "it is such a recommendation as if I should throw
you out of a two pair of stairs window, and recommend you to fall soft."

Happening one day to mention Mr. Flaxman, the doctor replied, "Let
me hear no more of him, sir; that is the fellow who made the index to my
Ramblers, and set down the name of Milton thus: 'Milton, *Mr.* John.'"

Goldsmith said that he thought he could write a good fable, mentioned
the simplicity which that kind of composition requires, and observed that,
in most fables, the animals introduced seldom talk in character. "For
instance," said he, "the fable of the little fishes, who saw birds fly over
their heads, and, envying them, petitioned Jupiter to be changed into birds.
The skill," continued he, "consists in making them talk like little fishes."
While he indulged himself in this fanciful reverie, he observed Johnson
shaking his sides and laughing. Upon which he smartly proceeded, "Why,
Dr. Johnson, this is not so easy as you seem to think; for if you were to
make little fishes talk, they would talk like WHALES."

He expressed a particular enthusiasm with respect to visiting the wall of
China. I caught it for the moment, and said I really believed I should go
and see the wall of China, had I not children of whom it was my duty to
take care. "Sir," said he, "by doing so, you would do what would be of
importance in raising your children to eminence. There would be a luster
reflected upon them from your spirit and curiosity. They would be at all
times regarded as the children of a man who had gone to view the wall of
China—I am serious, sir."

OLIVER GOLDSMITH.

THE VILLAGE PASTOR AND SCHOOL-MASTER.

[From *The Deserted Village.*]

Near yonder copse, where once the garden smiled,
And still where many a garden flower grows wild;
There, where a few torn shrubs the place disclose,
The village preacher's modest mansion rose.
A man he was to all the country dear,
And passing rich with forty pounds a year;
Remote from towns he ran his godly race,
Nor e'er had changed, nor wished to change, his place.
Unskillful he to fawn or seek for power
By doctrines fashioned to the varying hour;

Far other aims his heart had learned to prize,
More bent to raise the wretched than to rise.
His house was kuown to all the vagrant train—
He chid their wanderings, but relieved their pain;
The long-remembered beggar was his guest,
Whose beard, descending, swept his aged breast.
The ruined spendthrift, now no longer proud,
Claimed kindred there, and had his claims allowed;
The broken soldier, kindly bade to stay,
Sat by his fire and talked the night away;
Wept o'er his wounds, or tales of sorrow done,
Shouldered his crutch and showed how fields were won.
Pleased with his guests, the good man learned to glow,
And quite forgot their vices in their woe;
Careless their merits or their faults to scan,
His pity gave e'er charity began.
　　Thus to relieve the wretched was his pride,
And e'en his failings leaned to virtue's side. . . .
　　At church, with meek and unaffected grace,
His looks adorned the venerable place;
Truth from his lips prevailed with double sway,
And fools who came to scoff remained to pray.
The service past, around the pious man,
With steady zeal, each honest rustic ran;
E'en children followed with endearing wile
And plucked his gown to share the good man's smile.
His ready smile a parent's warmth expressed,
Their welfare pleased him, and their cares distressed;
To them his heart, his love, his griefs, were given,
But all his serious thoughts had rest in heaven.
As some tall cliff, that lifts its awful form,
Swells from the vale, and midway leaves the storm,
Though round its breast the rolling clouds are spread,
Eternal sunshine settles on its head.
　　Beside yon straggling fence that skirts the way,
With blossomed furze unprofitable gay,
There, in his noisy mansion, skilled to rule,
The village master taught his little school.
A man severe he was, and stern to view;
I knew him well, and every truant knew.
Well had the boding tremblers learned to trace
The day's disasters in his morning face;

Full well they laughed with counterfeited glee
At all his jokes (for many a joke had he);
Full well the busy whisper, circling round,
Conveyed the dismal, tidings when he frowned
Yet he was kind, or if severe in aught,
The love he bore for learning was his fault.
The village all declared how much he knew—
'Twas certain he could write and cipher too;
Lands he could measure, times and tides presage,
And e'en the story ran that he could gauge.
In arguing, too, the parson owned his skill,
For, e'en though vanquished, he could argue still,
While words of learned length and thundering sound
Amazed the gazing rustics ranged around;
And still they gazed, and still the wonder grew
That one small head could carry all he knew.

EDMUND BURKE.

THE DECAY OF LOYALTY.

[From *Reflections on the Revolution in France.*]

It is sixteen or seventeen years since I saw the queen of France,[1] then the dauphiness, at Versailles; and surely never lighted on this orb, which she hardly seemed to touch, a more delightful vision. I saw her just above the horizon, decorating and cheering the elevated sphere she just began to move in; glittering like the morning star, full of life and splendor and joy. O, what a revolution! and what a heart must I have to contemplate without emotion that elevation and that fall. Little did I dream, when she added titles of veneration to those of enthusiastic, distant, respectful love, that she should ever be obliged to carry the sharp antidote against disgrace concealed in that bosom; little did I dream that I should have lived to see such disasters fallen upon her in a nation of gallant men, in a nation of men of honor and of cavaliers. I thought ten thousand swords must have leaped from the scabbards to avenge even a look that threatened her with insult. But the age of chivalry is gone. That of sophisters, economists, and calculators has succeeded; and the glory of Europe is extinguished forever. Never, never more shall we behold that generous loyalty to rank and sex, that proud submission, that dignified obedience, that sub-

[1] Marie Antoinette.

ordination of the heart which kept alive, even in servitude itself, the spirit of an exalted freedom. The unbought grace of life, the cheap defense of nations, the nurse of manly sentiment and heroic enterprise is gone! It is gone, that sensibility of principle, that chastity of honor, which felt a stain like a wound, which inspired courage, whilst it mitigated ferocity, which ennobled whatever it touched, and under which vice itself lost half its evil by losing all its grossness. . . . On the scheme of this barbarous philosophy, which is the offspring of cold hearts and muddy understandings, and which is as void of solid wisdom as it is destitute of all taste and elegance, laws are to be supported only by their own terms, and by the concern which each individual may find in them from his own private speculations, or can spare to them from his own private interests. In the groves of their academy, at the end of every vista, you see nothing but the gallows. Nothing is left which engages the affections on the part of the commonwealth. On the principles of this mechanic philosophy, our institutions can never be embodied, if I may use the expresssion, in persons; so as to create in us love, veneration, admiration, or attachment. But that sort of reason which banishes the affections is incapable of filling their place. These public affections, combined with manners, are required sometimes as supplements, sometimes as corrections, always as aids, to law. The precept given by a wise man, as well as a great critic, for the construction of poems, is equally true as to states. *Non satis est pulchra esse poemata, dulcia sunto.* There ought to be a system of manners in every nation which a well-formed mind would be disposed to relish. To make us love our country, our country ought to be lovely.

THOMAS GRAY.

ODE ON A DISTANT PROSPECT OF ETON COLLEGE.

Ye distant spires, ye antique towers,
    That crown the watery glade,
Where grateful Science still adores
    Her Henry's [1] holy shade;
And ye, that from the stately brow
    Of Windsor's heights th' expanse below
Of grove, of lawn, of mead, survey,
Whose turf, whose shade, whose flowers among
Wanders the hoary Thames along
    His silver-winding way:

[1] Henry VI., founder of Eton College.

Ah happy hills, ah pleasing shade,
  Ah fields beloved in vain,
Where once my careless childhood strayed,
  A stranger yet to pain!
I feel the gales that from ye blow,
A momentary bliss bestow,
  As waving fresh their gladsome wing
My weary soul they seem to soothe,
And, redolent of joy and youth,
  To breathe a second spring.

Say, father Thames, for thou hast seen
  Full many a sprightly race,
Disporting on thy margent green,
  The paths of pleasure trace,
Who, foremost now delight to cleave
With pliant arm thy glassy wave?
  The captive linnet which enthral?
What idle progeny succeed
To chase the rolling circle's speed,
  Or urge the flying ball?

While some, on earnest business bent,
  Their morning labors ply
'Gainst graver hours, that bring constraint
  To sweeten liberty:
Some bold adventurers disdain
The limits of their little reign,
  And unknown regions dare discry:
Still as they run they look behind,
They hear a voice in every wind,
  And snatch a fearful joy.

Gay hope is theirs by fancy fed,
  Less pleasing when possest;
The tear forgot as soon as shed,
  The sunshine of the breast:
Theirs buxom health of rosy hue,
Wild wit, invention ever new,
  And lively cheer of vigour born;
The thoughtless day, the easy night,
The spirits pure, the slumbers light,
  That fly th' approach of morn.

Alas! regardless of their doom
  The little victims play.
No sense have they of ill to come,
  Nor care beyond to-day:
Yet see how all around them wait
The ministers of human fate,
  And black Misfortune's baleful train!
Ah, show them where in ambush stand,
To seize their prey the murth'rous band!
  Ah, tell them they are men!

These shall the fury Passions tear,
  The vultures of the mind,
Disdainful Anger, pallid Fear,
  And Shame that skulks behind;
Or pining Love shall waste their youth,
Or Jealousy with rankling tooth,
  That only gnaws the secret heart,
And Envy wan, and faded Care,
Grim-visaged, comfortless Despair,
  And Sorrow's piercing dart.

Ambition this shall tempt to rise,
  Then whirl the wretch from high,
To bitter Scorn a sacrifice,
  And grinning Infamy,
The stings of Falsehood those shall try,
And hard Unkindness' altered eye,
  That mocks the tear it forced to flow;
And keen Remorse with blood defiled,
And moody Madness laughing wild
  Amid severest woe.

Lo in the vale of years beneath
  A grisly troop are seen,
The painful family of Death,
  More hideous than their queen:
This racks the joints, this fires the veins,
That every laboring sinew strains,
  Those in the deeper vitals rage:
Lo, Poverty, to fill the band,
That numbs the soul with icy hand,
  And slow consuming Age.

To each his sufferings: all are men,
  Condemned alike to groan,
The tender for another's pain,
  The unfeeling for his own.
Yet ah! why should they know their fate?
Since sorrow never comes too late,
  And happiness too swiftly flies,
Thought would destroy their paradise.
No more; where ignorance is bliss,
  'Tis folly to be wise.

WILLIAM COWPER.

FROM LINES ON THE RECEIPT OF HIS MOTHER'S PICTURE.

O, that those lips had language! Life has passed
With me but roughly since I heard thee last.
Those lips are thine—thy own sweet smile I see,
The same that oft in childhood solaced me;
Voice only fails, else how distinct they say,
"Grieve not, my child; chase all thy fears away!"
  My mother! When I learnt that thou wast dead,
Say, wast thou conscious of the tears I shed?
Hovered thy spirit o'er thy sorrowing son,
Wretch even then, life's journey just begun?
I heard the bell tolled on thy burial day;
I saw the hearse that bore thee slow away;
And, turning from my nursery window, drew
A long, long sigh, and wept a last adieu!
Thy maidens, grieved themselves at my concern,
Oft gave me promise of thy quick return.
What ardently I wished I long believed,
And, disappointed still, was still deceived;
By expectation every day beguiled,
Dupe of *to-morrow* even from a child.
Thus many a sad to-morrow came and went,
Till, all my stock of infant sorrow spent,
I learnt at last submission to my lot;
But, though I less deplored thee, ne'er forgot.

WINTER EVENING.

[From *The Task.*]

Now stir the fire and close the shutters fast,
Let fall the curtains, wheel the sofa round,
And while the bubbling and loud hissing urn
Throws up a steaming column, and the cups
That cheer but not inebriate wait on each,
So let us welcome peaceful evening in. . . .
O winter! ruler of the inverted year,
Thy scattered hair with sleet-like ashes filled,
Thy breath congealed upon thy lips, thy cheek
Fringed with a beard made white with other snows
Than those of age, thy forehead wrapped in clouds,
A leafless branch thy sceptre, and thy throne
A sliding car, indebted to no wheels,
But urged by storms along its slippery way;
I love thee, all unlovely as thou seemest,
And dreaded as thou art.   Thou holdest the sun
A prisoner in the yet undawning east,
Shortening his journey between morn and noon,
And hurrying him, impatient of his stay,
Down to the rosy west; but kindly still
Compensating his loss with added hours
Of social converse and instructive ease,
And gathering, at short notice, in one group
The family dispersed, and fixing thought,
Not less dispersed by daylight and its cares.
I crown thee king of intimate delights,
Fireside enjoyments, homo-born happiness,
And all the comforts that the lowly roof
Of undisturbed retirement, and the hours
Of long uninterrupted evening know.

MAN'S INHUMANITY TO MAN.

[From *The Task.*]

O for a lodge in some vast wilderness,
Some boundless contiguity of shade,
Where rumor of oppression and deceit,
Of unsuccessful or successful war
Might never reach me more! My ear is pained,

My soul is sick with every day's report
Of wrong or outrage with which earth is filled.
There is no flesh in man's obdurate heart,
It does not feel for man; the natural bond
Of brotherhood is severed as the flax
That falls asunder at the touch of fire.

ROBERT BURNS.

TAM O'SHANTER.

When chapman billies[1] leave the street,
And drouthy[2] neebors neebors meet,
As market-days are wearing late
An' folk begin to tak the gate;[3]
While we sit bousing at the nappy,[4]
An' getting fou[5] and unco[6] happy,
We think na on the lang Scots miles,
The mosses,[7] waters, slaps,[8] and styles,
That lie between us and our hame,
Whare sits our sulky, sullen dame,
Gathering her brows like gathering storm,
Nursing her wrath to keep it warm.
　　This truth fand honest Tam O'Shanter,
As he frae Ayr ae[9] night did canter,
(Auld Ayr, wham ne'er a town surpasses,
For honest men and bonnie lasses.)
　　O Tam! hadst thou but been sae wise
As ta'en thy ain wife Kate's advice!
She tauld thee weel thou wast a skellum,[10]
A blethering,[11] blustering, drunken blellum;[12]
That frae November till October,
Ae market-day thou wasna sober;
That ilka melder,[13] wi' the miller,
Thou sat as lang as thou had siller;
That every naig was ca'd[14] a shoe on,
The smith and thee gat roaring fou on;

[1] Peddler fellows.　[2] Thirsty.　[3] Road home.　[4] Ale.　[5] Full.　[6] Uncommonly.
[7] Swamps.　[8] Gaps in a hedge.　[9] One.　[10] Good-for-nothing.　[11] Babbling.
[12] Gossip.　[13] Every time corn was sent to the mill.　[14] Driven.

That at the Lord's house, even on Sunday,
Thou drank wi' Kirten Jean till Monday.
She prophesy'd that, late or soon,
Thou would be found deep drowned in Doon,
Or catch'd wi' warlocks in the mirk,
By Alloway's auld haunted kirk.

Ah, gentle dames! it gars me greet,[1]
To think how monie counsels sweet,
How monie lengthened, sage advices
The husband frae the wife despises! . .

Nae man can tether time or tide;
The hour approaches Tam maun[2] ride;
That hour, o' night's black arch the key-stane,
That dreary hour he mounts his beast in;
And sic[3] a night he taks the road in,
As ne'er poor sinner was abroad in.

The wind blew as 'twad blawn its last;
The rattling showers rose on the blast;
The speedy gleams the darkness swallowed;
Loud, deep, and lang the thunder bellowed:
That night, a child might understand,
The Deil had business on his hand.

(Mounted on his gray mare Maggie, Tam pursues his homeward way in safety till, reaching Kirk-Alloway, he sees the windows in a blaze, and, looking in, beholds a dance of witches, with Old Nick playing the fiddle. Most of the witches are any thing but inviting, but there is one winsome wench, called Nannie, who dances in a "cutty-sark," or short smock.)

But here my muse her wing maun cower;
Sic flights are far beyond her power;
To sing how Nannie lap and flang[4]
(A souple jade she was, and strang),
And how Tam stood like ane bewitched,
And thought his very e'en enriched.
Even Satan glowered and fidged fu' fain,[5]
And hotch'd[6] and blew wi' might and main;
Till first ae caper, syne[7] anither,
Tam tint[8] his reason a' thegither,
And roars out, "Weel done, Cutty-sark!"

[1] Makes me weep. [2] Must. [3] Such. [4] Leaped and flung. [5] Stared and fidgeted with eagerness. [6] Hitched about. [7] Then. [8] Lost.

And in an instant all was dark:
And scarcely had he Maggie rallied,
When out the hellish legion sallied.
　As bees bizz out wi' angry fyke,[1]
When plundering herds assail their byke;[2]
As open pussie's mortal foes,
When, pop! she starts before their nose;
As eager runs the market-crowd
When " Catch the thief!" resounds aloud.
So Maggie runs, the witches follow
Wi' monie an eldritch skreech and hollow,
　Ah, Tam! ah, Tam! thou'll get thy fairin'![3]
In hell they'll roast thee like a herrin'!
In vain thy Kate awaits thy comin':
Kate soon will be a woefu' woman.
Now do thy speedy utmost Meg,
And win the key-stane of the brig;[4]
There at them thou thy tail may toss,
A running stream they dare na cross,
But ere the key-stane she could make,
The fient[5] a tale she had to shake,
For Nannie, far before the rest,
Hard upon noble Maggie pressed,
And flew at Tam wi' furious ettle;[6]
But little wist she Maggie's mettle—
Ae spring brought aff her master hale,[7]
But left behind her ain gray tail;
The carlin[8] claught[9] her by the rump,
And left poor Maggie scarce a stump.

JOHN ANDERSON.

John Anderson, my jo,[10] John,
　When we were first acquent,
Your locks were like the raven,
　Your bonnie brow was brent;[11]
But now your brow is beld, John,
　Your locks are like the snow;
But blessings on your frosty pow,
　John Anderson, my jo.

[1] Fuss.   [2] Hive.   [3] Deserts.   [4] Bridge.   [5] Devil.   [6] Aim.   [7] Whole.
[8] Hag.   [9] Caught.   [10] Sweetheart.   [11] Smooth.

John Anderson, my jo, John,
  We clamb the hill thegither;
And monie a canty [1] day, John,
  We've had wi' ane anither:
Now we maun totter down, John,
  But hand in hand we'll go,
And sleep thegither at the foot,
  John Anderson, my jo.

WILLIAM WORDSWORTH.

SONNET.

The world is too much with us; late and soon,
Getting and spending, we lay waste our powers:
Little we see in Nature that is ours;
We have given our hearts away, a sordid boon!
This sea that bares her bosom to the moon;
The winds that will be howling at all hours,
And are up-gathered now like sleeping flowers—
  For this, for every thing, we are out of tune;
It moves us not. Great God! I'd rather be
A Pagan, suckled in a creed outworn,
So might I, standing on this pleasant lea,
Have glimpses that would make me less forlorn;
Have sight of Proteus rising from the sea,
Or hear old Triton blow his wreathèd horn.

THE PRE-EXISTENCE OF THE SOUL.

[From Ode on the Intimations of Immortality from Recollections of Early Childhood.]

Our birth is but a sleep, and a forgetting:
The soul that rises with us, our life's star,
  Hath had elsewhere its setting,
    And cometh from afar;
  Not in entire forgetfulness,
  And not in utter nakedness,
But trailing clouds of glory do we come
  From God, who is our home.

[1] Merry.

Heaven lies about us in our infancy:
Shades of the prison-house begin to close
    Upon the growing boy;
But he beholds the light, and whence it flows,
    He sees it in his joy.
The youth, who daily farther from the east
   Must travel, still is Nature's priest,
    And by the vision splendid
    Is on his way attended;
At length the man perceives it die away,
And fade into the light of common day. . . .

    O joy! that in our embers
     Is something that doth live,
    That nature yet remembers
     What was so fugitive!
The thought of our past years in me doth breed
Perpetual benedictions: not, indeed,
For that which is most worthy to be blest;
Delight and liberty, the simple creed
Of childhood, whether busy or at rest,
With new-fledged hope still fluttering in his breast—
   Not for these I raise
   The song of thanks and praise;
   But for those obstinate questionings
   Of sense and outward things,
   Fallings from us, vanishings;
   Blank misgivings of a creature
Moving about in worlds not realized,
High instincts, before which our mortal nature
Did tremble, like a guilty thing surprised:
   But for those first affections,
   Those shadowy recollections,
   Which, be they what they may,
Are yet the fountain light of all our day,
Are yet a master light of all our seeing;
   Uphold us, cherish, and have power to make
Our noisy years seem moments in the being
Of the eternal silence: truths that wake
    To perish never;
Which neither listlessness, nor mad endeavor,

Nor man nor boy,
Nor all that is at enmity with joy,
Cau utterly abolish or destroy.
   Hence, in a season of calm weather,
    Though inland far we be,
Our souls have sight of that immortal sea
    Which brought us hither;
   Can in a moment travel thither,
And see the children sport upon the shore,
And hear the mighty waters rolling evermore.

LUCY.

She dwelt among the untrodden ways
   Beside the springs of Dove, ·
A maid whom there were none to praise,
   And very few to love.

A violet by a mossy stone
   Half hidden from the eye:
Fair as a star, when only one
   Is shining in the sky.

She lived unknown, and few could know
   When Lucy ceased to be;
But she is in her grave, and, oh,
   The difference to me!

THE SOLITARY REAPER.

Behold her, single in the field,
   Yon solitary Highland lass!
Reaping and singing by herself;
   Stop here, or gently pass!
Alone she cuts and binds the grain,
And sings a melancholy strain;
O listen! for the vale profound
Is overflowing with the sound.

No nightingale did ever chant
   More welcome notes to weary bands
Of travelers in some shady haunt,
   Among Arabian sands.

A voice so thrilling ne'er was heard
In spring-time from the cuckoo-bird,
Breaking the silence of the seas
Among the farthest Hebrides.

Will no one tell me what she sings?
  Perhaps the plaintive numbers flow
For old, unhappy, far-off things,
  And battles long ago:
Or is it some more humble lay,
Familiar matter of to-day?
Some natural sorrow, loss, or pain,
That has been, and may be again?

Whate'er the theme, the maiden sang
  As if her song could have no ending,
I saw her singing at her work,
  And o'er the sickle bending;
I listened, motionless and still,
And, as I mounted up the hill,
The music in my heart I bore,
Long after it was heard no more.

SKATING AT NIGHT.
[From the *Prelude.*]

So through the darkness and the cold we flew,
And not a voice was idle; with the din
Smitten, the precipices rang aloud;
The leafless trees and every icy crag
Tinkled like iron; while far distant hills
Into the tumult sent an alien sound
Of melancholy not unnoticed, while the stars
Eastward were sparking clear, and in the west
The orange sky of evening died away.
Not seldom from the uproar I retired
Into a silent bay, or sportively
Glanced sideway, leaving the tumultuous throng,
To cut across the reflex of a star
That fled, and, flying still before me, gleamed
Upon the glassy plain; and oftentimes,
When we had given our bodies to the wind,

And all the shadowy banks on either side
Came sweeping through the darkness, spinning still
The rapid line of motion, then at once
Have I, reclining back upon my heels,
Stopped short; yet still the solitary cliffs
Wheeled by me—even as if the earth had rolled
With visible motion her diurnal round!
Behind me did they stretch in solemn train,
Feebler and feebler, and I stood and watched
Till all was tranquil as a dreamless sleep.

SAMUEL TAYLOR COLERIDGE.

THE SONG OF THE SPIRITS.

[From *The Ancient Mariner*.]

Sometimes, a-dropping from the sky,
  I heard the skylark sing;
Sometimes all little birds that are,
  How they seemed to fill the sea and air
With their sweet jargoning!

And now 'twas like all instruments,
  And now like a lonely flute;
And now it is an angel's song
  That makes the heavens be mute.

It ceased; yet still the sails made on
  A pleasant noise till noon,
A noise like of a hidden brook
  In the leafy month of June,
That to the sleeping woods all night
  Singeth a quiet tune.

THE LOVE OF ALL CREATURES.

[From the same.]

O wedding guest, this soul hath been
  Alone on a wide, wide sea:
So lonely 'twas that God himself
  Scarce seemèd there to be.

O sweeter than the marriage feast,
  'Tis sweeter far to me,
  To walk together to the kirk
  With a goodly company.

To walk together to the kirk,
  And all together pray,
While each to his great Father bends,
Old men and babes and loving friends,
  And youths and maidens gay.

Farewell, farewell! but this I tell
  To thee, thou wedding guest;
He prayeth well who loveth well
  Both man and bird and beast.

He prayeth best who loveth best
  All things both great and small;
For the dear God who loveth us,
  He made and loveth all.

ESTRANGEMENT OF FRIENDS.

[From *Christabel*.]

Alas! they had been friends in youth
But whispering tongues can poison truth,
And constancy lives in realms above,
  And life is thorny and youth is vain,
And to be wroth with one we love
  Doth work like madness in the brain.
And thus it fared, as I divine,
With Roland and Sir Leoline.
Each spake words of high disdain
And insult to his heart's best brother;
But never either found another
  To free the hollow heart from paining.
  They stood aloof, the scars remaining,
Like cliffs that had been rent asunder:
  A dreary sea now flows between,
But neither heat, nor frost, nor thunder
Can wholly do away, I ween,
The marks of that which once has been.

WALTER SCOTT.

NATIVE LAND.

[From *The Lay of the Last Minstrel.*]

Breathes there the man, with soul so dead,
Who never to himself hath said,
  This is my own, my native land?
Whose heart hath ne'er within him burned,
As .home his footsteps he hath turned,
  From wandering on a foreign strand?
If such there breathe, go mark him well;
For him no minstrel raptures swell;
High though his titles, proud his name,
Boundless his wealth as wish can claim;
Despite those titles, power, and pelf,
The wretch concentred all in self,
Living, shall forfeit fair renown,
And, doubly dying, shall go down
To the vile dust from whence he sprung,
Unwept, unhonored, and unsung.

O Caledonia! stern and wild,
Meet nurse for a poetic child!
Land of brown heath and shaggy wood,
Land of the mountain and the flood,
Land of my sires! what mortal hand
Can e'er untie the filial band
That knits me to thy rugged strand?
Still, as I view each well-known scene,
Think what is now, and what hath been,
Seems as, to me, of all bereft
Sole friends thy woods and streams are left:
And thus I love them better still
Even in extremity of ill.
By Yarrow's stream still let me stray,
Though none should guide my feeble way;
Still feel the breeze down Ettrick break,
Although it chill my withered cheek;
Still lay my head by Teviot's stone,
Though there, forgotten and alone,
The bard may draw his parting groan.

SUNSET ON THE BORDER.

[From *Marmion*.]

Day set on Norham's castled steep
And Tweed's fair river, broad and deep,
  And Cheviot's mountains lone:
The battled towers, the donjon keep,
The loop-hole grates where captives weep,
The flanking walls that round it sweep,
  In yellow luster shone.
The warriors on the turrets high,
Moving athwart the evening sky
  Seemed forms of giant height:
Their armor, as it caught the rays,
Flashed back again the western blaze,
  In lines of dazzling light.

St. George's banner, broad and gay,
Now faded, as the fading ray
  Less bright, and less was flung;
The evening gale had scarce the power
To wave it on the donjon tower,
  So heavily it hung.
The scouts had parted on their search,
  The castle gates were barred;
Above the gloomy portal arch,
Timing his footsteps to a march,
  The warden kept his guard;
Low humming, as he passed along,
Some ancient border-gathering song.

PROUD MAISIE.

Proud Maisie is in the wood
  Walking so early;
Sweet Robin sits on the bush
  Singing so rarely.

"Tell me, thou bonny bird,
  When shall I marry me?"
—"When six braw[1] gentlemen
  Kirkward shall carry ye."

[1] Brave, fine.

" Who makes the bridal bed,
 Birdie, say truly ? "
" The gray-headed sexton
 That delves the grave duly.

" The glow-worm o'er grave and stone
 Shall light thee steady;
The owl from the steeple sing
 Welcome, proud lady."

PIBROCH OF DONUIL DHU.

Pibroch of Donuil Dhu, Pibroch of Donuil,
Wake thy wild voice anew, summon Clan-Conuil.
Come away, come away, hark to the summons!
Come in your war array, gentles and commons.

Come from deep glen and from mountain so rocky,
The war-pipe and pennon are at Inverlochy.
Come every hill-plaid and true heart that wears one,
Come every steel blade and strong hand that bears one.

Leave untended the herd, the flock without shelter;
Leave the corpse uninterred, the bride at the altar;
Leave the deer, leave the steer, leave nets and barges:
Come with your fighting gear, broadswords and targes.

Come as the winds come when forests are rended;
Come as the waves come when navies are stranded;
Faster come, faster come; faster and faster,
Chief, vassal, page and groom, tenant and master.

Fast they come, fast they come; see how they gather!
Wide waves the eagle plume blended with heather.
Cast your plaids, draw your blades, forward each man set!
Pibroch of Donuil Dhu, knell for the onset!

PERCY BYSSHE SHELLEY.

LINES TO AN INDIAN AIR.

I arise from dreams of thee
 In the first sweet sleep of night,
When the winds are breathing low
 And the stars are shining bright.

I arise from dreams of thee,
  And a spirit in my feet
Has led me—who knows how?—
  To thy chamber-window, sweet.

The wandering airs they faint
  On the dark, the silent stream:
The champak odours fail
  Like sweet thoughts in a dream;
The nightingale's complaint,
  It dies upon her heart,
As I must die on thine,
  O belovèd as thou art!

O lift me from the grass!
  I die, I faint, I fail!
Let thy love in kisses rain
  On my lips and eyelids pale.
My cheek is cold and white, alas!
  My heart beats loud and fast:
O! press it close to thine again,
  Where it will break at last.

VENICE.

[From *Lines Written in the Euganean Hills.*]

Sun-girt city, thou hast been
Ocean's child, and then his queen;
Now is come a darker day
And thou soon must be his prey,
If the power that raised thee here
Hallow so thy watery bier.
A less drear ruin then than now,
With thy conquest-branded brow
Stooping to the slave of slaves
From thy throne among the waves,
Wilt thou be, when the sea-mew
Flies, as once before it flew,
O'er thine isles depopulate,
And all is in its ancient state;
Save where many a palace gate
With green sea-flowers overgrown,
Like a rock of ocean's own

Topples o'er the abandoned sea
As the tides change sullenly.
The fisher on his watery way
Wandering at the close of day,
Will spread his sail and seize his oar
Till he pass the gloomy shore,
Lest thy dead should, from their sleep
Bursting o'er the starlight deep,
Lead a rapid masque of death
O'er the waters of his path.

A LAMENT.

O world! O life! O time!
On whose last steps I climb,
   Trembling at that where I had stood before,
When will return the glory of your prime?
   No more—O, never more!

Out of the day and night
A joy has taken flight;
   Fresh spring and summer and winter hoar
Move my faint heart with grief, but with delight
   No more—O, never more!

THE POET'S DREAM.

[From *Prometheus Unbound*.]

On a poet's lips I slept
Dreaming like a love-adept
In the sound his breathing kept.
Nor seeks nor finds he mortal blisses,
But feeds on the aerial kisses
Of shapes that haunt thought's wildernesses.
He will watch from dawn to gloom
The lake-reflected sun illume
The yellow bees in the ivy bloom,
Nor heed nor see what things they be;
But from these create he can
Forms more real than living man,
   Nurslings of immortality.

GEORGE GORDON BYRON.

ELEGY ON THYRZA.

And thou art dead, as young and fair
   As aught of mortal birth;
And form so soft and charms so rare,
   Too soon returned to earth:
Though earth received them in her bed,
And o'er the spot the crowd may tread
   In carelessness or mirth,
There is an eye which could not brook
A moment on that grave to look.

I will not ask where thou liest low
   Nor gaze upon the spot;
There flowers or weeds at will may grow,
   So I behold them not:
It is enough for me to prove
That what I loved and long must love
   Like common earth can rot;
To me there needs no stone to tell
'Tis nothing that I loved so well.

Yet did I love thee to the last
   As fervently as thou,
Who didst not change through all the past
   And canst not alter now.
The love where death has set his seal
Nor age can chill, nor rival steal,
   Nor falsehood disavow:
And, what were worse, thou canst not see
Or wrong, or change, or fault in me.

The better days of life were ours;
   The worst can be but mine:
The sun that cheers, the storm that lowers,
   Shall never more be thine.
The silence of that dreamless sleep
I envy now too much to weep,
   Nor need I to repine
That all those charms have passed away,
I might have watched through long decay.

The flower in ripened bloom unmatched
  Must fall the earliest prey;
Though by no hand untimely snatched,
  The leaves must drop away:
And yet it were a greater grief
To watch it withering leaf by leaf,
  Than see it plucked to-day;
Since earthly eye but ill can bear
To trace the change to foul from fair.

I know not if I could have borne
  To see thy beauties fade;
The night that followed such a morn
  Had worn a deeper shade:
Thy day without a cloud hath past,
And thou wert lovely to the last,
  Extinguished, not decayed;
As stars that shoot along the sky
Shine brightest as they fall from high.

As once I wept, if I could weep,
  My tears might well be shed,
To think I was not near to keep
  One vigil o'er thy bed;
To gaze, how fondly! on thy face,
To fold thee in a faint embrace,
  Uphold thy drooping head;
And show that love, however vain,
Nor thou nor I can feel again.

Yet how much less it were to gain,
  Though thou hast left me free,
The loveliest things that still remain,
  Than thus remember thee!
The all of thine that cannot die
Through dark and dread Eternity,
  Returns again to me,
And more thy buried love endears
Than aught, except its living years.

THE BALL AT BRUSSELS ON THE NIGHT BEFORE WATERLOO.

[From *Childe Harold*.]

There was a sound of revelry by night,
And Belgium's capital had gathered there
Her beauty and her chivalry, and bright
The lamps shone o'er fair women and brave men:
A thousand hearts beat happily; and when
Music arose with its voluptuous swell,
Soft eyes looked love to eyes which spake again,
And all went merry as a marriage-bell;
But hush! hark! a deep sound strikes like a rising knell!

Did ye not hear it? No; 'twas but the wind,
Or the car rattling o'er the stony street.
On with the dance! let joy be unconfined!
No sleep till morn when youth and pleasure meet
To chase the glowing hours with flying feet—
But hark! that heavy sound breaks in once more,
As if the clouds its echo would repeat;
And nearer, clearer, deadlier than before!
Arm! arm! it is—it is—the cannon's opening roar! . . .

Ah! then and there was hurrying to and fro,
And gathering tears, and tremblings of distress,
And cheeks all pale which but an hour ago
Blushed at the praise of their own loveliness;
And there were sudden partings, such as press
The life from out young hearts, and choking sighs
Which ne'er might be repeated: who could guess
If evermore should meet those mutual eyes,
Since upon night so sweet such awful morn could rise?

And there was mounting in hot haste: the steed,
The mustering squadron, and the clattering car
Went pouring forward with impetuous speed,
And swiftly forming in the ranks of war;
And the deep thunder peal on peal afar;

And near, the beat of the alarming drum
Roused up the soldier ere the morning star;
While thronged the citizens with terror dumb,
Or whispering, with white lips, "The foe! They come! they come!"

And wild and high the "Cameron's gathering" rose,
The war-note of Lochiel, which Albyn's hills
Have heard, and heard, too, have her Saxon foes:
How in the noon of night that pibroch thrills,
Savage and shrill!   But with the breath which fills
Their mountain pipe, so fill the mountaineers
With the fierce native daring which instils
The stirring memory of a thousand years;
And Evan's, Donald's fame rings in each clansman's ears.

And Ardennes waves above them her green leaves,
Dewy with nature's tear-drops, as they pass,
Grieving, if aught inanimate e'er grieves,
Over the unreturning brave—alas!
Ere evening to be trodden like the grass
Which now beneath them, but above shall grow,
In its next verdure, when this fiery mass
Of living valor rolling on the foe,
And burning with high hope, shall moulder cold and low.

JOHN KEATS.

ODE ON A GRECIAN URN.

Thou still unravished bride of quietness!
  Thou foster-child of Silence and slow Time,
Sylvan historian, who canst thus express
  A flowery tale more sweetly than our rhyme;
What leaf-fringed legend haunts about thy shape
    Of deities or mortals, or of both,
      In Tempe or the dales of Arcady?
  What men or gods are these?   What maidens loath?
What mad pursuit?   What struggle to escape?
    What pipes and timbrels?   What wild ecstasy?

Heard melodies are sweet; but those unheard
　Are sweeter; therefore, ye soft pipes, play on;
Not to the sensual ear, but, more endeared,
　Pipe to the spirit ditties of no tone:
Fair youth beneath the trees, thou canst not leave
　　Thy song, nor ever can those trees be bare;
　　Bold lover, never, never canst thou kiss,
Though winning near the goal—yet do not grieve:
　　She cannot fade though thou hast not thy bliss,
　Forever wilt thou love, and she be fair!

Ah, happy, happy boughs! that cannot shed
　Your leaves, nor ever bid the Spring adieu;
And happy melodist, unwearied
　Forever piping songs forever new;
More happy love! more happy, happy love!
　　Forever warm and still to be enjoyed,
　　Forever panting and forever young;
All breathing human passion far above,
　　That leaves a heart high sorrowful and cloyed,
　　A burning forehead, and a parching tongue.

Who are these coming to the sacrifice?
　To what green altar, O mysterious priest,
Lead'st thou that heifer lowing at the skies,
　And all her silken flanks with garlands drest?
What little town by river or sea-shore,
　Or mountain built with peaceful citadel,
　　Is emptied of its folk this pious morn?
Ah! little town, thy streets forever more
　Will silent be; and not a soul to tell
　　Why thou art desolate can e'er return.

O Attic shape! Fair attitude! with brede
　Of marble men and maidens overwrought,
With forest branches and the trodden weed;
　Thou, silent form, dost tease us out of thought
As doth eternity: Cold Pastoral!
　When old age shall this generation waste,
　　Thou shalt remain, in midst of other woe
　　Than ours, a friend to man, to whom thou say'st,
"Beauty is truth, truth beauty"—that is all
　Ye know on earth, and all ye need to know.

MADELINE.

[From *The Eve of St. Agnes.*]

Out went the taper as she hurried in;
Its little smoke in pallid moonshine died;
She closed the door, she panted, all akin
To spirits of the air and visions wide;
No uttered syllable, or, woe betide!
But to her heart her heart was voluble,
Paining with eloquence her balmy side;
As though a tongueless nightingale should swell
Her throat in vain, and die, heart-stifled in her dell.

A casement high and triple-arched there was,
All garlanded with carven imageries
Of fruits and flowers and bunches of knot-grass,
And diamonded with panes of quaint device,
Innumerable of stains and splendid dyes
As are the tiger-moth's deep-damasked wings;
And in the midst, 'mong thousand heraldries,
And twilight saints, and dim emblazonings,
A shielded scutcheon blushed with blood of queens and kings.

Full on this casement shone the wintry moon,
And threw warm gules on Madeline's fair breast,
As down she knelt for heaven's grace and boon;
Rose-bloom fell on her hands, together pressed,
And on her silver cross soft amethyst,
And on her hair a glory, like a saint:
She seemed a splendid angel, newly dressed,
Save wings, for heaven: Porphyro grew faint:
She knelt, so pure a thing, so free from mortal taint.

CHARLES DICKENS.

BOB SAWYER'S BACHELOR PARTY.

[From *Pickwick Papers.*]

After supper another jug of punch was put on the table, together with a paper of cigars and a couple of bottles of spirits. Then there was an awful pause; and this awful pause was occasioned by a very common occurrence in this sort of places, but a very embarrassing one, notwithstanding.

The fact is that the girl was washing the glasses. The establishment boasted four; we do not record this circumstance as at all derogatory to Mrs. Raddle, for there was never a lodging-house yet that was not short of glasses. The landlady's glasses were little thin blown-glass tumblers, and those which had been borrowed from the public-house were great, dropsical, bloated articles, each supported on a huge gouty leg. This would have been in itself sufficient to have possessed the company with the real state of affairs; but the young woman of all work had prevented the possibility of any misconception arising in the mind of any gentleman upon the subject, by forcibly dragging every man's glass away long before he had finished his beer, and audibly stating, despite the winks and interruptions of Mr. Bob Sawyer, that it was to be conveyed down-stairs and washed forthwith. . . .

The sight of the tumblers restored Bob Sawyer to a degree of equanimity which he had not possessed since his interview with his landlady. His face brightened up, and he began to feel quite convivial.

"Now, Betsy," said Mr. Bob Sawyer, with great suavity, and dispersing, at the same time, the tumultuous little mob of glasses that the girl had collected in the center of the table; " Now, Betsy, the warm water; be brisk, there's a good girl."

"You can't have no warm water," replied Betsy.

"No warm water!" exclaimed Mr. Bob Sawyer.

"No," said the girl, with a shake of the head which expressed a more decided negative than the most copious language could have conveyed. "Missis Raddle said you wasn't to have none."

The surprise depicted on the countenances of his guests imparted new courage to the host.

"Bring up the warm water instantly—instantly!" said Mr. Bob Sawyer, with desperate sternness.

"No; I can't," replied the girl. "Missis Raddle raked out the kitchen fire afore she went to bed, and locked up the kettle."

"O, never mind, never mind. Pray don't disturb yourself about such a trifle," said Mr. Pickwick, observing the conflict of Bob Sawyer's passions, as depicted on his countenance, "cold water will do very well."

"O, admirably," said Mr. Benjamin Allen.

"My landlady is subject to slight attacks of mental derangement," remarked Bob Sawyer, with a ghastly smile; "I fear I must give her warning."

"No, don't," said Ben Allen.

"I fear I must," said Bob, with heroic firmness. "I'll pay her what I owe her and give her warning to-morrow morning."

Poor fellow! How devoutly he wished he could! . . . It was at the end of the chorus to the first verse that Mr. Pickwick held up his hand in a listening attitude, and said, as soon as silence was restored, "Hush! I beg your pardon. I thought I heard somebody calling from up-stairs."

A profound silence immediately ensued, and Mr. Bob Sawyer was observed to turn pale.

"I think I hear it now," said Mr. Pickwick. "Have the goodness to open the door."

The door was no sooner opened than all doubt on the subject was removed.

"Mr. Sawyer—Mr. Sawyer," screamed a voice from the two-pair landing.

"It's my landlady," said Bob Sawyer, looking round him with great dismay. "Yes, Mrs. Raddle."

"What do you mean by this, Mr. Sawyer?" replied the voice, with great shrillness and rapidity of utterance. "'Aint it enough to be swindled out of one's rent, and money lent out of pocket besides, and abused and insulted by your friends that dares to call themselves men, without having the house turned out of window, and noise enough made to bring the fire-engines here at two o'clock in the morning? Turn them wretches away."

"You ought to be ashamed of yourselves," said the voice of Mr. Raddle, which appeared to proceed from beneath some distant bed-clothes.

"Ashamed of themselves!" said Mrs. Raddle. "Why don't you go down and knock 'em every one down-stairs? You would, if you was a man."

"I should if I was a dozen men, my dear," replied Mr. Raddle, pacifically; "but they've rather the advantage of me in numbers, my dear."

"Ugh, you coward!" replied Mrs. Raddle, with supreme contempt. "*Do* you mean to turn them wretches out, or not, Mr. Sawyer?"

"They're going, Mrs. Raddle, they're going," said the miserable Bob. "I'm afraid you'd better go," said Mr. Bob Sawyer to his friends. "I *thought* you were making too much noise."

"It's a very unfortunate thing," said the prim man. "Just as we were getting so comfortable, too." The fact was that the prim man was just beginning to have a dawning recollection of the story he had forgotten.

"It's hardly to be borne," said the prim man, looking round; "hardly to be borne, is it?"

"Not to be endured," replied Jack Hopkins; "let's have the other verse, Bob; come, here goes."

"No, no, Jack, don't," interposed Bob Sawyer; "it's a capital song, but I am afraid we had better not have the other verse. They are very violent people, the people of the house."

"Shall I step up-stairs and pitch into the landlord?" inquired Hopkins, "or keep on ringing the bell, or go and groan on the staircase? You may command me, Bob."

"I am very much indebted to you for your friendship and good-nature,

Hopkins," said the wretched Mr. Bob Sawyer, "but I am of opinion that the best plan to avoid any farther dispute is for us to break up at once."

"Now, Mr. Sawyer," screamed the shrill voice of Mrs. Raddle, "are them brutos going?"

"They're only looking for their hats, Mrs. Raddle," said Bob; "they are going directly."

"Going!" said Mrs. Raddle, thrusting her night-cap over the bannisters, just as Mr. Pickwick, followed by Mr. Tupman, emerged from the sitting-room. "Going! What did they ever come for."

"My dear ma'am," remonstrated Mr. Pickwick, looking up.

"Get along with you, you old wretch!" replied Mrs. Raddle, hastily withdrawing her night-cap. "Old enough to be his grandfather, you villain! You're worse than any of 'em."

Mr. Pickwick found it in vain to protest his innocence, so hurried downstairs into the street, whither he was closely followed by Mr. Tupman, Mr. Winkle, and Mr. Snodgrass.

WILLIAM MAKEPIECE THACKERAY.

Becky Goes to Court and Dines at Gaunt House.
[From *Vanity Fair*.]

The particulars of Becky's costume were in the newspapers—feathers, lappets, superb diamonds, and all the rest. Lady Crackenbury read the paragraph in bitterness of spirit, and discoursed to her followers about the airs which that woman was giving herself. Mrs. Bute Crawley and her young ladies in the country had a copy of the *Morning Post* from town, and gave a vent to their honest indignation. "If you had been sandy-haired, green-eyed, and a French rope-dancer's daughter," Mrs. Bute said to her eldest girl (who, on the contrary, was a very swarthy, short, and snub-nosed young lady), "you might have had superb diamonds, forsooth, and have been presented at court by your cousin, the Lady Jane. But you're only a gentlewoman, my poor dear child. You have only some of the best blood in England in your veins, and good principles and piety for your portion. I myself, the wife of a baronet's younger brother, too, never thought of such a thing as going to court—nor would other people if good Queen Charlotte had been alive." In this way the worthy rectoress consoled herself; and her daughters sighed, and sat over the *Peerage* all night. . . .

When the ladies of Gaunt House were at breakfast that morning Lord Steyne (who took his chocolate in private, and seldom disturbed the females of his household, or saw them except upon public days, or when they crossed each other in the hall, or when from his pit-box at the opera he surveyed them in their box in the grand tier)—his lordship, we say, appeared among the ladies and the children, who were assembled over the tea and toast, and a battle royal ensued apropos of Rebecca.

"My Lady Steyne," he said, "I want to see the list for your dinner on Friday; and I want you, if you please, to write a card for Colonel and Mrs. Crawley."

"Blanche writes them," Lady Steyne said, in a flutter. "Lady Gaunt writes them."

"I will not write to that person," Lady Gaunt said, a tall and stately lady, who looked up for an instant and then down again after she had spoken. It was not good to meet Lord Steyne's eyes for those who had offended him.

"Send the children out of the room. Go!" said he, pulling at the bell-rope. The urchins, always frightened before him, retired; their mother would have followed too. "Not you," he said. "You stop."

"My Lady Steyne," he said, "once more, will you have the goodness to go to the desk and write that card for your dinner on Friday?"

"My Lord, I will not be present at it," Lady Gaunt said; "I will go home."

"I wish you would, and stay there. You will find the bailiffs at Bare-acres very pleasant company; and I shall be freed from lending money to your relations, and from your own damned tragedy airs. Who are you, to give orders here? You have no money. You've got no brains. You were here to have children, and you have not had any. Gaunt's tired of you; and George's wife is the only person in the family who doesn't wish you were dead. Gaunt would marry again if you were."

"I wish I were," her ladyship answered, with tears and rage in her eyes.

"You, forsooth, must give yourself airs of virtue; while my wife, who is an immaculate saint, as every body knows, and never did wrong in her life, has no objection to meet my young friend, Mrs. Crawley. My Lady Steyne knows that appearances are sometimes against the best of women; that lies are often told about the most innocent of them. Pray, madam, shall I tell you some little anecdotes about my Lady Bareacres, your mamma?"

"You may strike me if you like, sir, or hit any cruel blow," Lady Gaunt said. To see his wife and daughter suffering always put his lordship into a good humor.

"My sweet Blanche," he said, "I am a gentleman, and never lay my hand upon a woman, save in the way of kindnesss. I only wish to correct little faults in your character. You women are too proud, and sadly lack humility, as Father Mole, I'm sure, would tell my Lady Steyne if he were here. You musn't give yourselves airs: you must be meek and humble, my blessings. For all Lady Steyne knows, this calumniated, simple, good-humored Mrs. Crawley is quite innocent—even more innocent than herself.

Her husband's character is not good, but it is as good as Bareacres's, who has played a little and not payed a great deal, who cheated you out of the only legacy you ever had, and left you a pauper on my hands. And Mrs. Crawley is not very well born; but she is not worse than Fanny's illustrious ancestor, the first de la Jones."

"The money which I brought into the family, sir," Lady George cried out—

"You purchased a contingent reversion with it," the marquis said, darkly. "If Gaunt dies, your husband may come to his honors; your little boys may inherit them, and who knows what besides? In the meanwhile, ladies, be as proud and virtuous as you like abroad, but don't give *me* any airs. As for Mrs. Crawley's character, I sha'n't demean myself or that most spotless and perfectly irreproachable lady, by even hinting that it even requires a defense. You will be pleased to receive her with the utmost cordiality, as you will receive all persons whom I present in this house. This house?" He broke out with a laugh. "Who is the master of it, and what is it? This temple of virtue belongs to me. And if I invite all Newgate or all Bedlam here, by —— they shall be welcome."

After this vigorous allocution, to one of which sort Lord Steyne treated his "Hareem" whenever symptoms of insubordination appeared in his household, the crestfallen women had nothing for it but to obey. Lady Gaunt wrote the invitation which his lordship required, and she and her mother-in-law drove in person, and with bitter and humiliated hearts, to leave the cards on Mrs. Rawdon, the reception of which caused that innocent woman so much pleasure.

GEORGE ELIOT.

PASSAGES FROM ADAM BEDE.

It was a wood of beeches and limes, with here and there a light, silver-stemmed birch—just the sort of wood most haunted by the nymphs; you see their white sun-lit limbs gleaming athwart the boughs or peeping from behind the smooth-sweeping outline of a tall lime; you hear their soft liquid laughter—but if you look with a too curious sacrilegious eye they vanish behind the silvery beeches, they make you believe that their voice was only a running brooklet, perhaps they metamorphose themselves into a tawny squirrel that scampers away and mocks you from the topmost bough. Not a grove with measured grass or rolled gravel for you to tread upon, but with narrow, hollow-shaped earthy paths, edged with faint dashes of delicate moss—paths which look as if they were made by the free will of the trees and underwood, moving reverently aside to look at the tall queen of the white-footed nymphs.

There are various orders of beauty, causing men to make fools of themselves in various styles, from the desperate to the sheepish; but there is one order of beauty which seems made to turn the heads not only of men, but of all intelligent mammals, even of women. It is a beauty like that of kittens, or very small downy ducks making gentle rippling noises with their soft bills, or babies just beginning to toddle and to engage in conscious mischief—a beauty with which you can never be angry, but that you feel ready to crush for inability to comprehend the state of mind into which it throws you. . . . It is of little use for me to tell you that Hetty's cheek was like a rose-petal, that dimples played about her pouting lips, that her large dark eyes hid a soft roguishness under their long lashes, and that her curly hair, though all pushed back under her round cap while she was at work, stole back in dark delicate rings on her forehead, and about her white shell-like ears; it is of little use for me to say how lovely was the contour of her pink-and-white neckerchief, tucked into her low plum-colored stuff bodice, or how the linen butter-making apron, with its bib, seemed a thing to be imitated in silk by duchesses, since it fell in such charming lines, or how her brown stockings and thick-soled buckled shoes lost all that clumsiness which they must certainly have had when empty of her foot and ankle—of little use unless you have seen a woman who affected you as Hetty affected her beholders, for otherwise, though you might conjure up the image of a lovely woman, she would not in the least resemble that distracting kitten-like maiden. I might mention all the divine charms of a bright spring day, but if you had never in your life utterly forgotten yourself in straining your eyes after the mounting lark, or in wandering through the still lanes when the fresh-opened blossoms fill them with a sacred, silent beauty like that of fretted aisles, where would be the use of my descriptive catalogue? I could never make you know what I meant by a bright spring day. Hetty's was a spring-tide beauty; it was the beauty of young frisking things, round-limbed, gambolling, circumventing you by a false air of innocence—the innocence of a young star-browed calf, for example, that, being inclined for a promenade out of bounds, leads you a severe steeple-chase over hedge and ditch, and only comes to a stand in the middle of a bog.

Family likeness has often a deep sadness in it. Nature, that great tragic dramatist, knits us together by bone and muscle, and divides us by the subtler web of our brains; blends yearning and repulsion, and ties us by our heart-strings to the beings that jar us at every movement. We hear a voice with the very cadence of our own uttering the thoughts we despise; we see eyes—ah! so like our mother's—averted from us in cold alienation; and our last darling child startles us with the air and gestures of the sister we parted from in bitterness long years ago. The father to whom we owe our best heritage—the mechanical instinct, the keen sensibility to harmony, the un-conscious skill of the modeling hand—galls us, and puts us to shame by his daily errors. The long-lost mother, whose face we begin to see in the glass as our own wrinkles come, once fretted our young souls with her anxious humors and irrational persistence.

It was to Adam the time that a man can least forget in after life—the time when he believes that the first woman he has ever loved betrays by a slight something—a word, a tone, a glance, the quivering of a lip or an eye-lid—that she is at least beginning to love him in return. . . . So unless our early gladness vanishes utterly from our memory, we can never recall the joy with which we laid our heads on our mother's bosom or rode on our father's back in childhood; doubtless that joy is wrought up into our nature, or as the sunlight of long-past mornings is wrought up into the soft mellow-ness of the apricot; but it is gone forever from our imagination as we can only *believe* in the joy of childhood. But the first glad moment in our first love is a vision which returns to us to the last, and brings with it a thrill of feeling intense and special as the recurrent sensation of a sweet odor breathed in a far-off hour of happiness. It is a memory that gives a more ex-quisite touch to tenderness, that feeds the madness of jealousy, and adds the last keenness to the agony of despair.

THOMAS CARLYLE.

MIDNIGHT IN THE CITY.

[From *Sartor Resartus.*]

"*Ach, mein Lieber!*" said he once, at midnight, when we had returned from the Coffee-house in rather earnest talk, "it is a true sublimity to dwell here. These fringes of lamp-light, struggling up through smoke and thousand-fold exhalation, some fathoms into the ancient reign of night, what thinks Boötes of them, as he leads his Hunting-Dogs over the Zenith in their leash of sidereal fire? That stifled hum of Midnight, when Traffic has lain down to rest; and the chariot-wheels of Vanity, still rolling here and there through distant streets, are bearing her to Halls roofed-in and lighted to the due pitch for her; and only Vice and Misery, to prowl or to moan like night-birds, are abroad: that hum, I say, like the stertorous, unquiet slumber of sick Life, is heard in Heaven! O, under that hideous coverlet of vapours and putrefactions and unimaginable gases, what a Fermenting-vat lies simmering and hid! The joyful and the sorrowful are there; men are dying there, men are being born: men are praying,—on the other side of a brick partition men are cursing; and around them all is the vast, void Night. The proud Grandee still lingers in his perfumed saloons, or reposes within damask curtains ; Wretchedness cowers into truckle-beds, or shivers hunger-stricken into its lair of straw: in obscure cellars, *Rouge-et-Noir* languidly emits its voice-of-destiny to haggard, hungry Villains; while Councillors of State sit plotting, and playing their high chess-game, whereof the pawns are Men. The Lover whispers his mistress that the coach is ready; and she, full of hope and fear, glides down to fly with him over the borders: the Thief, still more silently, sets-to his picklocks and crowbars, or lurks in wait till the watchmen first snore in their boxes. Gay mansions, with supper-rooms and dancing-rooms, are full of light and music and high-swelling hearts; but, in the Condemned Cells, the pulse of life beats tremulous and faint, and blood-shot eyes look out through the darkness, which is around and within, for the light of a stern last morning. Six men are to be hanged on the morrow: comes no hammering from the *Rabenstein ?*— their gallows must even now be o' building. Upward of five hundred thousand two-legged animals without feathers lie round us in horizontal positions; their heads all in night-caps and full of the foolishest dreams. Riot cries aloud, and staggers and swaggers in his rank dens of shame; and the Mother, with streaming hair, kneels over her pallid dying infant, whose cracked lips only her tears now moisten.—All these heaped and huddled together, with nothing but a little carpentry and masonry between them ;— crammed in, like salted fish in their barrel;—or weltering, shall I say, like an Egyptian pitcher of tamed Vipers, each struggling to get its *head above* the other: *such* work goes on under that smoke-counterpane!—But I, *mein Werther*, sit above it all; I am alone with the Stars."

GHOSTS.

[From the Same.]

Again, could any thing be more miraculous than an actual authentic Ghost? The English Johnson longed, all his life to see one; but could not, though he went to Cock Lane, and thence to the church-vaults, and tapped on coffins. Foolish Doctor ! Did he never, with the mind's eye as well as with the body's, look around him into that full tide of human Life he so loved ; did he never so much as look into himself? The good Doctor was a Ghost, as actual and authentic as heart could wish; well-nigh a million of Ghosts were travelling the streets by his side. Once more I say, sweep away the illusion of Time; compress the threescore years into three minutes: what else was he, what else are we ? Are we not Spirits, that are shaped into a body, into an Appearance; and that fade away again into air, and Invisibility?

This is no metaphor, it is a simple scientific *fact:* we start out of Nothing-
ness, take figure, and are Apparitions; round us, as round the veriest spec-
tre, is Eternity; and to Eternity minutes are as years and æons.   Come there
not tones of Love and Faith, as from celestial harp-strings, like the Song of
beatified souls?   And again, do not we squeak and gibber (in our discord-
ant, screech-owlish debatings and recriminatings); and glide bodeful and
feeble and fearful; or uproar (*poltern*), and revel in our mad Dance of the
Dead,—till the scent of the morning-air summons us to our still Home; and
dreamy Night becomes awake and Day?   Where now is Alexander of
Macedon: does the steel Host, that yelled in fierce battle-shouts, at Issus
and Arbela, remain behind him; or have they all vanished utterly, even
as perturbed Goblins must?   Napoleon too, and his Moscow Retreats and
Austerlitz Campaigns!   Was it all other than the veriest Spectre-hunt;
which has now, with its howling tumult that made Night hideous, flitted
away?—Ghosts! There are nigh a thousand million walking the Earth openly
at noontide; some half-hundred have vanished from it, some half-hundred
have arisen in it, ere thy watch ticks once. . . .

   Thus, like some wild-flaming, wild-thundering train of Heaven's Artillery,
does this mysterious Mankind thunder and flame, in long-drawn, quick-
succeeding grandeur, through the unknown Deep. Thus, like a God-created,
fire-breathing Spirit-host, we emerge from the Inane; haste stormfully
across the astonished Earth; then plunge again into the Inane.   Earth's
mountains are levelled, and her seas filled up, in our passage: can the Earth,
which is but dead and a vision, resist Spirits which have reality and are
alive?   On the hardest adamant some foot-print of us is stamped in; the
last Rear of the host will read traces of the earliest Van.   But whence?—O
Heaven, whither? Sense knows not; Faith knows not; only that it is
through Mystery to Mystery, from God and to God.

                    "We *are such stuff*
           As Dreams are made of, and our little Life
           Is rounded with a sleep!"

                    ————

                 ALFRED TENNYSON.
         The Days That Are no More.
              [From *The Princess.*]
        Tears, idle tears, I know not what they mean,
        Tears from the depth of some divine despair
        Rise in the heart and gather to the eyes,
        In looking on the happy autumn fields,
        And thinking of the days that are no more. . . .

Ah, sad and strange as in dark summer dawns
The earliest pipe of half-awakened birds
To dying ears, when unto dying eyes
The casement slowly grows a glimmering square;
So sad, so strange, the days that are no more.

Dear as remembered kisses after death,
And sweet as those by hopeless fancy feigned
On lips that are for others; deep as love,
Deep as first love, and wild with all regret;
O death in life, the days that are no more.

THE PASSING OF ARTHUR.

[From *Morte D'Arthur*.]

And slowly answered Arthur from the barge:
" The old order changeth, yielding place to new,
And God fulfills himself in many ways,
Lest one good custom should corrupt the world.
Comfort thyself: what comfort is in me?
I have lived my life, and that which I have done
May He within himself make pure! but thou,
If thou shouldst never see my face again,
Pray for my soul. More things are wrought by prayer
Than this world dreams of. Wherefore, let thy voice
Rise like a fountain for me night and day.
For what are men better than sheep or goats
That nourish a blind life within the brain,
If, knowing God, they lift not hands of prayer
Both for themselves and those who call them friend?
For so the whole round earth is every way
Bound by gold chains about the feet of God.
But now farewell: I am going a long way
With these thou seest—if indeed I go—
(For all my mind is clouded with a doubt)
To the island-valley of Avilion;
Where falls not hail, or rain, or any snow,
Nor ever wind blows loudly; but it lies
Deep-meadow'd, happy, fair with orchard-lawns,
And bowery hollows crowned with summer sea,
Where I will heal me of my grievous wound."

So said he, and the barge with oar and sail
Moved from the brink, like some full-breasted swan
That, fluting a wild carol ere her death,
Ruffles her pure cold plume, and takes the flood
With swarthy webs.   Long stood Sir Bedivere
Revolving many memories, till the hull
Looked one black dot against the verge of dawn,
And on the mere the wailing died away.

BUGLE SONG.

[From *The Princess*.]

The splendour falls on castle walls
    And snowy summits old in story:
The long light shakes across the lakes
    And the wild cataract leaps in glory.
Blow, bugle, blow, set the wild echoes flying,
Blow, bugle; answer, echoes, dying, dying, dying.

O hark, O hear ! how thin and clear,
    And thinner, clearer, farther going !
O sweet and far from cliff and scar
    The horns of Elfland faintly blowing !
Blow, let us hear the purple glens replying:
Blow, bugle; answer, echoes, dying, dying, dying.

O love, they die in yon rich sky,
    They faint on hill or field or river:
Our echoes roll from soul to soul,
    And grow for ever and for ever.
Blow, bugle, blow, set the wild echoes flying,
And answer, echoes, answer, dying, dying, dying.

BREAK, BREAK, BREAK.

Break, break, break
    On thy cold gray stones, O sea !
And I would that my tongue could utter
    The thoughts that arise in me.

O well for the fisherman's boy,
    That he shouts with his sister at play !
O well for the sailor lad,
    That he sings in his boat on the bay !

And the stately ships go on
   To their haven under the hill;
But O for the touch of a vanished hand,
   And the sound of a voice that is still!

Break, break, break
   At the foot of thy crags, O sea!
But the tender grace of a day that is dead
   Will never come back to me.

PEACE OR WAR?

[From *Maud*.]

Peace sitting under her olive, and slurring the days gone by,
   When the poor are hovelled and hustled together, each sex, like swine,
When only the ledger lives, and when only not all men lie;
   Peace in her vineyard—yes!—but a company forges the wine.

And the vitriol madness flushes up in the ruffian's head,
   Till the filthy by-lane rings to the yell of the trampled wife,
While chalk and alum and plaster are sold to the poor for bread,
   And the spirit of murder works in the very means of life.

And Sleep must lie down armed, for the villainous centre-bits
   Grind on the wakeful ear in the hush of the moonless nights,
While another is cheating the sick of a few last gasps, as he sits
   To pestle a poisoned poison behind his crimson lights.

When a Mammonite mother kills her babe for a burial fee,
   And Timour-Mammon grins on a pile of children's bones,
Is it peace or war? better, war! loud war by land and by sea,
   War with a thousand battles, and shaking a hundred thrones.

STANZAS FROM IN MEMORIAM.

I envy not in any moods
   The captive void of noble rage,
   The linnet born within the cage,
That never knew the summer woods:

I envy not the beast that takes
   His license in the fields of time,
   Unfettered by the sense of crime,
To whom a conscience never wakes;

Nor, what may count itself as blest,
  The heart that never plighted troth,
  But stagnates in the weeds of sloth;
Nor any want-begotten rest.

I hold it true, whate'er befall;
  I feel it when I sorrow most;
  'Tis better to have loved and lost
Than never to have loved at all.

SONG FROM MAUD.

Come into the garden, Maud,
  For the black bat, night, has flown;
Come into the garden, Maud,
  I am here at the gate alone;
And the woodbine spices are wafted abroad,
  And the musk of the roses blown.

For a breeze of morning moves,
  And the planet of Love is on high,
Beginning to faint in the light that she loves
  On a bed of daffodil sky,
To faint in the light of the sun she loves,
  To faint in his light, and to die.

All night have the roses heard
  The flute, violin, bassoon;
All night has the casement jessamine stirred
  To the dancers dancing in tune;
Till a silence fell with the waking bird,
  And a hush with the setting moon.

I said to the lily, "There is but one
  With whom she has heart to be gay.
When will the dancers leave her alone?
  She is weary of dance and play."
Now half to the setting moon are gone,
  And half to the rising day;
Low on the sand and loud on the stone
  The last wheel echoes away.

I said to the rose, " The brief night goes
  In babble and revel and wine.
O young lord-lover, what sighs are those
  For one that will never be thine?
But mine, but mine," so I swore to the rose,
  "For ever and ever mine."

ROBERT BROWNING.

INCIDENT OF THE FRENCH CAMP.

You know, we French stormed Ratisbon:
  A mile or so away
On a little mound, Napoleon
  Stood on our storming-day;
With neck out-thrust, you fancy how,
  Legs wide, arms locked behind,
As if to balance the prone brow
  Oppressive with its mind.

Just as perhaps he mused, " My plans
  That soar, to earth may fall,
Let once my army-leader Lannes
  Waver at yonder wall "—
Out 'twixt the battery-smokes there flew
  A rider, bound on bound
Full-galloping; nor bridle drew
  Until he reached the mound.

Then off there flung in smiling joy,
  And held himself erect
By just his horse's mane, a boy:
  You hardly could suspect—
(So tight he kept his lips compressed.
  Scarce any blood came through)
You looked twice ere you saw his breast
  Was all but shot in two.

" Well," cried he, " Emperor, by God's grace
  We've got you Ratisbon!
The Marshal's in the market-place,
  And you'll be there anon

To see your flag-bird flap his vans
Where I, to heart's desire,
Perched him !" The chief's eye flashed; his plans
Soared up again like fire.

The chief's eye flashed; but presently
Softened itself, as sheathes
A film the mother-eagle's eye
When her bruised eaglet breathes;
"You're wounded!" "Nay," the soldier's pride
Touched to the quick, he said:
"I'm killed, sire!" And his chief beside,
Smiling the boy fell dead.

THE LOST LEADER.

Just for a handful of silver he left us,
Just for a ribbon to stick in his coat—
Found the one gift of which fortune bereft us,
Lost all the others, she lets us devote;
They, with the gold to give, doled him out silver,
So much was theirs who so little allowed:
How all our copper had gone for his service!
Rags—were they purple, his heart had been proud!
We that had loved him so, followed him, honored him,
Lived in his mild and magnificent eye,
Learned his great language, caught his clear accents,
Made him our pattern to live and to die!
Shakspere was of us, Milton was for us,
Burns, Shelley were with us—they watch from their graves!
He alone breaks from the van and the freemen,
He alone sinks to the rear and the slaves !

We shall march prospering—not through his presence;
Songs may inspirit us—not from his lyre;
Deeds will be done, while he boasts his quiescence,
Still bidding crouch whom the rest bade aspire:
Blot out his name, then, record one lost soul more,
One task more declined, one more footpath untrod,
One more devil's triumph and sorrow for angels,
One wrong more to man, one more insult to God!
Life's night begins: let him never come back to us!

There would be doubt, hesitation, and pain,
Forced praise on our part—the glimmer of twilight,
  Never glad confident morning again!
Best fight on well, for we taught him—strike gallantly,
  Menace our heart ere we master his own;
Then let him receive the new knowledge and wait us,
  Pardoned in heaven, the first by the throne!

MEETING AT NIGHT.

The gray sea and the long black land,
And the yellow half-moon large and low;
And the startled little waves that leap
In fiery ringlets from their sleep,
As I gain the cove with pushing prow
And quench its speed in the slushy sand.

Then a mile of warm sea-scented beach;
Three fields to cross till a farm appears;
A tap at the pane, the quick sharp scratch
And blue spurt of a lighted match,
And a voice less loud, through its joys and fears,
Than the two hearts beating each to each!

WORK AND WORTH.

[From *Rabbi Ben Ezra*.]

Not on the vulgar mass
Called "work" must sentence pass,
  Things done, that took the eye and had the price;
O'er which, from level stand,
The low world laid its hand,
  Found straightway to its mind, could value in a trice:

But all, the world's coarse thumb
And finger failed to plumb,
  So passed in making up the main account;
All instincts immature,
All purposes unsure,
  That weighed not as his work, yet swelled the man's amount:

Thoughts hardly to be packed
Into a narrow act,
   Fancies that broke through language and escaped;
All I could never be,
All men ignored in me,
   This I was worth to God, whose wheel the pitcher shaped.

HOME THOUGHTS FROM ABROAD.

O, to be in England
Now that April's there,
And whoever wakes in England
Sees, some morning, unaware,
That the lowest boughs and the brush-wood sheaf
Round the elm-tree bole are in tiny leaf,
While the chaffinch sings on the orchard bough
In England—now !

And after April, when May follows,
And the white throat builds, and all the swallows !
Hark where my blossomed pear-tree in the hedge
Leans to the field and scatters on the clover
Blossoms and dew-drops—at the bent spray's edge--
That's the wise thrush; he sings each song twice over.
Lest you should think he never could recapture
The first fine careless rapture !
And though the fields look rough with hoary dew,
All will be gay when noontide wakes anew
The buttercups, the little children's dower,
Far brighter than this gaudy melon-flower !

INDEX.

An index to the English authors and writings and the principal English periodicals mentioned in this volume.

Absalom and Ahitophel, 131.
Account of the Greatest English Poets, An, 129.
Adam Bede, 206, 207.
Addison, Joseph, 112, 129, 134, 136, 139, 140, 184, 204, 207, 209.
Address to the Unco Guid, 161.
Adeline, 214.
Adonais, 192, 193.
Adventures of Five Hours, 128.
Adventures of Philip, 204.
Ae Fond Kiss, 160.
A King and No King, 95, 97, 98.
Aella, 146.
A Man's a Man for a' that, 163.
Aeneid, translated by Surrey, 48.
Agincourt, 72.
Aids to Reflection, 175.
Akenside, Mark, 143.
Alastor, 190, 192.
Albion's England, 71.
Alchemist, The, 90.
Alexander and Campaspe, 76.
Alexander's Feast, 130.
Alfred, King, 7, 8, 12, 44.
All for Love, 124, 125.
All's Well that Ends Well, 84.
Amelia, 154.
Amoretti, 55, 69.
Anatomy of Melancholy, The, 100, 101.
Ancient Mariner, The, 168, 175, 176.
Ancren Riwle, The, 17.
Anglo-Saxon Chronicle, The, 10, 11.
Annus Mirabilis, 131.
Anthony and Cleopatra, 86, 124.
Antiquary, The, 183.
Araby's Daughter, 189.
Arcadia, The Countess of Pembroke's 61, 62, 65.
Areopagitica, 115.

Argument against Abolishing Christianity, An, 142.
Arnold, Matthew, 16, 20, 172.
Art of English Poesy, The, 65.
Artificial Comedy of the Last Century, The, 127, 180.
Ascham, Roger, 38, 45, 46, 50, 105.
Astrophel and Stella, 62, 69.
As You Like It, 60, 66, 84, 85.
Auld Farmer's New Year's Salutation, The, 162.
Auld Lang Syne, 162.
Austen, Jane, 183.
"Authorized Version," The, 23, 46.
Ayenbite of Inwyt, The, 17.

Bacon, Francis, 63, 67, 68, 80, 114, 207, 209.
Ballad upon a Wedding, 110.
Banished Cavaliers, The, 126.
Bard, The, 130, 144, 149.
Baron's Wars, The, 71.
Bartholomew Fair, 89, 123.
Battle of the Baltic, The, 184.
Battle of Hastings, The, 146.
Battle of Otterbourne, The, 41.
Baviad, The, 143, 165.
Beattie, James, 144, 147, 160.
Beaumont, Francis, 69, 75, 81, 89, 93–99, 127.
Beaux' Stratagem, The, 126.
Beggar's Opera, The, 143.
Behn, Aphra, 126.
Beppo, 187.
Bible, Translations of the, 23, 46, 47.
Biographia Literaria, 174, 175.
Biographical History of Philosophy, A, 205.
Biographical Sketches, De Quincey's 178.
Bishop Orders his Tomb, The, 219.

Blackwood's Magazine, 165, 166, 176, 206.
Bleak House, 178, 199, 202, 207.
Blot in the Scutcheon, A, 220.
Boke of the Duchesse, The, 25, 31.
Book of Common Prayer, The, 47, 115.
Book of Martyrs, Fox's, 133.
Boswell, James, 149–152.
Bourchier, John, 38.
Bowge of Court, 39.
"Break, break, break," 216.
Bride of Abydos, The, 184.
Bride of Lammermoor, The, 183.
Brief Appraisal of the Greek Literature, A, 178.
Britannia's Pastorals, 70.
Broken Heart, The, 98.
Brontë, Charlotte, 197, 203.
Brook, The, 215.
Brooke, Arthur, 70.
Brougham, Henry, 165.
Browne, Thomas, 67, 100–103, 106, 133.
Browne, William, 70.
Browning, Elizabeth, 159.
Browning, Robert, 191, 214, 215, 217–220.
Brut, The, 15.
Bugle Song, 215.
Bunyan, John, 22, 55, 133, 209.
Burke, Edmund, 150, 157, 165.
Burns, Robert, 40, 157, 159–163, 171, 193, 210.
Burton, Robert, 100, 101, 180.
Butler, Samuel, 122, 123.
Byron, George Gordon, 70, 143, 159, 164, 169–171, 176, 179, 184–193, 195.

Cain, 185.
Caliban upon Setebos, 217.
Campaign, The, 140.
Campbell, Thomas, 184.
Canterbury Tales, The, 20, 22, 26–29, 32, 34, 129.
Capgrave's Chronicle, 12.
Captain Singleton, 152.
Carew, Thomas, 108, 110, 111.
Carlyle, Thomas, 150, 155, 160, 162, 166, 182, 183, 190, 207, 210–213.
Castle of Indolence, The, 147.
Castle of Otranto, The, 144, 183.
Casuistry of Roman Meals, The, 178.
Catiline, 86.
Cato, 140.
Cavalier Tunes, 218.

Caxton, William, 36–38, 40, 44.
Cenci, The, 191.
Chances, The, 95.
Chapman, George, 70, 71, 194.
Characteristics, 210.
Chartism, 211.
Chatterton, Thomas, 144, 145, 180.
Chaucer, Geoffrey, 8, 10, 19, 22, 24–29, 31–34, 39, 41, 44, 48–50, 70, 72, 129, 132, 144, 169, 194, 214.
Cheke, John, 45.
Chesterfield's Letters, 135.
Chevy Chase, 41.
Childe Harold, 184, 185, 187, 189.
Christabel, 174–176.
Christian Year, The, 107.
"Christopher North," 165.
Christ's Victory and Triumph, 118.
Chronicle of England, Capgrave's, 12.
Church and State, 175.
Church History, Fuller's, 24, 103.
Clannesse, 20.
Claribel, 214.
Clarissa Harlowe, 152, 153.
Cœlum Britannicum, 110.
Coleridge, S. T., 87, 95, 101, 153, 155, 162, 164, 166–168, 172–176, 178–180, 188, 209.
Colet, John, 45, 47.
Colin Clout's Come Home Again, 51.
Collar, The, 107.
Collier, Jeremy, 127.
Collins, William, 144, 147–149, 152, 156, 180.
Colombe's Birthday, 220.
Colonel, The, 90.
Comedy of Errors, 77, 83.
Comic Dramatists of the Restoration, 209.
Committee, The, 126.
Complaint of the Decay of Beggars, 180.
Complaints, 52.
Compleat Angler, The, 104.
Comus, 15, 98, 112, 113, 119.
Conduct of the Allies, 134.
Confessio Amantis, 29.
Confessions of an English Opium Eater, 177.
Confutation of the Animadversions, etc., A, 115.
Congreve, William, 126, 136, 143.
Conquest of Granada, The, 125.
Constable, Henry, 69.
Cooper's Hill, 129.
Coriolanus, 86.
Corsair, The, 184.

Cotter's Saturday Night, The, 160.
Country Wife, The, 125, 126.
Court of Love, The, 31.
Coverdale, Miles, 46.
Cowley, Abraham, 105, 106, 109, 110, 121, 128, 130, 133.
Cowper, William, 71, 148, 157-160, 171, 172.
Crabbe, George, 171, 172.
Cradle Song, 215.
Crashaw, Richard, 105, 109, 110.
Critic, The, 127.
Cromwell's Letters, 211.
Crowne, John, 125.
Cuckoo and the Nightingale, The, 31.
Curse of Kehama, The, 176.
Cursor Mundi, 17.
Cymbeline, 15, 85, 147.
Cynthia's Revels, 90.

Dame Siriz, 27.
Daniel Deronda, 207.
Daniel, Samuel, 69, 71, 72.
Daphnaida, 52.
Davenant, William, 121, 124, 128.
David and Bethsabe, 78.
David Copperfield, 199.
Davideis, The, 110.
Davison's Poetical Rhapsody, 69.
Death and Dr. Hornbook, 161.
Decline and Fall of the Roman Empire, 157.
Defense of Chimney Sweeps, A, 180.
Defense of Poesy, 62.
Defensio pro Populo Anglicano, 115.
Defoe, Daniel, 134, 141, 152.
Denham, John, 129.
De Quincey, Thomas, 101, 164, 176-178, 209.
Derby, Earl of, 71.
Description of England, 71.
Deserted Village, The, 156.
Destruction of Jerusalem, The, 125.
Diary of Samuel Pepys, 127.
Diary of H. C. Robinson, 178.
Dickens, Charles, 178, 197-207.
Dictes and Sayings of the Philosophers, 36.
Dictionary of the English Language, Johnson's, 151.
Difference between Absolute and Limited Monarchy, 35.
Dirge in Cymbeline, 147.
Discoveries, 77.
Discovery of the Empire of Guiana, 64.
Divine Emblems, 108.
Divine Weeks and Works, 117.

Doctor Faustus, 77, 78, 87.
Dombey and Son, 199.
Don Juan, 187.
Donne, John, 104, 107, 110, 128, 131, 132.
Dora, 215.
Dowie Dens of Yarrow, The, 42.
Dramatic Lyrics, 218.
Dramatis Personæ, 218.
Drayton, Michael, 61, 69, 71, 72, 104.
Dream Children, 180.
Dream of Fair Women, A, 214.
Dream of the Unknown, A, 192.
Drummond, William, 69.
Dryden, John, 27, 46, 56, 94, 109, 111, 115, 122, 124-126, 128-134, 136, 138, 141, 143, 148, 157.
Duchess of Malfi, The, 98.
Duke of Lerma, The, 125.
Dunciad, The, 135, 136.
Dyer, John, 147, 149, 152.
Dying Swan, The, 214.

Earle, John, 207.
Eastward Hoe, 88.
Easy and Ready Way to Establish a Free Commonwealth, An, 115.
Ecclesiastical Polity, 66, 67.
Edgeworth, Maria, 183.
Edinburgh Review, The, 165, 208, 210.
Edward II., 77.
Edwin Morris, 215.
Elaine, 214.
Eleanore, 214.
Elegy on Thyrza, 188.
Elegy to the Memory of an Unfortunate Lady, 188.
Elegy written in a Country Churchyard, 147, 148.
"Eliot, George," 68, 183, 198, 205-207.
Elixir, The, 108.
Elliott, Jane, 44.
Empress of Morocco, The, 125.
Encouragements to a Lover, 111.
Endymion, 193, 194.
England's Helicon, 69.
England's Heroical Epistles, 71.
English Bards and Scotch Reviewers, 143.
English Humorists, 204.
Enid, 216.
Epipsychidion, 192.
Epistle of Eloisa to Abelard, 138.
Epistle to Dr. Arbuthnot, 136.
Epistle to the Countess of Cumberland, 72.
Epithalamion, 54, 55.

Essays, Bacon's, 67.
Essays of Elia, 180.
Essay of Dramatic Poesie, 124, 132.
Essay on Criticism, 129.
Essay on the Genius and Writings of Pope, 148.
Essay on Man, 135.
Essay on Poetry, 129.
Essay on Satire, 129.
Essay on Translated Verse, 129.
Etherege, George, 126, 127.
Euphues, 59, 60, 65.
Evans, Mary Ann, 198.
Eve of St. Agnes, The, 194.
Evelyn Hope, 219.
Evening's Love, An, 125.
Evergreen, The, 44.
Every Man in his Humor, 89, 90.
Every Man out of his Humor, 89.
Excursion, The, 168, 171.

Fables, Dryden's, 132.
Fair and Happy Milkmaid, The, 68.
Fair Helen of Kirkconnell, 42.
Faerie Queene, The, 12, 88, 50, 51-54, 103, 133, 147, 194.
Faithful Shepherdess, The, 98.
Faits of Arms, 36.
Fall of Robespierre, 166.
Fall of the Bastile, 166.
Falls of Princes, 32, 50.
Famous Victories of Henry V., 83.
Farquhar, George, 126.
Fatima, 214.
Felix Holt, 206.
Ferdinand, Count Fathom, 154.
Ferguson, Robert, 160.
Fielding, Henry, 153-157, 183, 203, 204.
Fingal, 145.
First Epistle to Davie, 163.
"First Folio," The, 80, 81.
Flaming Heart, The, 109.
Fleece, The, 147.
Fletcher, Giles, 118.
Fletcher, John, 69, 75, 79, 81, 83, 93, 99, 114, 127.
Fletcher, Phineas, 105.
Flower and the Leaf, The, 31.
Ford, John, 98, 99.
Foreign Review, The, 210.
Forest, The, 91.
Forsaken Bride, The, 42.
Fortescue, John, 35.
Fountain, The, 169.
Four Georges, The, 204.
Fox and the Wolf, The, 28.
Fox, George, 133.

Fra Lippo Lippi, 219.
Franklin's Tale, The, 28.
Fraser's Magazine, 166, 202, 212.
Frederick the Great, Carlyle's, 211.
Frederick the Great, Macaulay's Essay on, 209.
French Revolution, Carlyle's, 212.
French Revolution as it Appeared to Enthusiasts, The, 167.
Friar Bacon and Friar Bungay, 78.
Fuller, Thomas, 24, 102, 103, 180, 207.

Gardener's Daughter, The, 215.
Garden of Cyrus, The, 101.
Gascoigne, George, 58.
"Gather ye Rosebuds While Ye May," 109.
Gay, John, 137, 204.
Gobir, 179.
Geoffrey of Monmouth, 14, 15.
Gertrude of Wyoming, 184.
Giaour, The, 184.
Gibbon, Edward, 157, 209.
Gifford, William, 143, 165.
Girl Describes her Fawn, The 120.
Glove, The, 218.
"Go, Lovely Rose," 111.
Goddwyn, 146.
Golden Legend, The, 19, 36.
Goldsmith, Oliver, 121, 127, 150, 155, 157, 183, 204.
Good Thoughts in Bad Times, 103.
Goody Blake and Harry Gill, 169.
Gorboduc, 15, 50.
Gosson, Stephen, 60.
Götz von Berlichingen, translated by Scott, 181.
Governail of Princes, The, 31.
Gower, John, 29, 33.
Graham, James, 111.
Grammarian's Funeral, The, 217.
Gray, Thomas, 121, 130, 144, 146-149, 152, 156, 180.
Great Expectations, 200.
Great Hoggarty Diamond, The, 202.
Greene, Robert, 60, 66, 76, 78.
"Green Grow The Rashes, O," 160.
Groat's Worth of Wit, A, 66.
Grocyn, William, 45.
Grongar Hill, 147.
Guest, Charlotte, 216.
Guinevere, 216, 217.
Gulliver's Travels, 141.

Hakluyt, Richard, 64.
Hales, Thomas de, 17.
Hall, Joseph, 69, 131, 132.

Hamlet, 12, 85, 87, 164, 220.
Handlyng Sinne, 17.
Harp of Tara, The, 189.
Harrison's Description of England, 71.
Harvey, Gabriel, 51.
Hawes, Stephen, 38, 39, 49, 50.
Hazlitt, William, 190.
Heads of the People, 68.
Heart of Midlothian, The, 183.
Hellenics, 179.
Henry IV., 82.
Henry V., 82.
Henry VI., 81, 82.
Henry VIII., 57, 81, 82.
Henry Esmond, 183, 203, 204.
Henry of Huntingdon, 12.
Herbert, George, 104, 105, 107, 109.
Hereford, Nicholas, 23.
Heretic's Tragedy, The, 219.
Hero and Leander, 70.
Heroes and Hero Worship, 207, 211.
Herrick, Robert, 105, 108, 109.
Hesperides, The, 108.
Hind and the Panther, The, 132.
Historia Britonum, 15.
History, Essay on, 210, 212.
History of Edward V., 47.
History of England, Macaulay's, 208, 209.
History of Frederick the Great, 211.
History of the Civil Wars, 71.
History of the World, 64.
Histrio-mastix, 95.
Hobbes, Thomas, 115, 121.
Hohenlinden, 184.
Holinshed's Chronicle, 66, 71.
Holy and Profane State, The, 103, 207.
Holy Dying, 103, 104.
Holy Fair, The, 161.
Holy Living, 103.
Holy Tulzie, The, 161.
Holy Willie's Prayer, 161.
Homer, translated by Chapman, 71, 194.
Homer, translated by Pope, 135.
Homer and the Homeridæ, 178.
Hooker, Richard, 66, 104.
Horatian Ode upon Cromwell's Return, 120.
Hous of Fame, The, 25, 26.
Howard, Henry, 48, 49.
Howard, Robert, 125, 126.
How to Keep a True Lent, 108.
How we Brought the Good News from Ghent, 215.
Hudibras, 122, 123.
Hume, David, 209.
Humphrey Clinker, 155.

Hunt, Leigh, 68, 191.
Hunting of the Cheviot, The, 41.
Hurd, Richard, 144,
Hydriotaphia, 101.
Hymns on Love and Beauty, 52, 55.
Hymn to Diana, 90.
Hymn to the Spirit of Nature, 192.
Hypatia, 183.
Hyperion, 193.

Idiot Boy, The, 169.
Idler, The, 140, 151.
Idyllia Heroica, 179.
Idyls of The King, 16, 214, 216.
Iliad, The, translated by Chapman, 71.
Il Penseroso, 113, 147.
Imaginary Conversations, 179.
Impressions of Theophrastus Such, 68, 207.
In a Balcony, 220.
In Memoriam, 216.
Incident of the French Camp, 219.
Indian Emperor, The, 125.
Irish Melodies, 189.
Irish Sketch-Book, The, 202.
Isabel, 214.
Isabella, 194.
Isle of Palms, The, 176.
Isles of Greece, The, 188.
Ivanhoe, 183.

James I. of Scotland, 32, 33.
Jeffrey, Francis, 165, 209.
Jerrold, Douglas, 68.
Jock O'Hazeldean, 182.
John Barleycorn, 161.
John Gilpin, 159.
Johnson, Samuel, 68, 101, 105, 107, 117, 130, 132, 135, 140, 143, 147, 149-152, 156, 165, 204.
Jolly Beggars, The, 40, 161.
Jonathan Wild, 154, 201.
Jonson, Ben, 50, 60, 62, 69, 72, 77, 80, 81, 83, 86, 88-91, 94, 98, 106, 108, 112, 122, 123, 201.
Joseph Andrews, 153.
Journal of the Plague, 152.
Julius Cæsar, 85, 86, 129.

Keats, John, 54, 71, 164, 188, 193-195.
Keble, John, 107.
Kenilworth, 58, 183.
Killigrew, Thomas, 126.
"King James's Bible," 23.
King John, 82, 83.
King Lear, 12, 15, 85, 97, 129.
Kingsley, Charles, 175, 183, 197.

King's Quhair, The, 32, 33.
King's Tragedy, The, 33.
Knight of the Burning Pestle, The, 98.
Knight's Tale, The, 25, 27, 32, 34.
Kubla Khan, 174, 176.
Kyd, Thomas, 76.

La Belle Dame sans Merci, 194.
Lady of Shalott, The, 214.
Lady of The Lake, The, 182.
Lalla Rookh, 189.
L'Allegro, 113, 147.
Lamb, Charles, 54, 127, 140, 164, 179, 180, 207.
Lament for Flodden, 44.
Lamia, 194.
"Landlady, Count The Lawin'," 162.
Land of Cokaygne, The, 18, 27.
Landor, W. S., 164, 169, 178, 179.
Langland, William, 21, 22, 25, 28, 42.
Lara, 184.
Last Ride Together, The, 219.
Last Rose of Summer, The, 189.
Latimer, Hugh, 47.
Latter Day Pamphlets, 211.
Layamon, 15.
Lay of The Ash, 27.
Lay of The Last Minstrel, 182.
Lays of Ancient Rome, 210.
Leben Jesu, translated by George Eliot, 205.
Lectures on Shakspere, Coleridge's, 175.
Lee, Nathaniel, 125.
Legend of Good Women, The, 25, 214.
Leonora, translated by Scott, 181.
Lessing, DeQuincey's Essay On, 178.
L'Estrange, Roger, 110.
Letters from Italy, (Addison's), 184.
Letters from Italy (Wotton's), 104.
Letters on Chivalry and Romance, 144.
Letters on Toleration, 115.
Lewes, G. H., 205.
Lewis, M. G., 183.
Liberty of Prophesying, 115.
Life of Johnson, Boswell's, 149.
Life of Nelson, Southey's, 176.
Life of Schiller, Carlyle's, 210.
Life of Scott, Lockhart's, 165.
Light of Other Days, The, 189.
Lilian, 214.
Lily, William, 45.
Linacre, Thomas, 45.
Lines to an Indian Air, 192.
Lines written near Tintern Abbey, 168.
Little Dorrit, 207.
Lives of Saints, 19.

Lives of the Poets, Johnson's, 148, 151.
Lives, Walton's, 104.
Locke, John, 115, 121.
Lockhart, J. G., 165.
Locksley Hall, 216.
Locrine, 15.
Lodge, Thomas, 60, 66, 76.
London, 143.
London Lyckpenny, 32.
London Magazine, The, 177, 186.
Lord Clive, 209.
Lord of the Isles, 182.
Lost Leader, The, 218.
Lotus Eaters, The, 214, 215.
Lovelace, Richard, 110.
Love's Labours Lost, 77, 83.
Love's Triumph, 90.
Luck of Barry Lyndon, The, 202.
Lucy, 169.
Luria, 220.
Luve Ron, A, 17.
Lycidas, 51, 113, 114.
Lydgate, John, 31–33, 50.
Lyly, John, 59–61, 66, 69, 76.
Lyrical Ballads, 168, 171, 172.
Lytell Geste of Robin Hood, A, 144.

Mabinogion, The, 216.
Macaulay, T. B., 123, 127, 150, 151, 207–210.
Macbeth, 12, 85, 87, 98, 128.
Mac Flecknoe, 131.
Macpherson, James, 144, 145, 180.
Madeline, 214.
Mæviad, The, 143, 165.
Maid's Tragedy, The, 95.
Malory, Thomas, 17, 37, 216.
Mandeville, John, 34, 35.
Manfred, 185.
Manly Heart, The, 111
Map, Walter, 16.
Margaret, 214.
Margaret Nicholson's Remains, 190.
Mariana, 214, 215.
Mariana in the South, 214.
Marlowe, Christopher, 70–72, 76–79, 87, 98.
Marmion, 182.
Marston, John, 131.
Martin Chuzzlewit, 199.
"Martin Marprelate," 66, 92.
Marvel, Andrew, 120, 131.
Mason, William, 144, 146.
Master Humphrey's Clock, 199.
Matthew of Westminster, 12.
Maud, 216.

May Queen, The, 215.
Measure for Measure, 84, 214.
Medal, The, 131.
Meeting of the Waters, The, 189.
Memorials of a Tour in Scotland, 170.
Men and Women, 214, 218.
Menaphon, 60.
Merchant of Venice, The, 84.
Merry Wives of Windsor, The, 70, 89, 90, 127.
Microcosmographie, Earle's, 207.
Middlemarch, 206, 207.
Midsummer Night's Dream, A, 57, 72. 84, 87.
Mill, J. S., 174.
Mill on the Floss, The, 206.
Miller's Daughter, The, 215.
Milton, John, 15, 51, 56, 67, 78,, 87, 93, 98, 103, 104, 111–121, 123, 132, 133, 147–149, 152, 164, 168, 178, 188, 191, 194, 195, 208.
Minstrel, The, 144, 147.
Minstrelsy of the Scottish Border, 182.
Mirrour for Magistrates, 50.
Miser, The, 125.
Mistress, The, 110.
Modern Painters, 207.
Modest Proposal, A, 142.
Monastery, The, 59.
Monk, The, 183.
Monk's Tale, The, 27.
Moore, Thomas, 164, 189.
Moral Essays, 136.
More, Thomas, 45–47.
Morning Post, The, 164.
Morris, William, 20.
Morte Darthur, 17, 37, 38, 216.
Mr. Sludge, the Medium, 217.
Much Ado About Nothing, 76, 84.
Muispotmos, 55.
Mulgrave, Earl of, 129.
Murder Considered as One of the Fine Arts, 178.
My Heart's in the Highlands, 162,
My Last Duchess, 217.
Mysteries of Udolpho, 183.

Nash, Thomas, 45, 66.
Necessity of Atheism, The, 189.
Nero, 125.
Newcomes, The, 203.
Nicholas Nickleby, 199, 202.
Noble Numbers, 108.
Noctes Ambrosianæ, 165.
Nonne Preste's Tale, The, 19, 27.
North, Thomas, 66.
Northern Farmer, The, 317.

Nut-brown Maid, The, 41.
Nymphidia, 72.

Observations on the Faerie Queene.
Occleve, Thomas, 31, 33.
Ode on a Distant Prospect of Eton College, 148.
Ode on a Grecian Urn, 194.
Ode on the Intimations of Immortality, 108, 168.
Ode on the Superstitions of the Scottish Highlands, 144.
Ode to Autumn, 194.
Ode to Evening, 147.
Ode to France, 166.
Ode to Memory, 213.
Ode to a Nightingale, 194.
Ode to Simplicity, 147.
Ode to the West Wind, 192.
Odyssey, The, translated by Chapman, 71.
Œnone, 214.
Old Benchers of the Inner Temple, The, 180.
Old China, 180.
Old Curiosity Shop, The, 199.
Oliver Twist, 199, 207.
Olney Hymns, 157.
On a Girdle, 111.
On a Picture of Leander, 194.
On First Looking into Chapman's Homer, 71, 194.
On Receipt of My Mother's Picture, 158.
On Seeing a Harp in the Shape of a Needle-Case, 171.
On Seeing the Elgin Marbles, 194.
On the Death of Thomson, 148.
On the Morning of Christ's Nativity, 113, 119, 147.
Order of Chivalry, 36.
Ordericus Vitalis, 12.
Ormulum, The, 17.
Ossian, Poems of, 144–146.
Othello, 85, 128.
Otway, Thomas, 125, 191.
Our Mutual Friend, 199, 200.
Over the Water to Charlie, 163.
Overbury, Thomas, 68.
Owl and the Nightingale, The, 18.

Pacience, 20.
Palace of Art, The, 215.
Palace of Pleasure, Paynter's, 66.
Pamela, 152, 153.
Pandosto, 66.
Pap with a Hatchet, 66.

Paracelsus, 218.
Paradise Lost, 116–119, 133, 139, 164, 191, 208.
Paradise Regained, 118, 119.
Parisina, 184.
Paris Sketch-Book, The, 202.
Parlament of Foules, The, 25, 26, 31.
Parson's Wedding, The, 126.
Passetyme of Pleasure, The, 38, 50.
Passing of Arthur, The, 16, 216, 217.
Passionate Pilgrim, The, 69.
Passionate Shepherd to his Love, The, 70.
Past and Present, 211.
Pastorals, Pope's, 138.
Patience, 90.
Paynter, William, 66.
Peacock, Reginald, 35.
Peele, George, 76, 78.
Pendennis, 203.
Pepys, Samuel, 122, 123, 127, 128.
Percy, Thomas, 44, 144, 180.
Peregrine Pickle, 154.
Pericles and Aspasia, 179.
Pericles, Prince of Tyre, 81.
Perle, The, 20.
Peter Bell, 169.
Peterborough Chronicle, The, 10, 11.
Pet Lamb, The, 169.
Philaster, 95, 97.
Philips, Ambrose, 143.
Phyllip Sparrowe, 40.
Pickwick Papers, The, 198, 201, 207.
Pied Piper, The, 219.
Piers Penniless' Supplication, 66.
Piers the Plowman's Crede, 22.
Piers the Plowman, Vision of William concerning, 20–22.
Pilgrimage, The, 65.
Pilgrim's Progress, The, 21, 133.
Pippa Passes, 220.
Plain Dealer, The, 125.
Pleasures of Hope, 184.
Pleasures of Imagination, 143.
Plowman's Tale, The, 22.
Plutarch's Lives, translated by North, 66.
Poems chiefly in the Scottish dialect, 159.
Poems chiefly Lyrical, 213.
Poetaster, The, 90.
Poetical Rhapsody, Davison's, 69.
Polyolbion, The, 71, 72, 104.
Poor Relations, 180.
Pope, Alexander, 71, 111, 123, 128–130, 132, 134–138, 141, 143, 148, 152, 156, 166, 178, 184.

Popular Tales, 183.
Prayer in Prospect of Death, A, 161.
Prayer under the Pressure of Violent Anguish, A, 161.
Predictions of Isaac Bickerstaff, 142.
Prelude, The, 168, 171.
Pricke of Conscience, The, 17.
Pride and Prejudice, 183.
Princely Pleasures of the Court of Kenilworth, 58.
Princess, The, 215, 216.
Prior, Matthew, 134.
Prisoner of Chillon, The, 184.
Progress of Poesy, The, 130, 149.
Prometheus Unbound, 191, 192.
Prothalamion, Spenser's, 52, 54.
"Proud Maisie is in the Wood," 44, 182.
Pseudodoxia Epidemica, 100.
Public Spirit of the Whigs, 134, 165.
Pulley, The, 107.
Punch, 202.
Purple Island, The, 105, 118.
"Purvey's Revision," 23.
Puttenham, George, 65.

Quarles, Francis, 105, 108.
Quarterly Review, The, 165.
Queen Mab, 190.
Queen Mary, 217.

Radcliffe, Anne, 183.
Raleigh, Walter, 51, 53, 57, 63–65, 70, 81.
Rambler, The, 140, 151.
Ramsay, Allan, 44, 160.
Rape of Lucrece, The, 70, 80.
Rape of the Lock, The, 136, 137, 143, 148.
Rapture, The, 110.
Rasselas, 151.
Reade, Charles, 197.
Recluse, The, 171.
Recollections of the Arabian Nights, 214.
Reflections on the Revolution in France, 165.
Rehearsal, The, 125, 131, 151.
Relapse, The, 126.
Religio Laici, 132.
Religio Medici, 101, 102.
Reliques of Ancient English Poetry, 44, 144, 180.
Remarks on the Tragedies of the Last Age, 128.
Repressor, etc., The, 35.
Resolution and Independence, 169.
Retreat, The, 108.

Reverie of Poor Susan, The, 169.
Revolt of Islam, The, 190.
Revolt of the Tartars, The, 178.
Reynard the Fox, 25, 36.
Richard II., 77, 82.
Richard III., 66, 82.
Richardson, Samuel, 152–154, 157, 204.
Rime of Sir Thopas, The, 27.
Ring and the Book, The, 219.
Rival Queens, The, 125.
Rivals, The, 127.
Roast Pig, 180.
Rob Roy, 183.
Robert of Gloucester, 12.
Robin Hood, 41–44.
Robinson Crusoe, 134, 141, 152.
Robinson, H. C., 178.
Rochester, Earl of, 130.
Roderick Random, 154.
Rokeby, 182.
Romaunt of the Rose, 25, 38, 53.
Romeo and Juliet, 70, 85.
Romola, 183, 206.
Rosalynde, 60, 66.
Roscommon, Earl of, 129.
Rossetti, D. G., 33.
Roundheads, The, 126.
Royden, Matthew, 63.
Ruins of Time, The, 63.
Rule a Wife and Have a Wife, 95.
Ruskin, John, 207.
Ruth, 169.
Rymer, Thomas. 128.

Sackville, Charles, 130.
Sackville, Thomas, 15, 50.
Sad Shepherd, The, 91, 98.
Samson Agonistes, 56, 78, 118–120.
Sartor Resartus, 212, 213.
Satires, Pope's, 136.
Scenes of Clerical Life, 206.
School of Abuse, The, 69.
School for Scandal, The, 127.
School-master, The, 46, 50.
School-mistress, The, 147.
Scornful Lady, The, 95.
Scotch Drink, 161.
" Scots wha hae wi' Wallace bled," 162.
Scott, Walter, 44, 58, 59, 141, 164, 165, 160, 170, 180–184, 186, 203, 205, 209, 210, 215.
Seasons, The, 143, 149.
Sedley, Charles, 130.
Sejanus, 86.
Selden, John, 104.
Sense and Sensibility, 183.
Sentimental Journey, The, 155.

Settle, Elkanah, 125.
Shadwell, Thomas, 125, 128, 131, 136.
Shakespeare, William, 15, 28, 56–58, 60, 62, 64, 66, 69, 70, 72–77, 79–90, 93, 98, 111, 113, 117, 124, 125, 127, 128, 137, 138, 147, 148, 151, 164, 173, 175, 183, 194, 195, 201, 205, 210, 213, 214, 218.
She Stoops to Conquer, 127.
" She walks in beauty," 188.
" She was a phantom of delight," 169.
She Would if She Could, 126.
Shelley, P. B., 164, 186–193, 195.
Shenstone, William, 147, 152.
Shephard's Calendar, The, 50, 51, 56.
Shepherd's Pipe, The, 70.
Sheridan, R. B., 127, 156.
Shirley, James, 100.
Short View of the English Stage, A, 127.
Short View of Tragedy, 128.
Shortest Way with Dissenters, The, 134.
Sidney, Philip, 38, 41, 51, 53, 57, 58, 60–63, 69, 81, 103.
Siege of Corinth, The, 184.
Siege of Rhodes, The, 124.
Signs of the Times, 210.
Silas Marner, 206, 207.
Silent Woman, The, 83, 90.
Simeon of Durham, 12.
Simon Lee, 169.
Sir Charles Grandison, 152, 203.
Sir Galahad, 216.
Sir Gawayne, 20.
Sir Launcelot and Queen Guinevere, 216.
Sir Martin Marall, 125.
Sir Patrick Spence, 44.
Skelton, John, 39, 49, 49.
Sketches by Boz, 198.
Sleeping Beauty, The, 214.
Smith, Sydney, 165.
Smollett, Tobias, 154, 155, 157, 204.
Snob, The, 202.
Soliloquy of the Spanish Cloister, 219.
Solitary Reaper, The, 169.
Song of the Exiles in Bermuda, 120.
Sonnets, Shakespeare's, 80.
Sonnets, Wordsworth's, 169.
Sordello, 218.
Southey, Robert, 164, 166, 167.
Spanish Curate, The, 95.
Spanish Friar, The, 125.
Specimens of English dramatic poets, 180.
Spectator, The, 139, 140, 197.
Speculum Meditantis, 29.

Speke, Parrot, 40.
Spenser, Edmund, 12, 38, 41, 50–57, 59, 63, 69, 81, 103, 114, 147–149, 194.
St. John, Henry, 135.
Stanzas to Augusta, 188.
Stanzas Written in Dejection, 192.
State of Innocence, The, 133.
Steele, Richard, 134, 135, 139, 204.
Sterne, Lawrence, 101, 135, 140, 155–157, 204, 210.
Story of Thebes, The, 32.
Stow, John, 71.
Strafford, 219.
Strauss, translated by George Eliot, 205.
Style, De Quincey's Essay on, 178.
Suckling, John, 110.
Survey of London, 71.
Surrey, Earl of, 48, 49.
Swift, Jonathan, 134–136, 140–142, 165, 203–205, 212.
Swinburne, A. C., 16, 176.
Sylvester, Joshua, 114, 117.

Table Talk, Coleridge's, 173.
Table Talk, Cowper's, 159.
Table Talk, Selden's, 104.
Tale of a Tub, 141, 212.
Tales of the Hall, 171.
Tales of Wonder, 183.
Talisman, The, 183.
Tam O'Shanter, 160, 161.
Tamburlaine, 77.
Taming of the Shrew, 81, 83, 85.
Task, The, 158, 159.
Tate, Nahum, 128.
Tatler, The, 139, 197.
Taxation no Tyranny, 165.
Taylor, Jeremy, 103, 104, 115, 133.
Tea-Table Miscellany, The, 44.
Temora, 145.
Tempest, The, 64, 84, 87, 128.
Temple, The, 107.
Temple, William, 133, 140.
Tennyson, Alfred 8, 15–17, 37, 202, 213–217.
Testament of Love, The, 34.
Thackeray, W. M., 137, 141, 142, 155, 183, 186, 198, 201–206.
Thalaba, 176.
Thierry and Theodoret, 95.
Thomas Lord Cromwell, 83.
Thomas of Ersyldoune, 42.
Thomson, James, 143, 144, 147–149, 159.
Thorn, The, 169.
Those Evening Bells, 189.
Thoughts in a Garden, 120.

Timbuctoo, 202.
Times, The, 164.
Timon of Athens, 81, 86, 128.
Tithonus, 215.
Titus Andronicus. 81, 85.
To a Highland Girl, 169.
To Althæa, 110.
To a Mountain Daisy, 162.
To a Mouse, 162.
To a Skylark, 192.
To Corinna, 109.
To Homer, 194.
To Lucasta, 110.
To Mary in Heaven, 160.
To Mary Unwin, 158.
To the Cuckoo, 169.
Toilet of a Hebrew Lady, 178.
Tom Jones, 154.
Tottel's Miscellany, 48, 49.
Tourneur, Cyril, 99.
Toxophilus, 38, 46, 105.
Tragical Tales, 66.
Tristram Shandy, 155.
Troilus and Cresseide, 26.
Troilus and Cressida, 85, 86, 128.
Tunnyng of Elynoure Rummyng, The, 40.
Turberville, George, 66.
Twa Corbies, The, 42.
Twa Dogs, The, 163.
Twa Herds, The, 161.
Twelfth Night, 84, 96, 97.
Two April Mornings, The, 169.
Two Gentlemen of Verona, 84.
Two Voices, The, 216.
Tyndale, William, 23, 46, 47.
Tyrannic Love, 125.
Tyrwhitt's Chaucer, 144.

Ulysses, 215, 216.
Underwoods, 71.
Unloveliness of Love-locks, The, 94.
Urn Burial, 101, 102.
Utopia, 47.

Valentinian, 95.
Van Brugh, John, 126.
Vanity Fair, 202.
Vanity of Human Wishes, The, 143.
Vaughan, Henry, 105, 108.
Venice Preserved, 125.
Venus and Adonis, 70, 80.
Vicar of Wakefield, The, 156.
Village, The, 171.
Villiers, George, 121, 125, 131, 151.
Virginians, The, 204.
Virtue, 107.

Vision of Mirza, The, 139.
Vision of Sin, The, 216.
Vision of Sudden Death, The, 177.
Visions of Bellay, translated by Spenser, 50.
Visions of Petrarch, translated by Spenser, 50.
Visit to the Hebrides, A, 151.
Vittoria Corombona, 99.
Voiage and Travaile of Sir John Mandeville, 34.
Volpone, 90.
Vox Clamantis. 29.
Voyages, Hakluyt's, 64.

Wagoner, The, 169.
Wallenstein, translated by Coleridge, 173.
Waller, Edmund, 110, 121.
Walpole, Horace, 144, 146, 149, 183.
Walton, Izaak, 104.
Warner, William, 71.
Warren Hastings, Macaulay's Essay on, 209.
Warton, Joseph, 147-149.
Warton, Thomas, 58, 144, 147.
Wat Tyler, 166.
Watson, Thomas, 69.
Waverley, 182.
Waverley Novels, The, 181-183.
Way of the World, The, 126.
We are Seven, 169.
Webster, John, 79, 80, 98, 99.

Westminster Review, The, 205.
"When Januar Winds," 160.
"When we two parted," 188.
Whitsunday, 107.
Why Come Ye not to Court, 40.
Wiat, Thomas, 48, 49.
Wiclif, John, 23, 24, 28.
Wife of Bath's Prologue, The, 26.
Wife of Bath's Tale, The, 28, 84.
Wilde Jäger, Der, translated by Scott, 181.
Wilhelm Meister, translated by Carlyle, 210.
William and the Werewolf, 20.
William of Malmsbury, 12.
"Willie brewed a peck o' maut," 161.
Wilson, John, 165, 176.
Windsor Forest, 138.
Winter's Tale, The, 66, 85.
Wishes for His Unknown Mistress, 109
Wither, George, 111, 120, 131.
Woodville, Anthony, 86.
Wordsworth, William, 44, 70, 108, 116, 148, 164, 166-173, 175, 176, 178, 179, 181, 188, 193, 195.
Worthies of England, The, 103.
Wotton, Henry, 104.
Written in the Euganean Hills, 192.
Wycherley, William, 121, 125-127.

Yarrow Unvisited, 169.
Ye Mariners of England, 184.
Yellowplush Papers, 202.